THE EVIDENCE
NEVER LIES

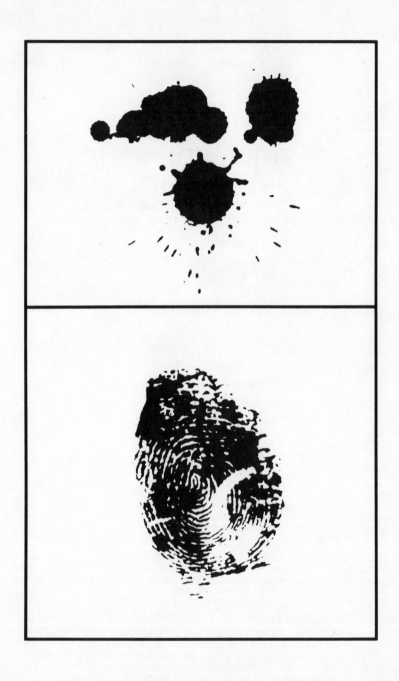

THE
EVIDENCE
NEVER LIES

THE CASEBOOK OF A MODERN
SHERLOCK HOLMES

ALFRED ALLAN LEWIS with
Herbert Leon MacDonell

HOLT, RINEHART AND WINSTON   NEW YORK

Published by Holt, Rinehart and Winston,
383 Madison Avenue, New York, New York 10017.
Published simultaneously in Canada by Holt, Rinehart and
Winston of Canada, Limited.

Library of Congress Cataloging in Publication Data
Lewis, Alfred Allan.
The evidence never lies.
1. Criminal investigation—United States—Case studies.
2. Evidence, Expert—United States—Case studies.
3. MacDonell, Herbert Leon. 4. Forensic scientists—
United States—Biography. I. MacDonell, Herbert Leon.
II. Title.
HV8073.L49 1984   363.2'5'0926   84-3834
ISBN 0-03-071856-2

First Edition

Designer: Kate Nichols
Printed in the United States of America
1 3 5 7 9 10 8 6 4 2
ISBN 0-03-071856-2

You can lead a jury to the truth, but you can't make them believe it. Physical evidence cannot be intimidated. It does not forget. It doesn't get excited at the moment something is happening—like people do. It sits there and waits to be detected, preserved, evaluated, and explained. This is what physical evidence is all about. In the course of a trial, defense and prosecuting attorneys may lie, witnesses may lie, the defendant certainly may lie. Even the judge may lie. Only the evidence never lies.

—HERBERT LEON MACDONELL

CONTENTS

Acknowledgments   ix

Preface   xi

1 A Moonlighting Criminalist   1

2 A Spattering of Evidence   31

3 The Black Panther Shoot-out/in   66

4 Portrait in Blood   100

5 A Serpent's Tooth   132

6 A Corpus Delicti Is Not a Corpse   177

7 The Piper Pays   221

ACKNOWLEDGMENTS

This book would not have been possible without the help of the extensive personal files of Herbert Leon Mac-Donell, his detailed recounting of the cases on which he has worked, and the recordings of his telephone conversations. Also invaluable were the complete transcripts of all of the trials and hearings that are discussed in the book. The work would have been immeasurably more difficult, if not impossible, to complete without access to the back issues, libraries, "morgues," and microfilm copies of the following publications: the *Albany Times-Union, Corning Leader, Chicago Sun-Times, Chicago Tribune, Elmira Star-Gazette, Florida Times-Union, Orlando Sentinel Star, Miami Herald, Miami News, New York Times, Minneapolis Tribune, St. Paul Pioneer Press, Duluth News-Tribune, St. Paul Dispatch, Oregon Statesman, Clatskanie Chief, The Oregonian, Oregon Journal, Columbia Herald*, and *Longview Daily News*, as well as articles relating to MacDonell that have appeared in *Life, Time*, and *Playboy* magazines.

Among the many people contacted and interviewed, those who proved particularly helpful are Ronald I. Meshbesher, Bruce Hartigan, Donald Larson, Kenneth Callahan, James Montgomery, William Kunstler, Phyllis MacDonell, Sara Moore, Donald Frye, Gerald Lefcourt, Gary Greene, Robert Ferry, Betty Ferry, and Myron Tillman.

Certain scenes in this book have necessarily been reconstructed. Their contents are based completely on the above sources.

The real names of some of the characters have been changed to protect the innocent, the guilty, and the author.

My deepest gratitude must go to Marian Wood for her invaluable editorial work, as well as to Jane Mollman and Dona Munker. I would also like to thank Mal Rintoul for his legal advice and, last but not least, my agent, Clyde Taylor, for his continued faith in and enthusiasm for this project through some rather trying times for both of us.

Alfred Allan Lewis
February 21, 1984

PREFACE

Criminalistics: Application of scientific techniques in collecting and analyzing physical evidence in criminal cases.

—*Webster's Ninth Collegiate Dictionary*

Until well after World War II, a criminalist was simply defined as "a specialist in criminal law," and criminalistics was often confused with criminology. It is true that both are concerned with a scientific approach to criminal investigation, but that is where they part company. Briefly, criminology is a social science, and criminalistics is a physical science.

A criminalist is not only a forensic scientist, he is the newest breed of detective; his milieu is more the laboratory than it is the scene of the crime. He interprets evidence by applying the laws of chemistry, biology, and physics. The best of these new sleuths have also become experts in giving courtroom testimony and both the defense and the prosecution call upon them to give credence to their arguments and often to solve the crimes.

Herbert Leon MacDonell is a criminalist. Attorneys and lawmen come from all over the world to attend his seminars and lectures. MacDonell's three major areas of expertise are:

Bloodstain Evidence. He wrote the major book on the subject and has been called "the Sherlock Holmes of bloodstain evidence."

Firearms Identification and Ballistics. His knowledge of firearms and ammunition is encyclopedic.

Fingerprint Identification. His invention, the MAGNA Brush, has both simplified the method of processing fingerprints that have been left at the scene of a crime and broadened the number of types of surface and substance on which fingerprints can be processed.

MacDonell is always on the lookout for new areas of exploration that may become legitimate parts of criminal investigation. He has taken to saving fingernail parings because he has become increasingly certain that, like fingerprints, no two sets of fingernails are alike in their markings. He has a twenty-five-year collection.

The criminalist is not interested in editorializing; that is for the media. He is not interested in motives; that is for the law enforcers. He is not interested in emotional, often biased, pleas for or against the defendant; that is for the lawyers. If he is not what MacDonell calls "a liar for hire," he is interested only in a scientific analysis of the evidence, which he regards as synonymous with the truth.

Because objectivity is so germane to his work, the criminalist cannot allow winning for his client to be a prime consideration. Men like MacDonell are not involved in a game that can be won or lost; they are involved with the truth as substantiated by their scientific experience and research. This often puts them at odds with public opinion, something that has happened with astonishing regularity in MacDonell's career.

Starting with the Chicago Black Panther shoot-out and coming right up through the death of Dr. Herman Tarnower at the hands of his mistress, Jean Harris, MacDonell has been consulted on almost every criminal case of national significance, including the assassinations of Robert F. Kennedy and Martin Luther King, Jr., as well as the trial of Joanne Chesimard. His findings can always be validated but that does not mean that his clients are vindicated. The truth may be revealed, but it is not always understood; it is not always believed. It has something to do with the double edge of our system. The defendant is entitled to, indeed, demands a trial by a jury of his or her peers. That jury is seldom the peer of the expert witness with his specialized education, technical expertise, and sometimes incomprehensible jargon. The evidence never lies, the truth does out, but it often speaks in an alien tongue.

1

A MOONLIGHTING CRIMINALIST

It was 4:45 P.M. on Tuesday, December 7, 1965. In the early winter dusk, the long shadows of the trees striped the woodland. Only fifteen minutes remained of the deer hunting season. On this last day, a hunter was permitted to shoot a doe as well as a buck, which meant that he did not have to waste precious time looking for a pair of antlers.

Bob Ferry could not believe his luck when he spotted a doe moving down into the gully. He lifted his shotgun, took careful aim at her, and pulled the trigger. It was not the howl of a wounded animal that reached his ears but the astonished cry of another hunter.

Ferry did not understand what had happened. He had spotted a deer. He had taken aim at a deer—not a man. He could not have hit a man. His pulse was racing, and he was paralyzed in place. The empty shell still lay at his feet marking the spot from which he had fired. A low wire fence separated him from the action that sped around him like a fast-motion movie. The other members of the hunting party were converging on a spot about 155 feet in front of him and to the right. Somebody was shouting, "Roxbury! It's Roy Roxbury! He's been shot in the throat."

Ferry did not think that he had fired in that direction at all and yet his was the only shot that had been fired. And what, in God's name, was Roxbury doing over there anyway? Every man in the party had his assigned position, and an experienced hunter knew that it was dangerous to move away from it. Yet, there was Roxbury all that distance away from where he was supposed to be. It made no sense. Roxbury and the others were all local fellows, part of a hunting party that went out together season after season. He should have known better.

They rushed Roxbury to the nearest hospital, which was some twenty miles away in the Steuben County seat of Bath. The shooting actually had taken place in Schuyler County in the Finger Lakes district of central New York State. Schuyler was a small, rural, insular county with no more than fifteen thousand inhabitants and no county facilities adequate to the needs of the wounded man.

Roy Roxbury died shortly after being admitted to the hospital. Everybody in the hunting party agreed that Robert Ferry had not deliberately set out to harm him. The two hunters had met for the first time that very morning. They had exchanged laconic but amiable greetings. Certainly, there had been no bad feelings expressed on either side. The only real impression that the younger man had made on Ferry was in the way he was dressed. Sporting a red beard, Roxbury wore fawn-colored trousers, jacket, and cap. Ferry had thought that it was a mighty peculiar outfit to wear to go hunting for deer. At any distance, this young hunter might easily be mistaken for the hunted.

Schuyler County Sheriff Maurice Dean took charge of

the still dazed Robert Ferry. When none of the other hunters admitted to having seen a deer, Dean became convinced that Ferry had not seen one either. Dean was a hunter and, from his own experience, was certain that Ferry had heard a noise and, without looking, had fired at it. On the last day of the season, some men were known to become trigger-happy.

The sheriff presented his argument so forcefully that, in his confusion, Ferry began to wonder if the lawman might not be right. He never had been in trouble before, and rarely if ever questioned anybody in authority. The "higher-ups" knew better than he did, or they would not have attained their positions.

It was this point of view that had brought him to Schuyler in the first place. Ferry lived in Steuben County, where he was employed by Corning Glass Works. It was only at the urging of his immediate superior, Robert Sawdey, that he had agreed to join the hunting party that day. He usually did his hunting in Steuben, where the deer were actually more plentiful and where he would have been a good deal closer to home. His wife, Betty, was entering the eighth month of her pregnancy, and he did not like to be too far from her.

Sheriff Dean brought him before Justice of the Peace Victor Allyn in nearby Orange, a hamlet so insignificant that it is often overlooked by cartographers of the area. Allyn was not informed of the purpose of the arraignment nor did he question the actions of the county sheriff. His job was to take down Ferry's statement.

Dean did most of the talking, occasionally turning for assent to Ferry, who was still in too much of a state of shock to understand what was happening. He asked, "There was only fifteen minutes left to the end of the season, is that right?"

Ferry replied, "Yes, sir."

3

"It was getting dark. You were eager to bag yourself some game."

"Everybody was."

"Did you hear a noise—like a deer coming down into the woodland?"

Ferry nodded.

"Didn't you shoot in the direction of that sound?"

"Yes," Ferry mumbled without adding that he had also seen a deer.

When Allyn was finished typing the statement, Ferry signed it, assuming that this was only a formality. He looked at the sheriff expecting to be told that he was free to go home. After all, it had been a tragic accident, and certainly nobody was to blame. Dean said: "Robert Ferry, I arrest you for criminal negligence in the homicide of Roy Roxbury."

Ferry stared at him as if he had not understood, and Justice Allyn murmured, "That's the same as manslaughter."

Dean weighed the document in his hand. "You confessed—it's right here in your statement. You're entitled to one phone call before I take you off to jail."

Betty Ferry knew about the shooting in Schuyler County before her husband's call. Her son had been a member of the hunting party and had raced home to tell her about it. Like Bob Ferry, she assumed it had been an accident and that he would be released as soon as he gave his statement. The call put an end to that. It seemed to her that it was ending a lot of things. Perhaps they had been too complacent about their good luck in finding each other, and now they were being punished for it. Betty Ferry was bewildered, and she was frightened.

She was expecting her baby the next month. It had

been a second marriage for both of them, and they were happier than either had been before, happier than either had thought that they ever would be.

Bob Ferry had traveled halfway around the world and returned again before this happiness could become a possibility for them. He had not yet completed high school when he went into the army during World War II. While stationed in Australia, he had met and married a local girl and, when peace came, had returned to make a life in her country. It did not work out. They divorced, and he came back to the place where he had been born. Like so many of his friends, he got a job with the local big industry, Corning Glass Works.

When Betty and Bob began to court, she was working as a waitress in the Poster restaurant in Painted Post, a small town to the west of Corning. She continued to work after they got married and during her pregnancy.

The Ferrys were hard-working and honest people. Their jobs were not grand, but they had a good and fulfilling life together and planned to make things better for their children, to provide them with good educations and encourage their ambitions. At least, that was how they thought it would be until that shot rang out across the Schuyler woodland just fifteen minutes before the hunting was due to stop for another season.

There was only one person to whom Betty Ferry thought that she could turn for help. Myron Tillman was one of her lunch regulars at the restaurant. He was a promising young attorney. She dialed his number and prayed.

The next morning, Tillman picked up Betty Ferry and they drove over to Watkins Glen, where Bob was being held. While she went to see her husband, he remained in the sheriff's office reading Ferry's statement. After he finished, he said, "This is a very impressive document."

Sheriff Dean smiled. "I think so."

"Why, it could serve as a textbook example of a negligent homicide confession."

"Well, it's a textbook case."

Tillman eyed him for a moment. "Is it? I'd like to see my client now."

The first thing that Tillman asked Ferry was if it was true that he had not actually seen anything. Ferry replied: "No, no. I swear—I saw a deer."

"In your statement, you said that you heard a noise and fired in the direction of it. You didn't say anything about seeing a deer."

"I was pretty shook up. They kept telling me what had happened. And I just listened. I didn't know what was going on. I figured—I'd just sign that piece of paper, and that would be that. I'd be free. I've never been through anything like this in my whole life."

"Okay. Take it easy. The first thing I'm going to do is arrange for bail. I'll have you out of here in a few hours."

After posting the bond, Tillman and his client picked up a copy of the local newspaper. Naturally, the shooting was the lead story. In the body of it, Sheriff Dean announced that there was too much careless shooting going on during the hunting season and that he was determined to make an example of the defendant in this case.

Tillman's thoughts coalesced, and he suddenly understood the county's eagerness to press the case. Schuyler was a tightly knit rural county with a fair degree of xenophobia. Tillman could even see some justification for this dislike of strangers. There were many cabins in Schuyler County that were owned by or rented to people who used them only during the hunting season. These men would come in from New York City, Buffalo, Rochester, or Syracuse sporting natty clothes and carrying expensive equipment. They would do a lot of partying and drinking and, from the local people's point of view, they were frivolous and undisciplined in their conduct of the hunt. They might tote fancy guns, but some of them knew very little about using them and seemed to see small difference between a pair of antlers and a pair of horns. Cattle were being shot along with the deer. Restitution might be made, but that was not the point. These outsiders behaved like an invading army. Something had to be done about them.

In the weeks following Roxbury's death, the local media hammered away at the story. There were photographs of Roxbury's widow and two small children at his funeral and an editorial screaming for action. Tillman despaired of being able to get a fair trial in Schuyler County. His only hope was for a change of venue. In February, he went before Judge Liston Coon and requested that the trial be moved to another county. Coon turned him down. Two weeks later, he was back before the judge to ask him to review the confession and how it was obtained. The judge politely threw him out of his court. Coon would hear the Ferry case on May 2 and, until then, he did not want to see the lawyer again.

Tillman persevered and, during the first week in March, he went to see the Schuyler County District Attorney, William Ellison. He told him that he agreed with a great deal of the local sentiment against outsiders. They did do damage. They disrupted the quality of rural life. He added: "If you want to make an example of somebody, Bob Ferry's the wrong man. He's hardly what you'd call a big city party boy. You ought to drop the case. Ferry's going to recant the confession. He's an experienced hunter and a good shot. If he says that he saw a deer, then he saw one."

The district attorney asked, "Did anybody else see it?"

"I'll bet Roxbury did."

Ellison smiled and commented that the dead man was hardly in a condition to give backup testimony. "A good try, Mike. But I'm going to court with this one. Local feeling is running too deep."

Tillman was stymied. He believed that Ferry was being railroaded, and it was up to him to come up with something that would get him off. But time was running out. It was already the middle of March.

Because of the way that the confession had been obtained, Tillman hoped to be able to persuade the jury not to place too much emphasis on it, but he needed more than that. Ellison could still build a strong case for criminal negligence: Ferry's admitted response to sound, the lateness of the hour, the hunter's zeal to bag something before the end of the season.

A case for the defense was building in his mind. What if he could prove that it was Roxbury who was negligent and not Ferry? The drive of a hunt is as precisely choreographed as a ballet. Every hunter is located in a position known to the other hunters. Any unannounced deviation is considered extremely bad form as well as dangerous, and it was Roxbury who had not been where he was supposed to be at the time that he was shot. Nor had he signaled to the others that he was changing positions.

By the end of the third week in April, Tillman had spoken privately to each member of the hunting party. Although they were local neighbors, they had not compared notes, but there was a general agreement that Roy Roxbury had violated a cardinal rule by leaving his assigned station. He was younger than the others and quick off the mark. Some

8

accused him of an arrogant disregard of their rights. Others thought that he was a greedy boy trying to get off the first shot before anybody else could spot the quarry. There was also a general agreement that the charge against Ferry was disproportionate to what actually had taken place.

Tillman was feeling better about Ferry's chances, but he was still far from secure. The only way to feel confident of a verdict of innocence was to prove irrefutably that his client had not only not intended to shoot Roxbury but actually had been aiming at the deer that he claimed to have spotted.

Aside from Ferry's confession, the only real piece of evidence in the case was the slug that had been removed from Roxbury's body. Tillman went back to the sheriff's office to have another look at it. It admittedly had come from Ferry's shotgun, but there was something peculiar about it. The lawyer hunted, and he knew that shotgun ammunition was composed of four basic parts: the outer shell, the powder charge, various cardboard and felt compression wads, and the actual metallic slug. After firing, Ferry ejected the cartridge case, which dropped immediately and was found at the spot where he claimed to have been standing. The wadding follows the slug for several inches before falling away, while the slug continues on alone for some distance to find its mark.

The peculiarity about the fatal bullet in this case was that the wadding had never fallen away. A shaving of the slug lead had reached up to hook around it, bonding the two together. Tillman reread the coroner's description of it in his autopsy report: "A metallic slug measuring $3/4$ by $1/2$ inch with a firmly attached piece of bloody wadding."

Tillman did not know what to make of it or if it had any bearing on the case. He decided that he had to consult a forensic scientist with unimpeachable qualifications in the field of firearms investigation. The problem was that such an outside expert usually commanded a fee and expenses far beyond anything that Ferry could afford to pay. Very little time remained before the trial. Tillman was personally acquainted with one man who he thought might be willing to take on the case despite the lack of money.

Herbert Leon MacDonell, known at times by the sobriquets of Bud, Mac, and Herb, fancying but not insisting upon the Scotch-Canadian pronunciation of his name, *Mac-do-nell,* made his living as a research chemist at Corning Glass Works. His avocation was criminalistics.

MacDonell was a Fellow of the American Academy of Forensic Sciences and a member of the American Chemical Society and the International Association for Identification. He had traveled across the country lecturing to these and related organizations. Since 1958, he had acted as consulting criminalist for law enforcement groups in Steuben as well as all of the neighboring counties, working on a range of cases from drunken driving to assault to burglary. Combining his professional expertise as a chemist with his insatiable curiosity in criminalistics, he had made the most significant advance in fingerprint technology in fifty years with his invention of the MAGNA Brush. This ingenious gadget, small enough to carry in a breast pocket, made it possible to develop fingerprints on an array of materials that previously had resisted processing. It was so easy to use that the fingerprint developed by a rookie cop using a MAGNA Brush was better than that developed by a technician who'd been working for thirty-five years with the conventional powder and feather duster. Naturally, this had not exactly endeared him to those who had made careers of using the old fingerprint technology.

At the time of the Ferry case, MacDonell believed that eight hours of sleep a night was a waste of five. When he was not working on a case, he was writing articles on firearms, photography, fingerprinting, and porous glass technology. He also taught a course in police science at Corning Community College that was open only to professional lawmen.

The one problem with all of this activity was that it was almost completely a labor of love. He needed his salary at Corning Glass Works to pay for his "habit" of criminalistics. He never accepted a fee for his work with the police departments. His articles were published in prestigious technical journals that paid as close to nothing as the traffic would allow. His MAGNA Brush was being pirated all over the world. Although professional criminalists regarded him as a "comer," his income tax return still listed him as a chemist.

On occasion, Lawyer Tillman and Chemist MacDonell had hoisted a few Scotches and discussed the state of the world and the idiosyncrasies of criminal justice. When Tillman called on the scientist on Wednesday, April 27, he already knew that MacDonell had the sort of off-center turn of mind and curiosity that would be aroused by the facts of the Ferry case. He outlined these and concluded: "Herb, I don't know if Ferry can pay you a fee. He's a poor man. In addition to everything else, his wife gave birth to a baby a month after the shooting, and he's got those expenses. If you're interested, the most I can promise is your expenses."

MacDonell did not remark that this was already an improvement on his other cases. He asked only, "Is he telling the truth?"

"I'll stake my reputation on it."

11

"Before we go any further, I've got to tell you that I'll call it the way I see it."

Tillman relaxed. He knew that he had his expert and one who would make a good impression on a conservative jury. No arrogant outsider, he was a local man who had always worked on the side of the law and had a reputation for scrupulous honesty, a man possessed of country good humor and shrewdness, one of their own. They would see a tall, bespectacled man in his late thirties, of medium build with neatly trimmed hair and mustache, dressed in a conservative suit, white shirt, and inconspicuous tie. He would remind them of one of the professional men from their own town, the type who went to lunch with the Rotary Club every Thursday noon, which, indeed, Mac-Donell did.

MacDonell said, "Let's get to work. What have you got for me?"

"Only the shot they dug out of Roy Roxbury."

"I suppose there's no doubt that it was fired by Ferry's gun?"

"None. But there's something very strange about it. When they removed it from the body, the wadding was still attached to the slug. Bonded. Do you know how that could've happened?"

"He must've been using a Brenneke shotgun slug. They're made in Germany, and the wadding is bonded to the base of the slug by a small screw. It's supposed to give them better flight characteristics."

"I've never heard of Brenneke. And I doubt if Bob Ferry has either. He was using Remington Peters ammunition."

"I'd better have a look at that slug."

"I kind of thought that you'd say that. I'll arrange it. When?"

"Tomorrow. I'll drive on up to Watkins Glen. There's nothing like spring in Schuyler County."

The next day, MacDonell skipped his lunch in order to leave the Corning Glass Works laboratory early. It was not much of a sacrifice. Except for Rotary, he considered lunch a waste of time and had not much greater feeling for breakfast. The road from Corning to Watkins Glen meandered for twenty miles along the pale gray-blue Post Creek. The mountains rose on all sides mottled with the pastel green of early spring. At that moment, he was as happy with the quality of his life as he had ever been. He loved the beauty of the countryside and he loved the challenge of this new case.

It did not take MacDonell long to reach the sheriff's office. Dean had given his consent for MacDonell to examine the slug that had killed Roxbury, and the moment he arrived he prepared to go to work. He opened an ordinary briefcase and took out a camera, a small balance with weights, a pair of tweezers, and a magnifying glass.

Dean brought him the badly deformed slug. "I don't know what you expect to find that our boys haven't found."

MacDonell examined it with the magnifying glass. He said slowly, "You never know, do you?"

Some of the sheriff's men watched him, wondering aloud who this research chemist from the Glass Works thought he was coming in and acting as if he knew more than the professionals. One of them muttered, "What is he—some kind of Sherlock goddam Holmes?"

Sheriff Dean was a highly skilled hunter who could justly claim to know all there was to know about shotguns and their ammunition. The wadding had traveled 155 feet through the woods, then had followed an irregular course of 2 feet through Roxbury's body, and it still had remained attached to the slug. Normally, the wadding should have separated from the slug within 18 to 36 inches from the place where the gun was fired.

MacDonell said, "You know, when I've dressed a deer that's been shot at this range, I've never found the wadding in the body—let alone, still attached to the slug. You've had much more experience at it. Have you?"

Dean admitted, "Well—no. I can't recall ever finding it."

"Don't you think that's interesting?" While Dean was pondering the question, MacDonell took his tweezers and removed what looked like a tiny particle of wood fiber that had become embedded in the slug. He carefully folded it in a clean sheet of paper from his pad.

The sheriff said, "I don't think it means a damned thing. You're wasting your time, MacDonell. It's an open-and-shut case."

"Could be. Could very well be just that." He went on weighing and measuring both the slug and the blood-soaked wadding and jotting down his findings. After photographing the evidence from all angles, he returned it with a smile.

"I'm finished now. Thank you. Oh. One last thing. Mind if I have a look at Ferry's shotgun? I'm told you impounded it."

The shotgun was a 16-gauge cylinder-bored Ithaca Deerslayer. MacDonell carefully went over the gun, particularly the barrel. He nodded and handed the weapon back to the sheriff. As Dean was showing him out, MacDonell asked, "Aside from the slug, did the autopsy turn up any significant traces of lead in Roxbury's body?"

"No. None. Why do you ask?"

"I thought not. Good day to you, Sheriff Dean. I'll be seeing you in court."

14

MacDonell paused outside the office to review the notes that he had just taken. From his knowledge of the specifications of Remington Peters cartridges, the weight and measurement of the slug removed from Roxbury's body indicated that some lead was missing. It was possible that the ammunition Ferry had used was defective, but it was extremely unlikely. He wondered about the origin of that minute particle of fiber that he had removed from the slug. He was only assuming that it was wood. Microscopic examination might prove that it was another substance.

He closed his notebook. The most significant piece of evidence remained the wadding and that strange hook of lead that bonded it to the slug so securely that it was still attached when removed from the dead man's body. An obstruction in the muzzle of the shotgun could have shaved the slug lead over to form the bond, but he just had examined Ferry's shotgun, and no such obstruction existed. Wadding was also known to enter a wound when a shot was fired at close range, but the undisputed fact was that Ferry was 155 feet away from Roxbury—hardly close range.

MacDonell's next priority was to investigate the scene of the shooting. He made a telephone call to Robert Ferry, who was still out on the bail that Mike Tillman had arranged. He said, "Ferry, I'd like you to come up here to Watkins Glen and take me out to where the accident happened. I want you to show me exactly where you were standing, where Roxbury was when he got hit, and where he was supposed to be."

Ferry grew agitated. "I went through enough at that place. Don't ask me to go back there. I won't. Not ever!"

MacDonell calmed the man and decided that he would go alone. Ferry gave him instructions on how to get there and described where he had stood, where Roxbury had fallen, and where Roxbury should have been.

Before hanging up, MacDonell asked, "Do you have any ammunition left from the lot you were using on that day?"

"Yeah. I haven't done any hunting since then, and I don't intend to."

"I can use it. I'll stop by on my way home and pick some up."

The drive to the woodlands was a short one. He pulled his car up on the shoulder of the road, where the hunters had been parked. He got out and climbed the slight rise to the area where he believed Ferry had been positioned. He studied the wooded vista and took some notes before climbing over a low wire fence and pacing over to where he thought Roxbury's body had been found. Then, he moved back through the woods and bellied under the wire fence to Roxbury's original position. He took some more notes and returned to his car. On the way home, he detoured to Ferry's house to pick up his unused Remington Peters shotgun ammunition. A theory was forming in his mind about what had actually happened when the fatal shot was fired, but it had to be tested before he could discuss it with Mike Tillman.

Herb MacDonell and his wife, Phyllis, shared a modest suburban home in Corning. It was located on Davis Road, which was named to honor the man who reputedly had invented the electric chair. After an early dinner, the dining-room table became his laboratory and the kitchen his darkroom. While the photographs taken that afternoon in the sheriff's office were drying, he set up his weighing and measuring instruments. Comparing the weights of slugs that he had brought from Ferry's unused ammunition with that of the evidence slug, he found that the latter was forty-five grains lighter in weight. The sheriff had admitted that no lead of any significance had been found in Roxbury's body and yet there was a measurable quantity of lead missing from the fatal slug. MacDonell was not surprised. The first part of his theory was proving valid.

Under his microscope he studied the particle of fiber he had removed from the death slug that afternoon. There was no doubt that it was wood. He looked up and smiled. Things were falling into place very nicely. Only one thing remained to be discovered. There was no information available about the flight characteristics of wadding in Remington Peters ammunition. He would have to conduct his own experiments to verify the pattern of the wadding under normal conditions, but that would have to wait until the following day.

The next morning, Phyllis MacDonell was awakened by the sound of gunfire. She was certain that it was her husband shooting in the yard and was unperturbed. When Herb was working on a case, anything was possible. They had been childhood sweethearts. No matter how eccentric some of his actions might seem to the rest of the world, there was no longer anything that he could do that would surprise her.

At the rear of house, MacDonell was firing off rounds of Remington Peters ammunition from a series of shotguns including the same model of Ithaca Deerslayer that Ferry had used. He looked for the wadding after each shot. It was exactly where he had expected it would be. In no case did the wadding become bonded to the slug, nor did it follow it for the entire flight. It consistently fell to the ground, having separated from the slug eighteen to thirty-six inches from the muzzle.

The puzzle was solved. The time had come to telephone Mike Tillman and make an appointment to reveal his findings.

17

The next morning, MacDonell, seated opposite Tillman in the lawyer's office, took out his notebook. "First of all, let's set the scene of the crime and add what I discovered when I went out there to look it over. Roxbury, Ferry, and a third man were positioned in the same area, with Ferry at the extreme left, Roxbury at the far right, and the third man between them. They were on a slight mound, the road ran behind them, and the woodland stretched before them. Because of the crest of the ground, the men could not see each other. Without telling the others, Roxbury apparently got down on his hands and knees, crawled under the wire fence, and snaked out into the shadowed woods. There was only one possible motivation for his actions. He saw—or thought he saw—a deer. Time was running out. And he was greedy to bag it before any of the others spotted it."

Tillman interjected, "Ferry also claims to have seen a deer in the same place."

"The crucial difference is that Ferry stayed put, and Roxbury stole toward it."

The lawyer looked dejected. "The question is, which of them was more negligent? The man who deserted his post or the man who fired at something without making absolutely sure of what it was? More important, will it matter to a jury? Or will a jury find that they were both negligent—only, my client has confessed to homicidal negligence?"

MacDonell smiled. "I think we ought to go over what else I have for you."

In 1966, Watkins Glen, the site of the trial, was a town of some three thousand people. Located at the southern tip of Seneca Lake, it played host to annual Grand Prix automobile races and to an occasional second-rate rock concert in the glen, but even these were resented by the locals because they brought in so many outsiders. As an attraction, the Ferry trial outclassed any daredevil driver or imitators of the Beatles. The townspeople were about to make a point about the dangers of letting strangers come among them.

The trial began on Tuesday morning, May 3. In his opening statement, William Ellison told the jury about Robert Ferry's signed confession to having shot at a noise. He said that this document constituted an admission of homicidal negligence and asked that they find the defendant guilty of manslaughter.

When Tillman's turn came to address the jury, he underscored the questionable means by which the alleged confession had been obtained. Less than an hour had passed since the tragic incident in which poor Ferry had accidentally shot Roy Roxbury, and the accused, who had never been in trouble before, was obviously in shock. He certainly had no reason to shoot Roxbury. He was aiming at a deer. Sheriff Dean had not even waited until he could get the dazed man to Watkins Glen. Instead, he had hauled him before the nearest justice of the peace. Ferry was never advised of his rights nor was he given the opportunity to seek counsel. Dean all but dictated the statement, and Ferry had signed it because his respect for the law was so great that he would never question even the most dubious actions of a law enforcement officer. Tillman ended his remarks by promising to prove that it was Roy Roxbury who was guilty of negligence and not Robert Ferry. It was a good opening address, but it was doubtful that anything Tillman said could counterbalance Ferry's damning confession, which he knew would later be admitted into evidence.

The prosecution opened its case. The coroner was called.

He testified that on the morning of December 8, 1965, he performed an autopsy on Roy Roxbury, who had been killed by a shotgun slug entering his throat and traveling through his chest and rib cage, and turning and coming to rest in his upper arm. He identified the fatal slug, which was marked as evidence. In cross-examination, Tillman got the coroner to admit that he never before had encountered a slug with the wadding bonded to it.

Sheriff Dean identified Ferry's Ithaca Deerslayer as the shotgun from which the slug in evidence had been fired. Under Ellison's questioning, he went on at great length about Ferry's statement, averring that it was a legal document and that no coercion had been used to obtain it.

When Ellison was finished with the witness, Tillman asked if Dean had informed Ferry of his right to counsel before making a statement or, for that matter, of any of his rights. The sheriff responded that there was no law that said that he had to give that information to a prisoner. (This was before the enactment of the Miranda rule, which made it compulsory.) Tillman asked, "Did Ferry ever mention having seen a deer?"

Dean admitted that Ferry had said something to that effect but, if he had wanted it in his statement, he should have put it in his statement. After all, the statement was being made by the accused and not the sheriff. Tillman was not getting very far. It was obvious that the jury agreed that it was Ferry's responsibility to state the facts for himself.

The defense did not begin to make any impression on the jury until after Ellison started calling the members of the hunting party as witnesses for the prosecution. In addition to Ferry, his stepson, and Roxbury, there had been eight other participants in the deer drive on the afternoon of December 7. They were called to establish the events leading up to the shooting and immediately following it.

When Tillman got them on cross-examination, his pre-trial questioning of the men paid off. He got each of them to state, with varying degrees of affirmation, that it was Roxbury who actually had been negligent and that Ferry was being unfairly prosecuted. The prosecutor was constantly on his feet objecting on the grounds of "personal opinion and not fact." Judge Coon, more often than not, sustained the objections and ordered the remarks stricken from the record. Nevertheless, Tillman had scored the point with the jury that some of their fellow townsmen felt Ferry was being treated unfairly.

The prosecution rested its case on Wednesday morning, May 4, with Ellison almost certain of winning. Tillman may have scored some points with the hunters, but the conclusive evidence remained the statement, Ferry's shotgun, and the slug that admittedly had been fired from it.

Herbert MacDonell was due to testify that afternoon. At lunch, he pushed the food around on his plate as he listened to Tillman and Betty Ferry. He could see the tears in the corners of her eyes as she expressed her pessimism about her husband's chances. This was MacDonell's first experience as a defense expert witness, and he believed in both the system and himself. He reached over and patted Mrs. Ferry's hand. "Don't you worry. By the time I get through giving my testimony, they're going to throw this case out."

Tillman was less hopeful, although he said nothing. There was not a defense attorney alive who had not seen instances of irrefutable evidence being totally ignored in the jury box. Beyond that, there was very little evidence upon which a good prosecutor could not cast some doubt.

MacDonell was sworn in and, after establishing his credentials as a forensic scientist and expert in the field of firearms, Tillman began a line of questioning relating to the specifics of the Ferry case. He asked MacDonell if he was familiar with the type of Remington Peters ammunition that Ferry had been using. The reply was in the affirmative, and the criminalist was then asked to describe a piece of this ammunition to the jury.

"The firing mechanism, called a primer, is at the base of the shell. Inside the shell, above the primer, is gunpowder, then wadding, and finally, the slug. After firing, the expended shell may be ejected and fall to the ground, which is admittedly what has happened in the case of Ferry. The wadding freely follows the slug and doesn't separate and fall away until within eighteen and thirty-six inches and usually travels freely not more than twenty-five feet after that."

"How can you be so certain of these measurements?"

"On the morning of April 30, 1966, in the backyard of my home, I test-fired a variety of shotguns, including the model of Ithaca Deerslayer that Ferry was using. In every instance, the separations took place within the distances I've just given." He smiled. "I happen to have all these weapons around the house because I'm a gun collector."

Tillman picked up the state's exhibit of the slug that had been removed from Roxbury's body. He asked if MacDonell had ever seen it before.

There was a stir in the courtroom when MacDonell lifted his regular glasses over his brow and held the slug within two inches of his eyes. He had been myopic since childhood and rather than bother to change to other glasses, he always held small objects at the distance from which he could comfortably see them without help.

"I examined and weighed this slug in the office of Sheriff Dean, on the afternoon of April twenty-eighth."

"Do you notice anything peculiar about it?"

"The first thing is that the wadding is still attached to it. This is only possible if Roxbury was hit within thirty-six inches of the gun that fired it."

Tillman turned to the jury. "And we know that Ferry was standing one hundred fifty-five feet from Roxbury when he fired." He turned back to his witness. "Is there any explanation that you can think of for this extraordinary bonding of slug and wadding?"

"It could happen if there was some sort of obstruction in the barrel or muzzle of Ferry's gun."

Tillman held up the state's exhibit of Ferry's shotgun. "Have you ever seen this before?"

"Yes. I examined it on the same afternoon in the sheriff's office. No such obstruction exists."

"Before we get to any other possibilities, you say that you weighed the slug. Why did you do that?"

"I wanted to find out if any lead was missing."

"How did you do that?"

"I obtained some ammunition from the same lot from Ferry. I removed the slugs and weighed them. I compared the weight of the unused slugs with the weight of the slug I'd examined in the sheriff's office. There was a significant difference. The slug that killed Roy Roxbury was missing fourteen percent of its lead."

Tillman faced the jury and read from the coroner's report. At the time of the autopsy, X rays were taken that revealed no significant traces of lead in Roxbury's body. He then asked if MacDonell had any other explanation for what had happened.

"If the slug had hit a cylindrical object within thirty-six inches of being fired and been deflected off it, this

23

collision might easily shave off fourteen percent of the lead while pushing up some of the remaining metal to form a hook around the wadding and make the bond."

"Mr. MacDonell, is there a name for the deflection of a bullet when it hits a cylindrical object?"

"Yes. It is called a ricochet."

"Were there any objects that could be described as cylindrical within thirty-six inches of the spot from which Robert Ferry fired his shot?"

"Yes. Trees."

"Do you have any evidence that tends to prove that the fatal slug did, indeed, ricochet off a tree?"

"On the afternoon that I examined the slug in the sheriff's office, I removed a tiny particle of fiber that had become attached to it. When I looked at it under a microscope, I discovered that it was a wood fiber."

Tillman picked up a photograph. "I offer in evidence this photograph taken by Mr. MacDonell showing a comparative microscopic view of the fiber from the slug and of a known wood fiber. I request permission that it be shown to the jury so that they may see that they are identical."

Judge Coon ordered the photograph marked in evidence and passed among the members of the jury. After they finished looking at it, Tillman returned to his witness. "Now, if you were to hit a tree, could the ricochet be controlled?"

"No, you cannot hit a tree, have the shot bounce off it, and then hit something or somebody intentionally."

"Then—if Mr. Ferry had been aiming in another direction entirely from where Roxbury was standing—say, at the deer he has always maintained that he saw and, in all probability, the same deer that impelled Roxbury to move negligently from his assigned position in order to bag it before the other hunters could get a shot at it—if Ferry, firing away from the dead man, accidentally had hit a tree, he would have had no control over where that shot went and certainly no responsibility for the death of Roy Roxbury?"

The prosecutor was on his feet shouting over the babble of the spectators. "Objection! Objection! The witness is being led."

Judge Coon said: "Objection overruled. The witness may answer."

MacDonell reiterated: "That is correct. Mr. Ferry no longer had any control over the flight of the slug. A ricochet cannot be controlled."

In cross-examination, the district attorney was not able to shake or cast doubt on any part of MacDonell's testimony. The defense rested its case. After the concluding arguments, the jury went out. It returned in less than two hours with a verdict of "not guilty."

Robert Ferry was a free man. Nobody ever questioned the justice of his acquittal. He returned to his family and his job and his respected position in the community. With time, the tragic incident almost completely faded from his mind. The only indelible difference that it made in his life was that, indeed, he never hunted again.

Aside from his expenses, the only fee that Herb Mac-Donell wanted was Ferry's shotgun. He wanted it to start an addition to his gun collection devoted to weapons that had figured prominently in his cases. Unfortunately, he asked too late. Ferry had wanted no part of the gun and had given it away the moment that the state returned it to him.

Fee or free, the case had been the most gratifying of MacDonell's sideline career as a criminalist. Until then, he had worked only with the police and prosecution, and he had enjoyed it. There was a satisfaction in seeing justice done and the guilty punished. But this was different. There was a headiness in helping to free an innocent man. It exhilarated him. Still, it was the evidence that excited him above all else. Uncovering it and making it speak to him was what he truly loved about the work, and he vowed that he would always let the evidence speak for itself, merely using him as the medium for its discovery and broadcast. He would never be one of those criminalists whom he classified as "quacks" who, for a fee, twisted and concealed evidence in order to make it do their unethical bidding. Evidence was beautiful and logical, leading, as it did, to objective truth.

It was precisely this almost rhapsodic dedication to evidence that made MacDonell slightly uneasy for almost two years after Robert Ferry had been cleared. It was not that he was dissatisfied with the verdict or his contribution to it, but the scientist in him longed for that last piece of indisputable evidence. In 1968, he finally overcame Ferry's refusal to return to the scene. The man said, "Even though I don't like it one little bit, I'll go out there with you. I guess it's the least I can do for you."

They climbed the low mound beside the wire fence. After a few moments of silence, Ferry said: "As near as I can remember, this is where I was standing."

MacDonell picked up a stick about the length of an Ithaca Deerslayer. "Would you show me where you were aiming with this?"

"Nope. I haven't hunted from that day to this, and I'm not even going to play-act hunting now."

He did agree to point out the direction in which MacDonell should aim and, after sighting, the sleuth climbed over the fence and entered the adjacent copse. He examined several of the trees. One of them had a dark scar unlike the broken branch markings that appeared like inverted Vs on all of the bark. It was at about Ferry's shoulder level and in the direction in which his gun had been pointed. MacDonell cut away that section of the bark and took it home to analyze in his laboratory.

The center contained some of the lead that had been missing from the fatal slug.

Had Ferry been willing to accompany him to the scene before the trial, this incontestable evidence would have been discovered and probably would have been sufficient to have the case dismissed before going to court. MacDonell speculated on what might have happened had the man been convicted and later been granted a second trial on the strength of this new evidence. How many judges and jurors might have suspected that it had been planted after the shooting? He wondered about the innocent men who may well have been convicted because, for one reason or another, nobody had bothered to look for the crucial evidence still there and waiting to be discovered. It was these speculations on the nature of justice and evidence that were slowly beginning to change the direction of Mac-Donell's life.

The conflict between the two careers of research chemist and criminalist was no new thing in MacDonell's life. It actually began to surface in the mid-1950s, when he was working toward his Master of Science degree in research chemistry at the University of Rhode Island. Dr. Harold Charles Harrison, his analytical chemistry professor, was giving the first course in criminalistics ever open to the law officers of Rhode Island, and he allowed MacDonell to sit in. Under Harrison's tutelage, he also began to work in the Rhode Island State Crime Laboratory. The analytical chemistry at school and the forensic science in the crime lab gave him the best of two worlds, and he was enjoying himself thoroughly, unaware of the fact that it was the start of a problem about choice of profession that would not be resolved for many years to come.

MacDonell was doing his master's thesis on the electrophoretic separation of some of the components of human blood. At about that time, Dr. Samuel Sheppard was on trial for the murder of his wife in a sensational but extremely circumstantial case. MacDonell was studying the characteristics of human blood, and it seemed to him that insufficient attention was being paid to the bloodstain evidence.

Sheppard was found guilty. His lawyer needed to find new evidence in order to petition for another trial. He engaged Dr. Paul Leland Kirk to examine the scene of the murder. Kirk was a nationally famous criminalist whose books on forensic science were dogma to young men who, like MacDonell, were fascinated by the new field of criminalistics.

On the basis of the bloodstain evidence, Kirk determined that the killer of Mrs. Sheppard was left-handed, which her husband was not, that a large blood spot on the bureau in the bedroom in which the murder took place was not left by either Dr. Sheppard or his wife, and that the convicted man's story was consistent with the evidence. The defense petitioned for a new trial but was turned down. The judiciary was not prepared to accept bloodstain evidence as the equal of fingerprints and firearms evidence. It was not until almost ten years later, in 1966, that Sheppard was given his new trial, and it was largely on the basis of the testimony of Dr. Kirk that he was acquitted.

Those same ten years had passed rewardingly for

MacDonell. He had received his degree; he enjoyed his work at the research laboratory at Corning Glass Works; his invention of the MAGNA Brush had revolutionized fingerprint technology; and the law enforcers were regularly calling on him for help. But for him, the most important thing was that his national reputation as a criminalist was expanding as a result of his speaking engagements and articles.

In January 1967, the National Institute of Law Enforcement sponsored its first conference on science and technology. MacDonell was scheduled to be one of the speakers, but the major address would be given by Dr. Paul Leland Kirk, whose subject was "Blood: A Neglected Criminalistics Research Area."

Kirk's speech at the conference would have been well attended under any circumstances but, when the subject of blood was posted only two months after his headline-making testimony at the second Sheppard trial, every seat was filled and the walls were ringed with standees. MacDonell was enthralled by the speaker, who once had been one of his distant gods and since had become one of his close friends. He would be able to quote from that speech for years after it was given. MacDonell went home determined to learn as much as possible about that neglected part of criminalistics: bloodstain evidence.

During the year after the Kirk speech, MacDonell devoted every spare minute that he could find to his study of blood as evidence. One of the first things that struck him was the lack of a vocabulary. Forensic scientists writing on the subject had no consistent terminology for the variety of bloodstains that could be found during the investigation of a case. Without a generally agreed-upon language, bloodstain evidence would never gain universal acceptance in courtrooms. Two experts might use different words to describe the same phenomenon, to the total confusion of a judge and jury.

MacDonell began to do some preliminary experiments on why blood fell, spattered, and flew in certain patterns. By the beginning of 1968, he had discerned some incontrovertible truths about the characteristics of blood in flight and about stain patterns. And he had begun to develop a sound technical vocabulary.

2

A SPATTERING
OF EVIDENCE

At 10:45 on Monday morning, April 15, 1968, Herbert MacDonell was in his office at Corning Glass Works when Dr. Joseph Spelman, the Philadelphia medical examiner, telephoned. Spelman was a highly respected forensic pathologist whom MacDonell had gotten to know at meetings of the American Academy of Forensic Sciences. He had recently been called in by the defense on a murder case. They wanted him to counter the prosecution, which was planning to use Dr. Milton Helpern as its expert. Helpern was the New York City medical examiner and probably the best-known forensic pathologist in the country, as well as the co-author of one of the most esteemed texts in the field, *Legal Medicine, Pathology, and Toxicology*.

Spelman said, "If you have the time, I'd like to bring you in as the criminalist."

MacDonell was very busy, and to take on a new case

he would have to rearrange his schedule. He said, "Before saying yes or no, I'd like to know a little about the case."

"Maybe you've read about it. The defendant's a veterinarian by the name of Gary Greene. He shot a young fellow, William Hodiak, over in Rockland County, New York. The case has had its share of headlines."

"Our newspapers aren't very interested in any homicides except our own."

"The evidence they need analyzed is firearms and bloodstain."

The word *bloodstain* hooked him, and he mentally began rescheduling his plans. He was longing to test the results of his recent research but had not dreamed that he would get the opportunity this quickly. He said, "I'm interested. Very interested."

"Good," Spelman responded. "I'll tell his lawyer to get in touch with you. His name is Lawrence Feitell. The firm's Edelbaum, Abrams, Feitell, and Edelbaum. New York City. Prestigious and very expensive."

MacDonell smiled at Spelman's unspoken message. At last, he was going to be paid for his work as a criminalist.

Just before 1:00 P.M., MacDonell received a call from Feitell, who gave him a general outline of the defense case. Greene claimed that shortly before the shooting, Hodiak had threatened him with violence during a heated telephone conversation. A few minutes later, Hodiak's Volkswagen microbus came to a screeching halt in front of Greene's house. Hodiak was actually trespassing. Greene grabbed a shotgun and went out to frighten him off. He had no intention of using the gun and did not even know that it was loaded.

Hodiak suddenly slammed the microbus door open, hitting the gun, which accidentally went off. The pellets broke the bus window and then hit Hodiak. The prosecution was maintaining that Greene had taken deliberate aim and fired through the window. He was being charged with premeditated murder.

The defense needed somebody to examine the weapon and the vehicle to verify Greene's story. Feitell concluded: "There's also blood on the outside of the microbus that's never been adequately explained. The prosecution says that it was spilled while Hodiak was being removed from the front seat. We think there's a lot more to it than that."

MacDonell thought that there was a lot more to the whole story. Spelman had mentioned that the case had made headlines. Nothing the lawyer had told him could be called a front-page story. But MacDonell was not impatient. Eventually, it would all be revealed. The details of most cases dropped one by one, like the oddly shaped pieces of a puzzle randomly scattered over a table. It was not until much later, after they were all down, that he could assemble them into the whole, often lurid picture.

Feitell wanted to know when they could get together. That always posed a problem to MacDonell. He could postpone a pending investigation, but he still had to finish a report on another case. There were never enough hours in the day to live his two lives. By 1968, he was spending more time at criminalistics than at his 37½-hour-a-week job at Corning, often managing no more than 3 hours of sleep a night.

He told Feitell that on the following Saturday morning, April 20, he would be giving a lecture in New Brunswick, New Jersey, at the Rutgers University College of Engineering School of Ceramics. "I'm on from nine-fifteen until twelve-fifteen. Perhaps we can get together after that."

"I wish you could make it sooner. The trial begins in a month."

Prosecutors or defense attorneys, they were alike in one respect. They were always rushing him, but often did not seek him out until it was almost too late. He said, "It would save time if you came up here to Corning."

"No, no. We'll meet in New Brunswick. I'll bring Greene along, and we'll talk over lunch."

Talk of wasting time, MacDonell thought, lunch again! Why did these fellows on expense accounts always insist upon lunch? It made such a hole right in the middle of the day. He said, "As we're in such a hurry, I'd like to bring in Andy Hart to help with the firearms investigation. He's got his own setup in Rensselaer, and he's one of the best."

Hart's qualifications as an expert were impeccable. For twenty years he had been the top firearms-identification officer in the New York State Police Crime Laboratory. He also had taught forensic ballistics at the New York State Police Academy. MacDonell suggested they collaborate on firearms, with MacDonell doing all the bloodstain investigation.

Feitell agreed to the arrangement. If a client could afford them, the more experts an attorney could bring in, the better. Fortunately, Greene could afford them.

There was nothing that MacDonell liked better than a large audience and, to his surprise and pleasure, Feitell and Gary Greene arrived in time to hear his entire three-hour lecture on porous glass chromatography and electrophoresis. The esoteric subject embraced the two halves of his professional life, as it related both to ink identification in criminal investigation and to the chemical properties of glass.

After the lecture, they repaired to a nearby restaurant, and Greene did most of the talking. He had the bantam macho of a jockey and a caustic sense of humor that he turned on himself as well as on others. As Greene related what had happened, MacDonell began to like him more and more, for the man insisted upon telling his own story in his own way rather than hiding behind his lawyer's interpretation of the facts.

Greene went back to the beginning of the series of events that were to lead to the death of William Hodiak on the night of May 12, 1967. It had all started five years earlier, in 1962, when Terry Lucca, a very attractive young woman, came to work as a general assistant in his animal hospital.

"Terry was thirty at the time and married. But she wasn't really working at it. She had two boys who were then eleven and seven. I was thirty-eight and separated from my wife. And the inevitable happened. We embarked upon a very satisfying relationship."

Greene also had two boys, younger than Terry's sons, only eight and four. He was going through a difficult divorce and had to be discreet, because his wife would have used any misstep to deprive him of the visitation rights for which he was fighting. At the start, Terry would stay over at his place only on those nights when his sons were not there.

She separated from her husband but did not get a divorce until 1966. Although quick-tempered, she was a warm and easygoing woman, and there was little of the bitterness in the breakup of her marriage that Greene had experienced in the disintegration of his. She developed the kind of free life-style that was characteristic of the times. Whenever one of her son's friends got into trouble with family or the law, he used her place as a crash pad. Greene observed that she was probably so good with the animals because she had a real feeling for strays.

At the beginning of 1966, William Hodiak, a nineteen-year-old drifter, wandered into Rockland County. He had come from California, where he had a criminal record for pushing drugs to high-school students. Although he had a preference for women, he was a muscular, sensual kid who took his sexual pleasures where he found them and was known not to be averse to the occasional one-night stand with a man. The drug culture was at its height, and it was not difficult for Hodiak to insinuate himself into its limited outpost in the small community. He met Terry's older son, who was only four years his junior. Hodiak eventually found his way to the older woman's door, where, with a combination of sexual come-on and youthful vulnerability, he easily won her sympathy. The story he told was the familiar litany of the flower child of the period. The Vietnam War was the pits. All he wanted was to do his thing and not hurt anybody, but the straight world would not give him a break. Because of one small slip, the establishment would not get off his back.

Terry tried to get Greene to help the boy and, in December 1966, he gave him a job cleaning out the kennels and horse barn and generally helping with whatever heavy work had to be done around the animal hospital. He was a good worker, and Greene had no reason to fire him even after the boy moved in with Terry the following month.

"If they were sleeping together, that was her business. Our thing had definitely begun to wane, and I was seeing other women. I only hoped that she wouldn't get hurt. She was doing all the giving. The kid was on the take. And he had a nasty streak."

For the next few months, Hodiak was living with Terry but she was still seeing Greene. It was a situation that could not have gone on much longer and, in March, there was a violent scene in which Hodiak accused Greene of

36

pushing him around because of his relationship with Terry. The boy went berserk and began to pull down shelves and tear apart one of the kennels. Greene, who had a black belt in karate, physically threw him off the premises. Despite the disparity in their sizes, the vet could take the kid in any physical contest.

"Terry left my employ that same month. But the kid had nothing to do with it. There was no anger between Terry and me. We went on seeing each other the same as before. We even had sex a couple of times. But we weren't lovers in any real sense of the word. We were intimate old friends. We liked each other. Terry always wanted everybody to like everybody else. She was a free spirit. Now, take the night of the accident—May twelfth—I won't forget that date. Early in the evening, Terry and Hodiak had dropped in for a drink with her ex-husband, Joe Lucca. It was like she was the head of some fraternal organization. Everybody who made love to her should at least like each other."

On that Friday night, Greene had custody of his two sons for the weekend. He had put them to bed before 10:00 and was feeling lonely. He wanted to be with somebody, to have a few laughs. Of all the people he knew, he wanted to see Terry Lucca. It would be a good opportunity to mend some fences, for there had been some altercations over Hodiak during the past few weeks. It was not jealousy, Greene maintained; he simply thought that the kid was bad news and had told her it was foolish for her to take in so many stray people. Terry later told the police that on two occasions, the conversation got so heavy that he had threatened to "punch Hodiak in the nose." Greene swore that he could not remember ever having used those words.

He called Terry at home at about 10:30 and asked her

to come around for a drink, but she refused, saying that she and Hodiak were busy painting her house. Things got heated between them and he hung up on her. She called back to tell him that nobody hung up on Terry Lucca. He hung up again. This went on for about ten calls during which he became increasingly vituperative about Hodiak and finally said, "If you'd rather spend your time with that no-good queer than with me, that's your problem."

The next call was from Hodiak, who told him that he was sick and tired of Greene cursing him out to Terry. Before hanging up, the boy shouted, "I'm coming right over there to beat the shit out of you."

Greene was not intimidated and replied: "Oh, just leave me alone."

He sat down to read his newspaper, certain that it was only an idle threat and that Hodiak would not appear. He had taken the boy before and could take him again, and the boy knew it. Unfortunately, he had reckoned without the challenge he had hurled at Hodiak's manhood.

A few minutes later, at shortly after 11:15, he heard a car come roaring down his driveway to his front door. It was Terry Lucca's Volkswagen microbus, and Hodiak was driving it. The last thing that Greene wanted was a scene. His sons were sleeping upstairs. Their mother always questioned them about everything that had happened during their weekends with him. She was still looking for a way to deprive him of his visitation rights. If she were to hear that he was brawling with some young man over his former mistress, there would be hell to pay. He took a shotgun from the coat closet near his front door. The only thing he wanted to do was to frighten Hodiak off the premises. The gun was kept there to shoot the weasels and raccoons that raided his chickens. He did not think that it was still loaded, because he had killed a weasel only the week before. He grabbed a shell and, without checking the weapon, he flung open the front door to confront the youth.

Greene was visibly troubled and paused in his narrative. "That's the part that gets me. I didn't intend to harm Hodiak. I swear I didn't. I just wanted to scare him. So, why did I take that shell?" He shook his head. "I don't know. I guess—I'll never know."

Greene seemed to be a man of some depth of feeling. What MacDonell could not understand was how, as a concerned father, he could have left a shotgun that might have been loaded in an unlocked closet with two small boys in the house. It was speculation that had no bearing on the facts or evidence, and so the criminalist said nothing.

Feitell was reassuring his client. "The only important point is that you didn't know the gun was loaded. And that you didn't load it. That you were holding a shell in your hand is of no consequence to what actually happened."

"To me, it is," Greene said. "I've got to live with it."

MacDonell asked, "At no point did you try to load it into the shotgun, is that right?"

"Never. They found it later. The same as if it had just come out of the ammo box."

MacDonell nodded. "Why don't you get on with the story?"

"I came down from the porch. The window of the bus was closed, so I came up real close to it, so he could hear me. I was holding the gun in front of me, pointed up— in the position they call in the army 'port arms.' At no time did I point it directly at him. I shouted for him to get out of there, to get that car off my land."

Hodiak began screaming, making "violent threats."

39

Suddenly, "he slammed his door open real fast." The gun hit the window, went off, and the barrel went through the window. Perhaps the barrel broke the window first and then went through before the shot. Things happened so fast that Greene had no way of telling.

"It seemed like the gun went off as it was hit by the door. I never intended to discharge the weapon, let alone shoot Hodiak."

The vehicle slowly backed off in a semicircle, and Greene did not think that Hodiak had been hurt until it struck a dog kennel some twenty-five yards away from the house. He dropped the shotgun and shell and raced over to the bus. Hodiak was lying with his head slumped over on the passenger side of the front seat.

Greene was certain that Hodiak was dead. As he rushed back to the house to notify the police, his thoughts were also on the well-being of his sons. There was bound to be an investigation. He might have to go to police head-quarters to make a statement. Somebody would have to be in the house to look after the boys. He telephoned the Orangeburg police station and reported the shooting to Officer Homer Wanamaker. He then called a good friend, an attorney named Jerry Tobias. Greene told him what had happened and asked him to bring over his wife to stay with the children. It might have been in the back of Greene's mind that it would be a good idea to have a lawyer present when he made his statement, but he swore that it was concern for his sons that was uppermost in his thoughts.

"And do you know, they're holding that call against me? The prosecution says that calling a lawyer in so early is a sure sign that I'm guilty."

MacDonell could see that from the prosecution's point of view the call would look bad for Greene, but he said nothing beyond asking Greene to continue with his story.

Greene had no sooner completed his call to Tobias when the phone rang. It was Terry Lucca. She said, "Bill's coming over to fight with you."

"Why didn't you give me some warning? He's already dead."

Terry Lucca and Greene lived less than two miles apart. After Hodiak drove off in a fury, she had waited a few minutes before attempting to call Greene. She then tried several times, but the line was busy. Once she learned of Hodiak's death, she was momentarily too dazed to do anything. Then she made one call to the police and another to her ex-husband, Joe, telling him what had happened and asking him to come by and drive her over to Greene's. But she was too nervous to wait, and started out on foot. On her way, she saw Officer Harry Uhlhorn's patrol car going in the same direction and flagged him down. Uhlhorn, who had received a radio call about the shooting, offered her a lift.

After Terry's phone call, Greene went back out to the yard. Two neighbor boys were walking toward him down the driveway. They had seen the microbus speeding in and then heard the shot. They wanted to know what had happened. He told them that the driver was dead and sent them away.

Greene returned to the bus for a closer investigation of the body and was startled to discover that Hodiak was still breathing. He raced back to the house to call for help. He reached Officer Wanamaker again, reported that Hodiak was still alive, and instructed him to get a neurosurgeon and an ambulance as quickly as possible. For some reason never satisfactorily explained, the police officer sent for neither ambulance nor doctor. Greene did not depend only on the police for help. He called his friend Dr. S. Sheldon Katz, a neurologic surgeon, and explained that there had been a terrible accident. He wanted Katz to get right over to Nyack Hospital and be prepared to treat the victim as soon as he arrived.

He then grabbed a blanket and some bandages and tore back to the bus. Sliding Hodiak's body out of the front seat, he covered him to keep him warm. He was giving mouth-to-mouth resuscitation and trying to stop the bleeding by applying pressure with a bandage when Uhlhorn's patrol car arrived. By this time Greene's face and chest were covered with Hodiak's blood. Terry Lucca leapt out of the car, shouting, "What are you doing to him? You killed him!"

Greene shook his head and looked at MacDonell.

"She was crazy. She kept screaming that I'd killed him, that I was always doing target practice with one of the guns from my collection, and that I'd killed him. I'd threatened to do him harm. I was a good shot. She yelled that I had to have killed him on purpose. She didn't know what she was saying and, after, she did say that she didn't mean any of it. By then, it was too late. Uhlhorn had been taking down her every word."

It seemed to Greene that the yard itself was going crazy—or was he? He did not know. People kept pouring in like voyeurs at a freak show. More police arrived; a man from the district attorney's office arrived; even Joe Lucca arrived. At least he helped by calming down his ex-wife. *But there was no ambulance.* The police kept distracting him from working on the kid by asking questions about the shooting and writing down everything he answered, and all he could really think was that the ambulance had not arrived.

He broke away and ran back to the house. He tried to divert Dr. Katz through his telephone service to tell him to come directly there to work on Hodiak instead of going to the hospital.

When he returned to the yard, he found that Jerry Tobias and his wife had arrived. Greene sent her upstairs to look after the children. "Make sure they don't come down here. I don't want them to see this."

The police went on pumping him with questions and still there was no ambulance in sight. Tobias took Greene aside. "As a lawyer, I'm advising you that you don't have to answer."

"Why shouldn't I? I've got nothing to hide."

Finally, a half-hour after Greene had asked the police to send for it, the ambulance did arrive. Dr. Katz had sent it, after arriving at the hospital and discovering that none had been dispatched.

For a moment, Greene was too overcome to go on with his story. He turned to MacDonell. "If it hadn't been for my calling Katz, there wouldn't even have been a surgeon at the hospital. Maybe that half-hour wouldn't have made any difference between Hodiak's life and death. But it might have. I don't understand the cops anymore. They seem more interested in the case than in the victim."

By 2:00 A.M. on May 13, Hodiak was dead, and Gary Greene was charged with homicide and ordered held without bail. Tobias was acting as if he was his lawyer, and the accused was too confused to assimilate what was happening to him. It was only after a few days in jail that Greene was able to understand he was as much a victim as Hodiak. The case even made the headlines in the *New York Daily News*. The district attorney, Robert Meehan, was basing his case on the alleged fact that the door was closed at the time the gun was fired. The bus was stopped and in reverse gear. The victim's foot had to be on the clutch. Meehan contended that Hodiak was obviously about to back out when Greene took careful aim and shot him. Greene swore that it had not happened that way. Hodiak, he insisted, had probably put the bus in reverse intending to make a quick getaway after knocking him down by slamming the door into him. The gun had gone off by accident.

While Greene was in jail, only his lawyer and some members of his family were allowed to see him. Jerry Tobias was acting as if he were the defense attorney. He was there every day.

Greene said: "Only he wasn't my lawyer. I never told him that he was my lawyer. But he was making sure that no other lawyer got to me. I sat in that jail for three weeks without him even trying to arrange bail. Finally, my family approached Maurice Edelbaum, a senior partner in the firm in which Feitell works. I was out on bail within an hour."

Feitell added, "Tobias claimed to have been collecting evidence. But he never let us see it."

Greene smiled grimly. "And now, we never will. Old Tobias was out doing the town one night in a local night-club. He got hit over the head in a brawl. He never recovered. Exit Jerry Tobias."

MacDonell asked, "Did he ever mention what kind of evidence he had?"

"He said that he'd collected some of the window glass from the ground outside the vehicle."

MacDonell thought that the glass from the ground would indeed have been interesting evidence, for it would have substantiated Greene's story that the door was opening and hit the gun. If the door had been closed, as the prosecution was charging, then after being shattered by the shot, most of the window glass would have been blown into the microbus.

There was one point that troubled the criminalist. He asked: "If you didn't think the gun was loaded and had no intention of using it, why did you release the safety catch?"

"I didn't. I didn't know that it wasn't on. I'm left-handed. The shotgun was made for a right-handed person. The safety was on that side. From my vantage point, there was no way that I could tell if it was on or off. Maybe I should have checked, but I didn't think of it. Maybe I should have checked to see if the gun was loaded. I didn't think of that either. You see, weasels are quicker than hell. You've got to be ready to shoot the minute one appears. I must have put the gun back that way, loaded and without the safety, after using it the week before. I didn't think of it. I didn't remember. I certainly wasn't thinking I'd ever use it on Hodiak. Everything happened so fast that night—"

There was an appealing mixture of bravado and sincerity in Greene's recitation of the facts. MacDonell wanted to believe him, but he suspended judgment until after the evidence yielded its story. He said, "I want you to know in advance that, if I discover you're lying, I'm reserving the right to go to the district attorney with my findings. If you won't accept those terms, I'm not your man."

He waited for a response and hoped that there would be no equivocation. Feitell and Andy Hart, who had come down for the meeting, were also watching the defendant.

Greene said, "I'm telling the truth. I haven't changed one thing since the night of the shooting. They offered a plea bargain. Manslaughter. Maybe a suspended sentence. Two or three years at the most. I turned them down. I've told it like it happened. I accept your terms."

His audience relaxed. Feitell said, "What we're most interested in your investigating are the blood spots on the outside of the microbus. The vehicle's been held in bond in a garage in Orangeburg. Nobody's touched it since the night of the accident. When can you come over?"

MacDonell took out his pocket calendar and silently cursed the job with Corning Glass Works. He could not get away on any weekday, and he was committed to something else on the following weekend. "I'm afraid I can't do it until two weeks from today. May fourth. I can come over on the evening of the third and be ready for you the first thing in the morning."

Feitell was visibly disappointed. "That cuts it very thin. We go to trial on the twentieth."

"Don't worry. That'll give me all the time I need."

"We have no choice. We'll make the arrangements for the morning of the fourth."

As they were shaking hands before parting, MacDonell studied Greene's eyes. The man unflinchingly returned his gaze. Their eyes would have remained locked until one or the other was forced to look away if Feitell had not started moving the party toward the door.

In the late afternoon of May 3, Phyllis MacDonell picked up her husband at Corning Glass Works, and they drove the more than two hundred miles to a motel in West Nyack, Rockland County. Here MacDonell met briefly with Andy Hart, who had made the hundred-mile journey down from Rensselaer. They agreed that the central point of their investigation would be to learn if the door of Mrs. Lucca's microbus was open, closed, or opening at the moment that Gary Greene's gun was fired. The only thing that they already knew for sure was that the window was closed, because it had been shattered by the shot.

The defense team assembled at Greene's animal hospital at 10:30 the next morning. MacDonell was introduced to the one stranger in the group. Greene said, "This is my friend Melvin Sokolsky. He's a great fashion photographer. His pictures are in all the magazines. He's going along to take whatever pictures you need."

MacDonell said that the man was free to come but that he preferred to do his own photography. It was one of the essential tools of his trade. A criminalist had to take his own pictures because only he knew what he was looking for and, from experience, how best to shoot it for his purposes.

He explained, "Photographing evidence isn't like shooting fashion. You've got to take it the way it is. No fancy angles or lighting. No prettifying or tricks. Just an exact reproduction of what you're looking for."

MacDonell, Hart, Feitell, and Sokolsky proceeded to the police station to pick up two detectives, who escorted them to the garage where the microbus was waiting. The vehicle had been kept for almost a year in the same condition in which it had been found on the night of the shooting. The first thing that MacDonell noticed was two bullet holes in the windshield on the passenger side. They had not been mentioned to him, and he wondered how they had got there. A closer inspection revealed that they were only decals, the kind of boyish prank that might have appealed to Hodiak or the Lucca boys. It was a grim and prescient joke.

The Volkswagen microbus was a squat two-door vehicle with a body that sat relatively high on its four wheels. On the driver's side, the door curved up and over the front left wheel. There were no fenders, and a bumper wrapped around the front of the vehicle and ran beneath the door, stopping at the point where the door quarter-circled up to accommodate the wheel. The window had three sections, each with separate panes of glass. The front one was a wind ventilator. The middle pane was a slider, which normally moved back over the third (stationary) pane.

The slider glass was missing as was the vertical strut that had held the third panel in place and had been protected on the outside by a glass overlap of the slider.

MacDonell and Hart requested that the missing strut be produced and reset in its original position. The strut was painted the same cream color as the bus and, at a point a little more than three inches down from its top, the metal and paint on the outer edge had been torn away by a great force striking it from outside the bus. It was apparent that the pellets had hit and shattered the middle glass panel and grazed the strut before hitting Hodiak.

Milton Helpern, the New York City medical examiner, had been called in to perform the autopsy. He had reported that the shot charge had entered Hodiak's left temple, tearing away part of the thin cranial shell to expose his brain. There was a large indentation on the left side of the bus's heater, which was located in the center of the ceiling. This was where the bulk of the shot had finally impacted after doing its deadly damage and passing out through the top of the victim's head.

What the defense wanted to establish was that the door was opening at the moment of the shot, possibly with the force of Hodiak's body pushing it out. Judging only by the dent in the strut and the point of impact at the edge of the ceiling heater, there was nothing to prove that the door was in motion. All that was indicated was the trajectory of the pellets from the time they hit the strut to their final destination in the side of the heater. It did nothing to help the defense's case and to prove that Greene was telling the truth.

MacDonell and Hart huddled for a whispered conference. Then Hart slid into the bus from the driver's side and closed the door after him. He held the end of a reeled tape at the impact point in the ceiling. MacDonell reached in through the broken pane and pulled it forward until it touched the dent in the strut. Asking Sokolsky to press the tape lightly against the dent with his finger, MacDonell continued to pull it out in a straight line, so that the tape ran down from the ceiling to touch the dent in the strut and on to the point where the tape reached the floor of the garage. The angle formed by the tape and the ground was the angle of trajectory, *if* the prosecution was right and the door had been closed.

MacDonell secured the tape measure to the ground with a piece of Scotch tape. He then rose and moved forward toward the bus door, his finger circling the tape, the tape running through his hands. It was as if he were holding Greene's shotgun with the barrel in his right hand and the index finger of his left hand on the trigger.

He said, "Let's imagine that the gun is in my hands, and I'm following the trajectory of the pellets that killed Hodiak. It could've been fired at any point along the way. But only if the door had remained shut."

MacDonell stopped short of the door and startled everybody in the garage by flinging it open. The tape snapped away from its mooring on the floor and hurtled through the air to shoot back into its case, which Hart was still pressing to the fatal bullet's impact point.

MacDonell calmly bent down to examine the frame and sill that had been concealed by the door when it was closed. He murmured, "Then again, Greene may have been telling the truth. The door was being pushed open, in which case the pellets did not travel that course at all."

MacDonell pored over the tiny reddish brown specks on the door frame and sill, some of which became visible only when he held a magnifying glass to them. He took extreme close-up photographs of them and then scraped some off the bus with a pocket knife, carefully folding the scrapings in a piece of paper. He repeated the process with some specks and larger spots that were on the bumper beneath as well as with a sunburst of spatter and spots that radiated from one focal point across the outside panel of the bus to the rear of the door.

He closed the door and went over the outside of it, nodding conclusively. He went around to the other side and carefully examined the passenger door. After finishing with the door, he got into the front seat and scanned both the windshield and floor on the driver's side, taking pictures all along the way. By the time MacDonell was finished, everybody in the garage was watching him. He said, "I now know that Dr. Gary Greene was telling the truth. Hodiak was opening the door when the shot that killed him was fired. And I can prove it."

They waited, the two police detectives perhaps more avidly than the others, but MacDonell would say no more in front of them.

What he did not explain was that the blood spatters he had discovered on the inside of the door frame as well as on the door sill could have gotten there only if the door was open. When the door was closed, those areas were covered by it and consequently could not be spattered. The prosecution was to maintain that the blood had come from the bleeding wound as Greene was removing Hodiak from the bus in his attempt to keep him alive. MacDonell knew that this was impossible. The spatters in question were as small and as fine as mist. They were high-velocity impact spatters and could have been made only by explosive impact as the shot entered Hodiak's body.

It was true that the blood that MacDonell found on the bumper might have gotten there with the door closed but only under one circumstance. Hodiak would have had to be leaning out of the window, perhaps in argument with

Greene, when the shot was fired. This was clearly not the case. The pellets broke the window before hitting Hodiak, thus, the window had to have been closed.

Furthermore, all of the spatters indicated that the head of the victim had to be in or just outside the frame of the opening door. This was underscored by the sunburst on the outside of the panel to the rear of the door. That bloody sunburst radiated back to one focal point, and that point was where the pellets had struck Hodiak's head, which was on a plane with or just outside the frame of the door. The blood could not have radiated to the outside panel from the head wound if he was shot while seated inside the bus, trying to back it away. To MacDonell, the sunburst proved Greene's case in three ways: (1) the door had to be open for the blood to appear on the outside of the bus; (2) the victim had to be leaning forward as if pushing open the door rather than well inside engaging the bus in reverse; and (3) that particular pattern of blood bursting forth from one point could be formed only if that point was where the bullet hit Hodiak.

The tape-measure experiment had actually substantiated the prosecution's case; the bullet could have been fired with the door closed. The characteristics of blood in flight were an unknown quantity to a jury. If the prosecutor's arguments were compelling enough, the jurors would not have sufficient knowledge to doubt his word that all of the blood on the outside of the bus got there when the body was being removed from the vehicle.

The defense had to prove that the door could have been opened wide enough for all of the blood on the bumper farthest from the wound to have been spilled at the moment of impact, with the charge hitting only the three established points of contact: dented strut, victim, and ceiling heater. To do this, MacDonell and Hart would

51

have to reenact the shot in flight with the door opening. To represent trajectory, they needed a stick of roughly the same diameter as the muzzle. It could be wider but it could not be narrower, or Hart, the firearms expert, would be open to challenge from the prosecution because the slimmer the object representing trajectory, the wider the door could open before the object came in contact with something other than the three known points. Although it was not the most scientific of objects, Hart found a mop handle in the garage that would fill the bill.

The strut dent and the heater impact point were again the constants, as they were in the tape-measure demonstration. With Hart's help, MacDonell placed one end of the mop handle in the heater indentation so that it also grazed the dent in the strut. The other end of the pole was held outside the bus in a manner that allowed it to move while keeping contact with the strut, as the door was being moved.

Hart slowly opened the door, and MacDonell watched the pole ride up without losing touch with its contact points. When the pole grazed the unmarked top of the door frame, MacDonell called: "Stop! That's it."

The door could have been opened to any distance up to that contact; it could not have been opened any wider at the instant that the gun was discharged or some of the pellets would have hit and marked the frame at the point where the pole touched it. MacDonell took photographs of the experiment while Hart measured the distance from the door frame to the outer edge of the door. The maximum opening was 9¼ inches.

MacDonell got into the car from the passenger side and slid over to the driver's seat. He used a flashlight to examine what he could see of the high-velocity spatters on the bumper through the door held at its maximum opening. He said, "There's something wrong."

The spatters on the bumper extended forward beyond the point where it was possible for them to have hit with the door opened to 9¼ inches. Not wishing to explain the problem in the presence of the police detectives, he merely asked Hart to remove the mop handle and continue to push open the door. When the door was opened to a certain point, MacDonell called, "Hold it right there. Now, measure the opening again."

At that point, the door was opened 25 inches. It had to have been opened that wide for the high-velocity blood spatters to have reached all of the places in which MacDonell had discovered them. If the gun had been fired when the door was opened no wider than 9¼ inches, while it had to have been opened a full 25 inches to accommodate the spatter from Hodiak's head to the bumper, he reasoned that there was only one plausible explanation. The door had to have been opening very rapidly and with great force when the shot was fired; it continued to open after Hodiak was hit. The speed and force jibed with Greene's account. MacDonell would have to find a way to prove this scientifically. If he failed, his entire testimony might well be discredited.

That afternoon, MacDonell met Robert Meehan for the first time. The defense team and the district attorney assembled in the grand jury room of the Rockland County courthouse in New City to examine the physical evidence and the photographs taken at the scene of the shooting. MacDonell found Meehan to be a self-confident man with an abrasive wit. Although his legal deportment was perfect, he did little to mask his disdain for his opponents. MacDonell recognized a formidable adversary.

There were two boxes containing pieces of glass from the shattered pane of the microbus. The box with less in it held the glass that had been collected from the ground outside the bus. There was considerably more glass in the other box; this had been collected from the interior. The glass was the prosecution's most compelling piece of physical evidence. It was the sort of exhibit that convinced a jury without the need of any complicated scientific explanation. All that Meehan needed to do was point out that most of the glass had fallen inside the bus, and therefore the door had to have been closed.

MacDonell had the more difficult job of justifying the two measurements for the door openings in a manner that both conformed to possible trajectory and confirmed his bloodstain evidence. Compounding the problem was the fact that he would have to use a vocabulary that was not familiar even to the majority of other criminalists, let alone to the members of a jury.

Back in Corning, MacDonell decided to see if he could throw some doubt on Meehan's physical evidence. His work in the research laboratory of Corning Glass Works made him much more knowledgeable than the police about the behavior of glass. He began to conduct experiments with German tempered glass of the same size and type as the microbus slider. In shattering it, he discovered that there should have been much more glass than he had seen in the grand jury room.

Greene's friend Jerry Tobias probably had been telling the truth when he said that he had collected some glass from the ground after the shooting, but nobody would ever know for certain. He was dead, and the glass had never turned up. MacDonell's experiments had proven that there was missing glass. But without Tobias's evidence, MacDonell could not testify whether it had fallen on the ground or inside the bus.

Tobias and the original glass would have been enough

to destroy Meehan's case. Without them, the bloodstain evidence was crucial. MacDonell had to learn if it was possible for Hodiak's blood to have spattered from his head to the bumper in the time it took for the door to open from $9\frac{1}{4}$ inches to 25 inches. The focal point of the sunburst of blood on the outside panel of the bus to the rear of the door had placed Hodiak's wound between 48 and 49 inches above the bumper. The problem was two-fold: MacDonell had to discover how long it had taken for the door to open those $15\frac{3}{4}$ inches and how long for the blood to drop the 48 to 49 inches to the bumper.

First deciding to tackle the time it took for the door to open, he borrowed a Volkswagen microbus of the same year as the one that Hodiak was driving and parked it in his garage. He then mounted a yardstick on two tripods so that it extended horizontally and parallel to the floor between them. He was improvising again. He did not yet have an extensively equipped laboratory in his home and often solved the problem of equipment in terms of what was at hand.

MacDonell moved his impromptu apparatus so that the yardstick was perpendicular to the driver's door and a fraction of an inch beyond its opening edge. In that way, as he opened the door, he could read the number of inches of the opening on the yardstick. He connected a micro-switch so that it activated a timer when the door reached $9\frac{1}{2}$ inches on the yardstick and turned it off at 25 inches.

MacDonell asked Terrance Igoe, a young associate from Corning Glass Works, to get behind the wheel. He said, "Greene claims that Hodiak slammed open the door quickly and with all of his strength. I want you to push it open normally and easily."

MacDonell was giving the prosecution the benefit of the doubt. The faster the door was opening, the more time blood had to reach the bumper, and Hodiak must have pushed much more swiftly than Igoe would.

The timer clicked on and off in the wink of an eye. It had taken 0.14 second for the door to open the given distance.

Igoe asked, "Are you going to bring this bus into court to demonstrate the experiment?"

MacDonell replied, "Of course not."

"Then how are you going to prove to the jury that the figure is accurate?"

"They'll have to take my word for that."

"Why should they?"

If anything was likely to raise MacDonell's temperature, it was the suggestion that anybody would not take his word on any scientific subject. He roared, "Because I'm the expert!"

They looked at each other and began to laugh. MacDonell thought for a moment and then said, "We'll prove it to them visually. I'll take a picture of it."

"How will a picture of a door opening prove how fast it's opening?"

"Watch and you'll learn." MacDonell mounted a high-intensity lamp on the edge of the microbus door. He set up his camera with the shutter operating at 0.10 second. He said, "Now, open the door the same way that you did before."

When Igoe opened the door, MacDonell snapped his picture. When the photograph was developed, everything in it was in sharp focus except the lighted bulb, which had become a streak. The distance that the streak measured on the mounted yardstick was the distance that the door had opened in the 0.10 second that the film was exposed. By using this figure as his base, he was able to calculate how long it would take for the door to open from 9¼ inches to 25 inches. It came to the same 0.14 second.

MacDonell smiled. "You see? I now have a photograph of distance in time."

Igoe said, "I just hope it doesn't confuse them. Some of those jurors may have flunked mathematics."

"I'll make some charts that will demonstrate the mathematical calculations involved."

Igoe did not say another word. He knew MacDonell well enough to realize that it would be useless. The man refused to believe that anybody could be impervious to the beauty of an equation.

MacDonell had the time it took for the door to open. Next, he had to learn the time it took for the blood to fall. He thought this would be a simple matter of looking the information up in Kirk or Helpern or one of the other standard reference books on criminalistics or hematology. To his amazement, it was not in the literature. Nobody had ever bothered to time the falling of a drop of blood. He recalled what Kirk had said in Chicago about the neglect of bloodstain evidence and said to himself, "If I only had the money to afford the time to do all the research."

He would have to time the blood himself. Obtaining fresh blood for the experiment posed no problem. It always came as something of a shock to a first-time visitor when, told to help himself to a beer in the refrigerator, he found plastic bags filled with human blood amid the litter of cans and bottles of his host's favorite brews and jars of his hostess's homemade pickles. MacDonell always stored blood for the research he was doing with it.

That night, after Corning Glass Works was officially closed, MacDonell met with Igoe and a group of other associates in the lobby of the administration building. The stairwell offered the only space in town where blood could be dropped freely almost 100 feet to the ground below.

This could be repeated every few feet as one slowly descended the steps.

Large sheets of white cardboard were first spread on the ground floor. Blood was then dropped from the very top of the stairs, and the time it took to reach the ground was meticulously clocked. This was done again every five feet all the way down. A draft at the third-floor landing blew some blood to the outer side of the stairs. To this day, the janitor has not been able to figure out how it got there.

When MacDonell finished his calculations, he knew that a normal 0.05 ml. drop of blood fell at the speed of 25.1 feet per second. Breaking this down in terms of the distance from Hodiak's head to the bumper of the microbus, the time it took for the blood to strike the bumper after the shot was 0.17 second. He already knew that it took 0.14 second for the door to open the necessary 15¾ inches. That meant that the blood reached the bumper with 0.03 second to spare, which is a very comfortable margin when working with such small fractions of time.

MacDonell had scientifically proven the veracity of Greene's story. He felt certain that the verdict had to be not guilty.

The trial opened on May 20, 1968, in New City, Rockland County. Maurice Edelbaum was handling the defense against Robert Meehan for the prosecution. Edelbaum, a senior partner in Lawrence Feitell's firm, was one of the most skilled trial attorneys in the country.

During the jury selection, Meehan used his objections wisely, and the panel was composed of jurors of modest means and education. It had been little more than a year since William Hodiak was shot and for most of that time Gary Greene had been free on bail. In his opening remarks to this very middle-class jury, the prosecutor kept underscoring the advantages of Greene's wealth. Not only did it enable him to post bond and pay handsome fees for his "experts," Meehan said, but "a person who could afford to hire Mr. Edelbaum would be far better off than a person who had a young lawyer, and that would not be fair. That would not serve the interests of justice."

The trial had to be recessed on June 6 because of the assassination of Senator Robert F. Kennedy. Edelbaum later claimed that this tragedy placed too heavy an emotional burden on a jury serving on a case involving the use of firearms. And Meehan lost little time in drawing parallels between the shootings of the two Kennedy brothers and the death of Hodiak. "William Hodiak was not a president or a leader," but he, too, had been slain by a man carrying a gun. Edelbaum tried to counter this by reminding the jury that Hodiak had not only threatened Greene but was also a trespasser on his property, and that any man had the right to bear arms in defense of his life and property.

None of this should have had any bearing on the basic question: Had Greene deliberately murdered Hodiak, or had the gun gone off accidentally? Nevertheless, it would take an adroit defense to overcome the jury's awareness that Greene was a wealthy and educated man who brandished a loaded shotgun at a time when national heroes were being slaughtered.

The brilliant forensic pathologist, Milton Helpern, had performed the autopsy on Hodiak and was called by the prosecution to testify on the condition of the body. In his cross-examination, Edelbaum interpolated some of the terms that he knew MacDonell would be using in his testimony. He asked: "In the type of wound inflicted and received by this individual [Hodiak], would you say that the blood would spatter?"

Helpern replied, "It certainly would. Yes."

"And do you call these 'high-velocity spatters'? Have you heard that expression?"

"You can have high-velocity spatter, and you can have low-velocity spatter, and there is considerable variation."

Edelbaum explained that he was speaking of this specific gunshot wound. "Wouldn't blood spatter in a high velocity?"

"It certainly would. Yes."

Edelbaum introduced Helpern's book, *Legal Medicine, Pathology, and Toxicology,* as a piece of evidence for the defense. He made reference to a specific photograph that Helpern had taken of a drop of blood. The picture had been made when a man shot himself, and the blood spattered back from his temple and hit his hand. Edelbaum asked: "It was what you call high-speed velocity . . . caused by the impact of a gunshot. Would, wouldn't that be—"

Helpern interrupted. He was not going to be pinned down. "I would say that it simply represents a drop of blood in motion. . . . It doesn't have to be high speed, but it could have been high-speed velocity. It is a splash, you see."

Edelbaum then got Helpern to agree that the microbus door could have been open when the shot was fired.

In redirect examination, Meehan tried to get Helpern to admit that the stains on the bumper and on the outside panel to the rear of the door had been made when the body was removed. Helpern would not commit himself.

MacDonell was the last witness for the defense, testifying after both Andrew Hart and Gary Greene. Edelbaum was convinced that this expert's testimony would clinch the case for the defense. MacDonell came equipped with slides illustrating his points to the jury. It was a very persuasive show, demonstrating how he had proven that the door was opening, and exactly what high-velocity blood spatters were. When MacDonell was finished, Meehan apparently felt unprepared to challenge this convincing performance in cross-examination. He asked for a recess for lunch.

Edelbaum objected. "I just had breakfast an hour ago."

The judge was also surprised by the request. "It's twenty-five to twelve. You want to break?"

Meehan finally admitted that he was not ready to cross-examine MacDonell. He needed some time. The judge granted the recess.

When the court reconvened, Meehan returned armed for battle by his experts. His first attack was on Mac-Donell's credentials as an expert. He had worked on relatively few homicide cases and never testified solely on bloodstain evidence.

During his direct examination, MacDonell had said that he had used Helpern's book in his course at Corning Community College. Meehan defied him to examine the volume and to find the terms "high velocity," "medium velocity," and "low velocity." Although Helpern had used the terms in his testimony, they did not appear in his book.

MacDonell explained that it was a question of nomenclature. There were many ways to describe the same phenomena. The science of bloodstain evidence was so new that a vocabulary had yet to be agreed upon by all the experts.

Meehan next questioned MacDonell's testimony on the nature of glass and on ballistics, but the witness was on solid ground and could not be shaken. Unfortunately, his testimony became so technical that many of the points being made were missed by the laypeople on the jury.

Meehan had one last trap for the witness. He showed MacDonell a photograph of blood droplets and asked him to describe how they had been made. The picture was still damp from having been so recently developed, and MacDonell observed, "You must have hurried."

The photograph had been taken during the recess. One of Meehan's men had cut his finger and flicked some blood on a white board propped against a file cabinet. MacDonell not only identified what the photograph was but told how it had been set up and how the bloodstains differed from those on the microbus bumper. He described the properties of blood with such precision, and at such great length, that Meehan cried, "He wants to go on forever."

MacDonell shrugged. "It's a very exact science."

By the time the case went to the jury, all that Meehan had been able to establish was that MacDonell's actual experience in homicide cases was meager compared with that of the prosecution experts, and that the latter did not believe that the interpretation of bloodstain evidence was an exact enough element of forensic science to be considered comparable to fingerprints and firearms. When this was added to the jury's lack of comprehension of MacDonell's often esoteric explanations, however, it was enough to make them doubt the validity of his findings.

Meehan did not get the murder conviction that he had asked for. Greene was found guilty of manslaughter. He was later sentenced to three and a half to ten years. By the time the case went through several appeals, all denied, Greene had spent well over $100,000 on his defense and ultimately he received the same punishment that he would have been given had he consented to the plea bargain that he had been offered a full year before he was put on trial.

MacDonell was stunned by the verdict. He knew that he had proven that Gary Greene was innocent but, somehow, the jury had not been convinced. He had failed. In the letters he began to exchange with Greene, it was as often the case that Greene was reassuring him as it was that he was comforting Greene.

After all of Greene's appeals were exhausted, Mac-Donell took it upon himself to write to the governor of New York State, Nelson A. Rockefeller:

In May of 1967 an accident occurred in Rockland County that took the life of one William Hodiak. Approximately one year later Dr. Gary Greene was convicted of manslaughter. It is quite possible that to a large extent I am responsible for the verdict in this case.

In any event I had pure scientific fact at my disposal that should have led any true jury to but one conclusion: Mr. Hodiak was responsible for his own death. Dr. Greene was Hodiak's instrument of death, not his assassin!

It is the responsibility of the expert witness to explain technical matters in lay terminology in such a manner that they in the jury understand and believe his testimony. I have to accept the fact that I may have failed to discharge this duty satisfactorily and, therefore, respectfully request that you carefully review Dr. Greene's case as you, and you alone, can correct what I believe has been a gross miscarriage of justice.

It is significant that my students of criminalistics . . . essentially all law enforcement officers, also agree that Dr. Greene should not have been found guilty of either murder or manslaughter.

I am well aware of the current status of Dr. Greene's case. He will go to prison this month. He has exhausted every legal avenue that originally was open to him. All were explored from the standpoint of law and procedure. Unfortunately, there seems to be no mechanism by which an erroneous verdict may be corrected. If the jury erred it appears irreversible. For this reason I respectfully request you to review this case in depth. Thereafter, if you agree that justice will not best be served by his incarceration, I pray that you will exercise executive clemency and grant Dr. Greene a full pardon.

MacDonell could not get the Greene case out of his mind. If bloodstain evidence had been fully understood and accepted in the courts, Greene would have been a free man. MacDonell became obsessed by the desire to persuade as many law officers and forensic scientists as he could reach of the need for this acceptance. Not only did he use the case in classes to illustrate the potential effectiveness of this type of evidence, but he presented it at most of the scientific meetings at which he spoke.

On June 5, 1969, MacDonell addressed the International Meeting for Forensic Scientists, in Toronto. He not only presented the Greene case, but he also described the bloodstain research that he had done before and after it. Dr. Kirk was in the audience and, after the talk was over, he told MacDonell, "You've done more bloodstain research on the Greene case than I did on the Sheppard case. You ought to get the government to sponsor more of it. They're running what they call 'Project Acorn' grants."

"Acorn?"

Kirk smiled. "You know—from little acorns mighty oaks grow."

MacDonell observed, "I guess the government has as great a constitutional right to whimsy as the rest of us."

The grants, for $5,000, were to be used to study some

aspect of criminal justice. They were administered by the National Institute of Law Enforcement and Criminal Justice under the Law Enforcement Assistance Administration. Kirk said, "I'm sure you'll get one. I'm on the advisory board."

As soon as he got home, MacDonell applied for and received his grant. The work to be done was so exhaustive and his time so limited that he knew that he could not do it alone. He asked another chemist at Corning, Lorraine Fiske Bialousz, to be his research associate on the project.

By the time they were finished, MacDonell believed that they had examined every aspect of the behavior of blood that might relate to the gathering of evidence at the scene of a violent accident, injury, or homicide. The result of this intensive research was their book, *Flight Characteristics and Stain Patterns of Human Blood*. This slim volume, first published in 1971 by the U.S. Department of Justice, Law Enforcement Assistance Administration, was in print for twelve years and is considered by many forensic scientists to be the "bible" of bloodstain evidence.

MacDonell had achieved what he set out to do. There finally existed a standard vocabulary and reference work on bloodstain evidence that elevated it to the status of a legal peer of fingerprint and firearms evidence. He hoped that there need never again be the kind of miscarriage of justice that had convicted Gary Greene.

3

THE BLACK PANTHER SHOOT-OUT/IN

At 4:45 on the morning of December 4, 1969, a group of Chicago policemen attached to the office of the Cook County State's Attorney, Edward V. Hanrahan, attempted to execute a routine search warrant at 2337 West Monroe Street in the black ghetto of Chicago. Two days earlier, an unidentified informer had told them that a militant organization, the Black Panther Party, was storing a large and illegal cache of weapons and ammunition at that address.

The newspaper and television accounts described what ensued as a "predawn shoot-out" between the Panthers and the police. In the course of the action, two policemen were superficially wounded; four teenage Panthers were the victims of multiple gunshot wounds, with two of them listed in "serious condition." Two Panthers, Fred Hampton, aged twenty-one, and Mark Clark, aged twenty-two, were killed. Hampton was the chairman of the Illinois branch of the party and one of the most effective leaders in the entire organization. Three other Panthers were taken prisoner. One of them, eighteen-year-old Deborah Johnson, was Hampton's girl. She was in the eighth month of pregnancy. The wounded and the prisoners were charged with a variety of offenses including attempted murder.

Police sergeant Daniel Groth was the leader of the fifteen-man raiding party. As he told it to the press, seven of his men surrounded the building, with two in the rear. These two, Officers John Ciszewski and Edward Carmody, were injured in the action: Ciszewski was nicked in the leg by a flying bullet, and Carmody cut himself on broken glass while attempting to enter through a back window. A second police group, wearing helmets and carrying rifles, was stationed on nearby rooftops; while a third set up a cordon around the block.

Groth, backed up by four of his men, entered the front door of the building, which led into a small foyer with two locked doors. One led to the upstairs apartment, and the other was the entrance to the ground-floor Panther apartment. When Groth knocked on Hampton's door, somebody inside shouted, "Who's there?" He identified himself as a police officer with a search warrant.

Groth told the press that this exchange was repeated several times before he ordered one of his men to kick open the door. They then found themselves in the entrance hall to the apartment, faced by another closed but not bolted door. As they pushed it open, a shot tore through it coming from the room beyond. Groth and his men pushed into the room, shining their flashlights through the darkness. The first thing they saw was a young woman (later identified as Brenda Harris) lying on a bed in the far corner, pointing a shotgun at them. She opened fire, and they were forced to shoot back in self-defense. Then bullets started flying from all over the apartment.

At several points during the battle, Groth said, he had

ordered a cease-fire and asked the occupants to surrender peaceably, but a voice from somewhere in the darkened flat had cried, "Shoot it out!"

Groth said, "There must have been six or seven of them firing. The firing must have gone for ten or twelve minutes. If two hundred shots were exchanged, that was nothing."

After the Panthers finally surrendered, the police found the dead: Mark Clark near the front door with a gun in his hand, and Fred Hampton in his bed with two bullet holes in his head and one in his left shoulder, a cocked .45 automatic on the floor near his right hand and a shotgun at his left side.

Groth told the press that the police had found large quantities of arms and ammunition. The wounded Officer Ciszewski added, "The whole front room was covered with shotguns and handguns."

Groth's account of the action was taken up by his superior, State's Attorney Edward Hanrahan. In a press conference held several hours after the raid, Hanrahan charged that the Panthers had made a vicious and totally unprovoked attack on police officers attempting to execute a legitimate search warrant. When one of the reporters brought up the question of race, the state's attorney responded that he could not understand how anybody could see racial overtones in the killing of Fred Hampton when five members of the raiding party were black, including Groth's second in command, Officer James "Gloves" Davis, who had admitted to firing the shot that had killed Mark Clark. None of the officers would take credit for the shooting of Hampton. Hanrahan went on to praise his officers for having exhibited "good judgment, considerable restraint, and professional discipline."

He also outlined some of the details leading up to the raid. On December 2, an unidentified informer within the

Panther organization had telephoned the state's attorney's office and reported that a small arsenal of illegal weapons was being stored in the West Monroe Street apartment. Instead of relaying the information to the regular police or the FBI, with whom his office cooperated on matters concerning the Panthers, Hanrahan had decided to stage the raid himself, using his Special Prosecution Unit (SPU), a hand-picked group of policemen and detectives who were assigned to his office.

The informer had suggested that 8:00 P.M. on the evening of December 4 would be a good time for the raid, because most of the Panthers would be away from the apartment attending a political-education class. When Sergeant Groth was put in charge of the operation, he decided to disregard this advice; an early morning hour would help to avoid incident and provide maximum security for his men and for innocent neighbors.

When one of the journalists pointed out that cordoning off the street and stationing armed men on rooftops seemed excessive precautions for the execution of a routine action, Hanrahan replied that there were very good reasons for them. He reminded the reporters that, during that same year, two policemen and two Panthers had been killed in Chicago in armed confrontation and that a score of others on both sides had been wounded.

These were the official accounts of the incident, and the first reports released to the press and public. Apart from minor alterations, Hanrahan and his men never deviated from this story. The attorney, a big, rugged, handsome Irishman, was one of Mayor Daley's protégés and had visions of following him into the office in City Hall. There was no better way of becoming Daley's designated heir than by being the man who had personally smashed the notorious Black Panther Party.

In the four years since its inception, this numerically

small band of militants had inspired a disproportionate amount of loathing in the leaders of the American establishment. Vice President Spiro Agnew had called them "a completely irresponsible anarchistic group of criminals."

The director of the FBI, J. Edgar Hoover, had said: "The Black Panther Party without question represents the greatest threat to the internal security of this country among violence-prone black extremist groups."

The assistant attorney general of the United States, Jerris Leonard, had summed up the official attitude in what might be regarded as the official prose of the Nixon administration: "The Black Panthers are nothing but hoodlums, and we've got to get them!"

Some of the basic tenets of the party could legitimately inspire this vituperation. The organization had been born of the disillusionment of black youth with the progress of the civil rights movement. The majority of its members were still in their early twenties or late teens. They had been children when the Supreme Court decision outlawing segregation in the public schools began a decade of promise.

By the mid-1960s, it was clear that progress was too slow for some. The time was right for a movement like the Panthers, and the party was founded on the West Coast in 1965. Its leaders did not ask for their civil rights, they demanded them with the proclamation that Martin Luther King's passive, nonviolent resistance was a thing of the past. They were self-professed Maoist revolutionaries, prophets of self-defense who openly carried weapons and promised to shoot back whenever the police opened fire. In the words of one black leader of the period, H. Rap Brown: "Violence is as American as cherry pie."

The Panther party attracted many of the best and brightest black youth. Fred Hampton was an example. In the Chicago suburb of Maywood in which he was raised, he had been an excellent student and star athlete. After high school, his intention was to study law. He became the president of the Youth Council of the local branch of the National Association for the Advancement of Colored People (NAACP), but he soon grew impatient with its gradualist programs. In 1967, Hampton moved to the black ghetto of Chicago. Exchanging his dream of a legal career for the activist role of a militant, he resigned from the NAACP to join the Panthers and he rapidly rose to the chairmanship of the Illinois branch. Six months before his death, Hampton wrote: "It is perfectly clear that the so-called law enforcement officials will stop at nothing including genocide."

The deaths of Hampton and Clark did not weigh heavily on the consciences of those who read the first accounts of the shoot-out in their newspapers. The public generally believed its elected officials and police. The Panthers were dedicated to the violent overthrow of the government. They were armed and they were dangerous. If several of their number had been killed and wounded, it was because of their provocative response to lawmen who were merely doing their duty. The majority believed that even decent acts of the Panthers, such as their free breakfast programs for needy ghetto children, were somehow contributing to the upheavals in the nation's black communities.

An extraordinary thing happened at 2337 West Monroe Street within three hours of the raid on December 4. After removing the Panther weapons and ammunition, the dead, the wounded, and their uninjured prisoners, after only the most cursory examination by the police crime laboratory mobile unit, the authorities simply abandoned the premises. No guards were left at the doors, no police or coroner's seal was put in place. The only thing that they left behind was the bulk of the evidence.

By 7:30 that morning, a group of attorneys for the Panthers, led by Francis "Skip" Andrew, had taken possession of the apartment. Word of the raid was sent out to the many lawyers engaged in defending the civil rights of party members in all of the cities in which there were chapters. That those rights might need defending could be assumed from a series of events, similar to the raid, that had preceded it. When Fred Hampton and Mark Clark were shot that morning, they were the twenty-seventh and twenty-eighth Black Panthers killed in clashes with the police since January 1968.

The lawyers working for the group, often without fee, included some of the most distinguished constitutional experts in the country. The New York City attorney Gerald B. Lefcourt was among them. Skip Andrew called him about a matter that needed immediate attention. They had to find an expert to examine and analyze the plethora of evidence that so unexpectedly had fallen into their hands. Hanrahan was calling the incident a shoot-out but, from what the prisoners had told him earlier at their arraignment, Andrew was certain that an objective analysis of the things in the apartment would prove that it was a shoot-*in*. He said, "This place looks like a firing range. And I'm telling you—the police did all the shooting."

Lefcourt knew that the expert would have to have verifiable criminalistic credentials with a particular knowledge of firearms evidence. Almost as important, he would have to be something of a political neutral. Anybody to the right might be tempted or persuaded to prove the official version, and anybody to the left would be suspect should he be able to establish that Hanrahan and his men were giving false testimony. As much as they might enjoy the luxury of somebody who was sympathetic to the Panther cause, they could not afford it.

Andrew had told Lefcourt that he could not be certain when the police would find a pretext for repossessing the apartment. Time was short, and the specific qualifications were not easy to fill. Most of the best-known criminalists and forensic scientists were working for some branch of the city, state, or federal government. Their jobs could make them vulnerable to official influence; beyond that, most of them were already engaged in other Panther cases and on the side of the prosecution. Lefcourt was not alone in his search. It was being duplicated by other attorneys in Chicago, Los Angeles, Berkeley, and Detroit.

The Panthers had sent out the word. "Man, find us a cat who's above suspicion. And on the double."

It was a cool, crisp Saturday morning. Some remnants of snow clung to the sides of Davis Road, a pretty, mean-dering rural road that Herb and Phyllis MacDonell were leisurely climbing from the spot on which their present house stood to a location farther up on which they thought they would one day build a new home. Phyllis, who was a crossword puzzle enthusiast and a collector of odd facts, noted that the next day would be the fifth time since the bombing of Pearl Harbor in 1941 that December 7 fell on a Sunday.

MacDonell said, "That's fine. I've got a perfectly good appointment book for 1942. I'll get it out to use next year." (One of MacDonell's idiosyncrasies was carrying appointment books for bygone years in which the dates fell on the same days of the week as in the current year. He enjoyed foiling "snoopers.")

Given MacDonell's full-time work at Corning and his

73

ever-expanding criminalistics practice, this kind of shared free time was rare and precious. It was also to prove short. Returning to their house before noon, they were greeted by a ringing telephone. It was Gerald Lefcourt. The attorney introduced himself and abruptly asked, "What do you know about the Black Panthers?"

"They're some sort of militants, aren't they? Always in trouble with the police."

"Have you heard about the raid that took place in Chicago two days ago?"

"It may have been in the papers. But I don't recall seeing it. That sort of thing is a little remote from us here in Corning. Why don't you tell me the facts?"

Lefcourt related the official police account of the raid. He concluded, "That's the story they're putting out. What's your first reaction to it?"

MacDonell considered for a moment before replying. "It seems like a very strange time for the police to be executing a search warrant. But the most important point is—*who fired first?* If that dead Panther fired first, then the police can make a very good case for shooting back in self-defense, no matter how excessive their response might seem to an outsider."

Lefcourt said: "There's much more to this case. The police have got to have fired first."

"Mr. Lefcourt, don't you tell me who fired first now. If you want to hire me—and I assume that's the purpose of this call—I'll tell you who fired and when. After I've completed my investigation."

"Stay near the phone. We'll be in touch with you."

Within fifteen minutes, the phone rang again. This time, it was another prominent but far more controversial civil rights attorney, William M. Kunstler. He was calling from Chicago where, at that moment, he was defending

74

the "Chicago 7," one of whom was West Coast Panther Bobby Seale. The group was on trial for having incited the riots during the 1968 Democratic convention in that city. Kunstler expanded on what Lefcourt already had told MacDonell. He explained that the Panthers were asleep at the time the police burst in with a barrage of gunfire. They were awakened by the shots. In their state of panic and confusion, it was highly unlikely that they had the presence of mind to reach for guns and start shooting back.

MacDonell asked, "Why? They did consider themselves at war with the police, didn't they? Besides, you've only got their word for the fact that they were asleep."

Kunstler said that even the police admitted the Panthers were in their beds. "An informer had tipped Hanrahan's office about an enormous cache of arms hidden in the apartment. They found only thirteen weapons on the premises. That hardly constitutes an arsenal, when you consider that there were nine Panthers there. If you want to talk about arsenals, there were fifteen members of the raiding party, and they were carrying twenty-eight weapons including one submachine gun, five high-power shotguns, and an illegal sawed-off shotgun."

"That is quite a bit of fancy hardware."

Kunstler asked, "Would you be interested in coming out to Chicago and examining the apartment? We're fairly sure that most of the evidence is still there. Of course, we'll pay for your time and expenses."

"That would depend on what was required of me in time—as well as in other things."

"Somebody will be back to you with all of the particulars."

MacDonell hung up and turned to Phyllis with a smile. "It's shaping up as a very interesting day."

She nodded, fully aware of the meaning of both his smile and his words. There would be no Christmas shopping that afternoon.

At 3:45, attorneys Dennis Cunningham and Skip Andrew called from Chicago. They explained that they represented the Panthers and that, on the advice of Kunstler and Lefcourt, they would very much like to employ MacDonell as their independent expert.

MacDonell said, "You know, the Chicago police crime laboratory has an excellent bunch of fellows in it. I've worked with them before, and I'd trust their findings." He paused for a moment to reflect on Mayor Daley's administration in that city, and then he added, "Unless, of course, the case is political."

Andrew replied, "Mr. MacDonell, this case is very political."

He explained that the West Monroe Street apartment was not the official Panther headquarters. It belonged to the party chairman, Fred Hampton, and was used as a crash pad by other members of the organization. The informer had to have given Hanrahan's office a detailed plan of the flat. Although the police had never been in it and were operating in the dark, they knew exactly where to move and what they were looking for—and it was not weapons. Andrew said, "They were looking for Fred Hampton. And they found him."

Hampton had been a charismatic and brilliant young man who had enjoyed the confidence of much of the black community. There was no doubt that he would have risen to a very high position among the leaders of his race. For that reason, there were those in power who considered him too dangerous to live. Political assassination was not an unlikely possibility.

MacDonell thought that what he was hearing about Hampton was probably fairly biased speculation. He was not interested in the political aspects of the case, but the criminalistic opportunity intrigued him. When Andrew asked if he would be willing to come to Chicago immediately, he replied, "I'm most interested. But before we make any arrangements, we've got to be in agreement on one point."

He repeated what was becoming his official philosophy. "I call them as I see them. If what I find proves that it happened the way Hanrahan and his boys claim it happened, then that's what my report will say."

Andrew said, "We'll take our chances on that. Number one: We believe our clients. Number two: We're very familiar with the tactics of the law enforcers out here. That rules out any faith in the findings of their crime lab."

MacDonell told him that it would be impossible for him to get out that evening, but that he would try to get reservations for the next day. He could only spend twenty-four hours in Chicago. That was all he had left of his vacation time from Corning Glass Works. Andrew replied that he would call again that evening to confirm the arrangements.

Flying almost anyplace from Corning was not the easiest thing to do, but MacDonell had become quite expert at playing the often frustrating game of connecting flights. He called the airport with several alternative routes and managed to book space out on the following afternoon. As he was collecting the gear that he would need in Chicago, he asked Phyllis, "Guess how I'm spending the fifth anniversary of the attack on Pearl Harbor?"

She gave him one of those looks that said that she had known the answer to that one since before noon of that day. She already had made a mental note to call the lab and let them know that he would not be coming to work on Monday.

By the time Andrew telephoned again shortly before

nine that evening, MacDonell had assembled everything that he thought would be of use, including some long, thin dowels and a box of plastic straws that mystified even Phyllis. After telling Andrew when he was scheduled to arrive in Chicago, he added, "But my flight can be canceled, if we're not in full agreement."

He knew that lawyers sometimes had selective hearing, and repeated his main point to make certain that it had sunk in. "My examination is going to be impartial. It'd make no difference to me if I'd been hired by Hanrahan instead of you. My conclusions would be the same. Mr. Andrew, if you don't want the whole truth, don't hire me."

Skip Andrew said, "You be on that plane. I'll meet you at O'Hare Airport tomorrow night."

When Andrew picked up MacDonell to drive him to his hotel, he said very little beyond generalizations and pleasantries. He respected MacDonell's request that there be no further attempt to prejudice him and no questions about the procedures he would employ on the following day.

Andrew showed him photographs and a sketchy floor plan of the West Monroe Street apartment. MacDonell wanted to know the exact location of each of the Panthers at the moment of the raid, and the nature of the wounds of those who had been injured and killed. He was most interested in the photographs of the door that led from the hallway into the living room. There was a large bullet hole in it almost an inch in diameter. The powder burns were on the living-room side, leading to the unmistakable conclusion that the shot had been discharged from inside the apartment. Hanrahan's men claimed that this was the first shot fired during the raid and that it had been fired by Mark Clark.

There were two things MacDonell would have to discover on the following day: (1) who shot first, and (2) how large the Panther response was, even if they did not get off the first shot.

Groth claimed he had called for a cease-fire several times, and that the Panther response was to shout, "Shoot it out!" If this was true, then the Panthers were still culpable. It was no longer self-defense if they ignored a truce offer. The Panthers swore that they had not shot back at all. That remained to be proven.

The sky was turning a gunmetal gray when Skip Andrew came to pick up MacDonell at 7:30 the next morning. It was a cold, damp, bleak day that belied the fact winter had not yet officially arrived, the sort of day for which Chicago has earned a dubious fame. Street by street, the neighborhood into which they were descending grew increasingly cheerless. The building at 2337 West Monroe Street was one of a row of two-family houses that looked as if they might have known better days even if their present occupants had not.

There was not a soul in sight, and the building appeared to be derelict. MacDonell waited in the car while Andrew went to the front door, which was partially open. He did not know if he was more surprised by the total lack of security or by the lawyer's matter-of-fact acceptance of it. Andrew decided that it would be safer to enter with a member of the Panther party. They went around the block to the official Panther headquarters on West Madison Street, found no one there, then cruised around futilely looking for a witness or guide or guard before returning alone to West Monroe.

At 8:30, the lawyer and the criminalist climbed the steps to the porch. The front door opened into a small foyer in which there were two doors. One led to a staircase to the upstairs flat, and the other to Hampton's ground-floor apartment. There were no bullet holes in Hampton's front door, but the condition of it left no doubt that there had been a forced entry. The lock hung limply from bolts loosened by the thrust of the raiders. The place was wide open for anybody to walk in and take or do exactly what they wanted. MacDonell thought that the Panthers and the police shared an equally cavalier attitude toward the scene of two killings.

The door led to a tiny entrance hall that was actually a part of the Hampton apartment. It was crammed with a roll-away bed and piles of clothing stacked like shabby merchandise in a thrift shop. Another door led to the living room. This was the significant door. In it, MacDonell could see the large hole made by the blast from Clark's shotgun that, Groth said, had opened the battle.

MacDonell helped Andrew connect some lights and ignite the space heater in the living room. It was a small rectangle of a room measuring no more than seventeen by thirteen feet and overcrowded with furniture. Mac-Donell had been told that the informer had given the raiders a layout of the apartment. That much had to be true for, without one, it would have been impossible for the police to maneuver in that place in the dark.

A double mattress took up most of the center of the room. A twin bed in the far right corner opposite the door was the one in which Brenda Harris was wounded and from which, Groth said, she had opened fire as he and his men were entering. A large round hassock was pulled up near it, and, circling the walls, there were chests, the heater, a television console, and a long wall unit that almost totally blocked the front windows so that nobody could see into the apartment from the porch. All manner of personal paraphernalia was stacked in corners and along every surface. Three chairs stood at haphazard angles. The most important of these was pulled up behind the door from the entry hallway. Mark Clark had been sitting in it when he discharged the shotgun blast that went through the door.

A short corridor led from the living room to the rear of the apartment. As MacDonell entered this hall, the bathroom door was to the right. The bathroom was cluttered with a miscellany of wearing apparel, furniture, and toiletries. The tub was filled with dirty ice-filmed water.

Facing the bathroom, a door on the left side of the corridor led to a small bedroom. It was furnished with twin beds, a folding chair, and a chest. A closet was filled with an assortment of old clothes. There were several cans of paint on the floor, one of which had been punctured by a shot causing a finger of pigment to curl over the floor. On the night of the raid, three people had been sleeping in this room: Verlina Brewer, aged seventeen, and Blair Anderson and Ronald Satchel, both aged eighteen. It was from this room that the police said they had heard the cry, "Shoot it out!" By the time the shooting was over, all three occupants were wounded. Verlina Brewer had received two gunshot wounds, Satchel had five, and Anderson, three. Both boys were listed in serious condition.

Whoever had done the firing, the amount of ammunition spent in that modest space was prodigious. MacDonell had never seen anything to equal it. The door and walls were pitted, scarred, and perforated by bullets. The next tenants would have to cut to the skeleton of the building to remove the evidence of violence etched in those walls.

MacDonell and Andrew moved on. The short corridor terminated in a windowless dining room containing a double bed among an odd assortment of articles, none of which pertained to dining. From the dining room, MacDonell could see into the quite ordinary kitchen. The window had been broken and the back door forced by Officers Ciszewski and Carmody when they rushed in to reinforce Groth's men in the front of the apartment.

Turning from the kitchen, MacDonell peered through a doorway that led off the dining room to the left. He saw a cluttered bedroom adjacent to the other bedroom and of approximately the same dimensions. Fred Hampton had been killed in the blood-soaked queen-sized bed in this room. When the raid opened, he had been sleeping with his pregnant mistress, Deborah Johnson. Two other Panthers, Harold Bell and Louis Truelock, had raced back from the living room to warn him of the intruders. They were able to rouse Johnson but could not awaken Hampton, who slept through the raid and into his death.

After Andrew finished describing the scene, MacDonell asked, "Was he drugged?"

"There was an informer. The police knew exactly where Fred was sleeping. They even knew that he slept with his head toward the foot of the bed and that's where most of the bullets in the mattress are concentrated. He was shot twice in the head. Were those lucky shots? Was he drugged? With all that shooting, he never awakened. You're the criminalist. What do you think?"

MacDonell did not reply. His job was to examine the evidence, and he had very little time. He could not afford to waste any of it in speculation. Andrew had been true to his word and had volunteered no information unless asked a direct question. MacDonell would make no more queries that did not relate to his work.

The glass in one of the windows in Hampton's bedroom had been shattered by gunfire, allowing the cold wind to rattle through the room. MacDonell was grateful for the gray mouton hat that he had bought the previous winter when he was in Canada for a lecture. He and Andrew found a door panel and, as they were placing it in front of the broken window, a group of young black men appeared in the bedroom doorway. One of them pointed at MacDonell's hat and said, "Dig the man in the muff hat."

Andrew introduced them as representatives of the Black Panther party. Throughout MacDonell's investigation, they would remain distant, polite, and unobtrusive but always there, with opaque dark eyes observing every move he made. He looked at them and decided it was time to get to work.

He left Hampton's bedroom and went back through the apartment: down the short corridor past the other bedroom, across the living room into the cluttered hallway, through the foyer, and out onto the front porch. He was ready to retrace Groth's steps at the beginning of the raid.

He reentered the foyer. There was nothing of any interest in it except for the battered door with its dangling lock. He stepped into Hampton's hallway and, pushing aside the stacks of clothes and the roll-away bed, he slowly beamed his flashlight over the walls and ceiling. Turning to Andrew, who had been following along, he smiled and said, "It begins to get interesting here."

The small space had several evidential treasures that had been completely overlooked by the police. He unpacked his equipment, including the mysterious long, thin dowels and the plastic straws.

A shotgun had been fired point-blank in the hallway. The shot had struck the wall adjacent to the door leading in from the foyer. Judging by the impact, the muzzle could not have been more than twelve inches away. There was no way of telling when the shot had been fired. He asked

Andrew if either the police or the Panthers had mentioned any shots fired in that area in addition to those exchanged through the door separating it from the living room. The answer was negative. Still, things had happened so quickly on the morning of the raid that MacDonell thought anything was possible. On the other hand, the shot could have been fired at an earlier date. Hampton and his friends were violent young people for whom gunfire was a fact of life. In that case, it was likely that there would not be any corroborating evidence still around. Still, he thought he would have a look just to satisfy his own curiosity.

Poking in the dust on the hall floor, MacDonell found two wads from 12-gauge shotgun shells and a few pellets. They were in a corner directly beneath the impact hole. There had to be more pellets, and MacDonell probed the hole until he released them. The police had been carrying a sawed-off shotgun, and it was probable that this had been fired in the raid and that it had been fired by a nervous police officer. Ironically, this evidence would mean little in a courtroom. The police would never admit that they had fired first, and the Panthers would stick to their story that the police had fired the first shot, without provocation, through the closed door into the living room.

MacDonell crossed the hallway to study that door leading to the living room. There was a large bullet hole in it that had been made by Clark's shot coming from inside. The slug had exited into the hallway in which MacDonell was standing. It had not hit one of the raiders, and so it had to have impacted somewhere in this tiny room. With the aid of his flashlight, he carefully searched the walls until he found what he was seeking.

There was a large bullet hole about eighteen inches down from the ceiling at the juncture of two walls in the corner opposite the living-room door. An examination proved that this hole went clear through the wall into the stairway leading to the upstairs apartment. The tenants gave him permission to have a look at it.

Slowly climbing the stairs, he squinted past the beam of the flashlight that he ran along the left wall until he found the exit hole. Using a microspatula, he was able to probe back through to the Hampton hallway. The slug had pierced the wall and kept on going across the stairway. MacDonell moved to the other side and gently ran his fingers over the opposite wall. Like a blind man reading braille, he let his fingertips transmit the message to him. He found what he thought was an entrance hole diagonally opposite and slightly higher than the entrance hole in the other wall. Closer investigation proved that it was not a hole at all but only an impact point. The bruised plaster covered a solid outside wall in which no slug was embedded. He started to grope around on the tread. Cleanliness might be next to godliness, but MacDonell was hoping that the quantity of filth on those steps might prove to be on the side of the angels. It was extremely unlikely that they had been swept at any point in the last four days or even four weeks. It was there. He picked up the large lead shotgun slug that had been fired from Clark's gun. The projectile had struck the wall and, having lost energy in flight and by passage through the other wall, had not had the force to penetrate it. It struck and then it fell to the ground.

In the better light of Hampton's apartment, Mac-Donell examined the slug with his magnifying glass. It had both plaster and copper or bronze paint clinging to its nose. There was no metallic paint in the apartment, and the grime on the stairway walls concealed their hue. He wondered aloud where the specks had come from.

One of the Panthers smiled. "Next door. Man, a lotta

stairways in this neighborhood were painted gold, 'cause they were the stairways to paradise leading to those hot mamas upstairs."

In what could only have been more prosperous times, the area had served as one of Chicago's better-known red-light districts. It was doubtful that any police raid in those bygone days had been accompanied by anything approaching the bloodshed of the Panther raid. Indeed, the madam's stairway had probably led to the paradise of police protection and been lined with gold as well as painted gold.

MacDonell made a closer investigation of the living-room door. Although the police admitted to having found only one bullet hole in it, he found two. The larger hole unmistakably had been made by the slug that he had just retrieved. The smaller hole was the one in which he was interested. The supervising sergeant of the police mobile crime laboratory had not thought that it was significant enough to probe when examining the door less than two hours after the shots were fired. MacDonell did not agree with him. He went over the bruise on the hallway side of the door. The plywood fibers had almost knit back together again as they would if a .38 revolver, of the type that was standard police issue, had been fired at close range.

If that unreported bullet had been fired by the police at the start of the raid, from the hallway, through the closed or opening door, it would have terminated in the far wall of the living room, unless it had hit some obstruction in flight. The wounded Brenda Harris and the dead Mark Clark were the only obstructions in the room that had been hit, and the police admitted to having shot them after crossing the threshold.

MacDonell dashed across the room like a broken-field

runner dodging the obstacles of chairs, mattress, and hassock. His eyes and hands scanned that far wall. About thirty inches up from the floor, he found a hole measuring approximately one inch in diameter. He carefully examined it, gently probing with his spatula, fully expecting to find the bullet. There was none. He could not understand. The beam of his light was penetrating the hole, and he was peering in, nose to wall. He looked up and asked, "Do you mind if I cut away a piece?"

Andrew replied dryly, "So long as you don't make a mess of the place."

MacDonell cut out a section of wall just below the bullet hole and above the high baseboard. He reached in and nodded, as he brought forth a small metal object. "As pretty a .38 slug as I've ever seen."

One of the Panthers asked, "How'd you know it was there?"

"When I looked into the hole, I could see that the plasterboard was being held away from the solid outside wall. What I know about construction indicated that it had to be separated by wooden laths. The bullet passed between two of them, hit the concrete outer wall, and fell. After figuring that out, it wasn't hard to find the slug."

The Panther asked, "If it was as easy as that, how come the pigs didn't find it?"

MacDonell was studying the .38 slug with his magnifying glass, and Andrew answered for him. "Because they weren't looking."

MacDonell noted that there were many wood fibers embedded in the base of the slug. He was certain they would prove to be a part of the plywood panel of the door that had adhered to the bullet after the police fired it from the hallway.

Andrew was watching him, obviously stifling a question about what he was doing, and MacDonell explained that his latest discoveries proved that two bullets had passed through the door during the opening stage of the raid. One had been fired by Clark and the other by the police. He concluded, "My next problem is to find out who fired first."

"Do you think you can?"

"I'm going to try. Let's go back into the stairway next door."

MacDonell attached a long string to the impact point in the far wall of the stairway, the last thing struck by Clark's slug before it fell to the tread where he had found it. He stretched the string across the stairs and threaded it through the hole in the opposite wall that led back into Hampton's hallway. They returned to the apartment.

The string was dangling from the bullet hole in the corner of the hallway. MacDonell pulled it across and threaded it through the larger bullet hole in the door. He went into the living room and slowly opened the door until he could tighten the string to make a straight line from the impact point through the holes in the hallway wall and door and into the living room. It was a descending line, and he continued letting it out until the string struck the floor directly behind the chair in which Clark had been sitting. He tacked it down. The door was almost wide open, and the string was taut and straight.

MacDonell said, "The string is the trajectory of Clark's shot, and that's the position the door was in when it was struck by it."

MacDonell was about to repeat the process from the point where the police bullet had entered the far wall of the living room back through the hole it had made in the door, when two young white men carrying a movie camera and lights slid through the open door into the room, causing the string that ran through it to tremble. They were a team of filmmakers shooting a documentary on Hampton prior to his death. They asked if MacDonell minded if they filmed him at work. He turned to Andrew, who nodded. MacDonell did not like it, but all he said was, "If you can keep me in focus and keep out of my way at the same time, then I suppose it's all right. Now, if you don't mind, I'm going to run the second string."

A Panther said, "You can't do that yet."

"Why not?"

"The people are about to start coming through here."

"What people?"

A Panther led MacDonell behind the large wall cabinet that almost obscured the windows. He pointed out. There was an orderly queue of neatly dressed, somber-looking people, mostly black but with a sprinkling of whites. MacDonell asked, "Who are they?"

The Panther repeated, "The people. We take them through here to show them what the pigs did and to tell them about Fred and his work."

MacDonell could not believe what he was hearing. The Panthers were trying to turn the house on West Monroe into the Lourdes of Saint Fred Hampton, and they had a movie crew to document them doing it. It was a propaganda circus. Trying to control his anger, he asked, "You let mobs—maybe souvenir hunters—tramp through this place before all the evidence is collected?"

"We know what happened here."

MacDonell finally exploded. "You only *think* you know what happened here. The police also think they know what happened here. But nobody can *prove* what happened here until after I've finished my work—*if* I can finish my work under these circumstances."

One of the Panthers said, "You do your thing. We'll

do ours. The people won't bother you. I'll see to that."

When one of those fellows said that he would see to something, MacDonell had the feeling that it would be seen to. He sighed. "As long as you keep them out of my way."

He returned to the hallway to examine the small hole made by the police .38 high on the left side of the middle panel of the door. He made a gun of his finger and aimed at the door. It was impossible for the officer who opened the door also to have fired the shot, unless he was in two places at one time, because he could not shoot from the left while opening the door from the right.

He crouched behind the wall to the left of the door as if taking cover from shots that might come out of the living room. He made a gun of his finger again and reached over to fire it through the door while still remaining shielded by the wall. The bullet hole was in the right place. The police shot had been fired by an officer protecting himself from retaliation by keeping away from the door.

Officer "Gloves" Davis had flung open the door, while Sergeant Groth crouched to his left and fired into the room as the door was opening. Part of Davis's original report was true. He had not fired until he had hurled himself into the living room. It was then that he had wounded Brenda Harris and killed Mark Clark. It was Groth who probably got off the police shot through the door.

MacDonell had reconstructed the actions of the police at the start of the raid, but the original problem remained. He still did not know which side had fired first. The answer to that all-important question would have to wait until he returned to Corning. He turned to Andrew and said, "You're going to have to make an exact scale floor plan of the apartment. If I'm going to figure out who fired first, the plan must be precise. There cannot be even the slightest deviation from scale. It's got to be drawn and sent to me in Corning as soon as possible. Sooner."

Andrew made a note of the request. "You'll have it before the end of the week."

MacDonell returned to the living room and went over to the wall that separated it from the bedroom in which the three wounded Panthers had been sleeping. It was riddled with bullet holes, forty-five by MacDonell's count, some undoubtedly made by the firing of a submachine gun. The only such gun known to be on the premises during the raid had been brought in by the police. Beyond that, it was highly unlikely that a Panther had fired those shots, because the only lives endangered by them were those of his or her comrades.

MacDonell walked into the corridor to examine the door to that adjoining bedroom. It was scarred by more than two dozen bullet holes. The shots had all entered the door from the bedroom side and, on first impression, bolstered the police contention of a shoot-out. It would seem that, while attempting to enter the bedroom from the corridor, they had been greeted by a barrage of shots fired by the three Panthers inside, and were thus justified in returning the fire.

MacDonell slowly turned around in the narrow corridor. He studied it from every angle. He examined the bathroom door directly opposite the bedroom door, as well as the interior of the bathroom. He did not find a single bullet hole. If the shots had been fired out by the Panthers in the bedroom, after going through the door they had to have lodged in or hit something. They had not hit anything in the corridor or bathroom, nor had they hit any of the raiders.

The door opened into the bedroom toward the bullet-sprayed wall that separated it from the living room.

MacDonell slowly inched the door back to an open position. It covered twenty-five of the holes in the dividing wall. His eyes moved from the holes in the wall to those in the door, and he nodded as if something that might be of importance had just occurred to him.

He returned to the living room and started rummaging through his equipment. He took out the box of clear plastic straws and grabbed a handful of the mysterious thin dowels. Mentally aligning the holes in the section of the wall nearest to the corridor with those in the open bedroom door directly behind it, he inserted a straw in each of them. The straw probes were made with a gentle precision so that they did not disturb the angle of trajectory that was preserved in each hole. He started passing dowels through the holes in the straws until they cleared the wall and entered the bedroom.

He had an audience for this operation. Not only were the filmmakers recording it with their camera, but the first group of people had been led in by the Panthers. Curious about what the man in the muff hat was doing, they had stopped listening to the political litany of their guide and were watching him.

After placing a dowel in the last straw, MacDonell went around into the bedroom. He pulled the dowels toward him one at a time and passed them through corresponding holes in the door. Those holes had not been made by Panthers shooting out of the bedroom but by a police officer shooting in through the living room wall. The dowels represented the exact trajectories of his bullets. Scars and holes in the opposite wall and bedroom closet facing the open door told MacDonell where they had gone after entering from the living room.

He looked at Andrew and said, "The door was wide open at the time of the raid. All of the bullets that went through it were fired in from the living room."

Andrew nodded noncommittally, and MacDonell continued. "As far as I can see, there wasn't one shot fired out of this room."

That statement reached Andrew. "Are you willing to testify to that in court?"

"If no counterevidence turns up. Not only that. See these holes?" He used a spare dowel to point out several slug scars in the other walls. "These had to have been made by firing in from the doorway. There were a lot of bullets coming into this room, but none were going out from it."

The Panther guide shouted for the benefit of his group, "Three innocent young people were shot in this room."

MacDonell silently walked past him back into the corridor. He was not about to make any comments about the relative guilt or innocence of either the Panthers or the police. Those evaluations were too often based upon the biases of the people making them. His conclusions would be based on an objective analysis of the evidence.

The bedroom in which Hampton had been killed yielded no information that altered what MacDonell had already learned in the other rooms. Again, there was no proof that anybody had fired out and overwhelming evidence of shooting in.

Most of the room was filled by a queen-sized bed. When the shooting started, there were three other people on that bed with Hampton: his mistress, Deborah Johnson, and the two men who had raced in from the living room to warn him, Louis Truelock and Harold Bell. All tried frantically to awaken him.

MacDonell mentally reconstructed what had happened. After failing to rouse Hampton, the other three had sprung back against the rear wall of the room when the shooting started. Bullets were flying from the doorway and through the walls, and yet not one of the three was so much as grazed by a shot. In that darkened room, it was extraordinary how much of the fire was centered on Hampton's head, especially as he had been sleeping in the unusual position of head to the foot of the bed. Everything that Andrew had told him was verified by the evidence. The lawyer could make an excellent circumstantial case for political assassination. An equally good case could be made for one of the Panthers having been an undercover agent and informer.

By the time MacDonell completed his investigation at 11:00 P.M., the dowels and strings tracing trajectories had converted the cheerless flat into a modern sculptural environment. Except for a quick lunch and a snack that had been brought in for him at 8:00 P.M., he had been at work steadily since 8:30 that morning and had located and analyzed every slug crucial to the case—excluding those that were in the bodies of the wounded and dead. Only one mystery still remained to be solved. He did not know who had fired first. He was taking the living-room door panel that contained the bullet holes from the opening shots and several important slugs from elsewhere in the apartment back to Corning with him, where many more hours and days would be spent examining them.

Andrew instructed him not to tell anybody about the evidence in his possession until after he received word from Chicago. MacDonell's last words before leaving were, "Don't forget to get that precise floor plan to me as soon as possible. I can't complete my investigation without it."

In Corning, MacDonell was using the glass works lab after hours, his own kitchen and dining-room tables, his yard, and whatever other space he could find to put the evidence through a range of forensic tests. There may have been a great many muttered asides about the need for a proper laboratory facility in his own home, but he was able to substantiate his conclusions. With the exception of the slug from Clark's shotgun, all of the other ammunition had come from police arms.

Once the floor plan arrived, he was able to get to work on solving the last remaining mystery of the case: Who was the first to fire through the living-room door? He had already traced Clark's shot with string in the apartment and found that the door was almost wide open when the bullet went through it. This was confirmed by a minute examination of the direction of the trajectory embedded in the hole in the door panel that he had brought home with him.

The smaller .38 hole gave him the exact direction from which the police had fired from the hallway. The scale floor plan showed exactly where that shot hit the far wall of the living room. By making geometric calculations based on the trajectory angle, he was able to draw the line of flight on the plan and pinpoint the position of the door when it was struck. The door was only partially open when the police fired and, as he had already concluded, almost wide open when Clark fired.

The police admitted to having pushed the door open, which meant that, at the point the shots rang out, the door was moving from closed to ajar to wide open. The bullet that struck when the door was ajar was, therefore, the first to be fired during the exchange, and that was the .38. The police had been the first to fire.

MacDonell's investigation provided the evidential foundation for the Panther defense. The police in Hanrahan's special prosecution unit had not told the truth in their reports. The raiders had fired first; they had entered the apartment shooting. The only response was Clark's single shot, and he had paid for it with his life. All of the more than one hundred rounds of ammunition subsequently expended had been discharged by the police. The Panthers never had a chance to defend themselves.

On December 17, the apartment at 2337 West Monroe Street was officially sealed by the police. By then, all of the important pieces of evidence had been removed and well over twenty-five thousand blacks and whites had tramped through to view the scene of the crime and to hear the Panther version of the Fred Hampton story. Public indignation was rising, and Hanrahan and his raiders were on the defensive.

On January 6, 1970, a Cook County grand jury was convened for the purpose of determining if the Panthers had acted illegally during the raid and, if they had, of handing down indictments against the survivors. The defense team was extremely optimistic because of the results of MacDonell's investigation. They decided on a strategy of allowing the police to get as many of their evasions, mistakes, and lies on the record before putting their criminalist on the stand to disprove them.

Pursuing this plan, Skip Andrew and James Montgomery, one of his colleagues on the team, asked MacDonell to delay in Corning for as long as possible before responding to the grand jury subpoena. It was not difficult for him to arrange. The judge who was instructed to order him to testify was his sister-in-law's uncle. That was one of the neighborly things about living in a place like Steuben County. Eventually, everybody married into everybody else's family.

MacDonell finally did testify on January 16. Although he did not share the Panthers' optimism about their case, he did his best for them on the stand. But looking at and listening to that jury, he suspected that they were out to get the blacks, and he was right. On January 30, the seven surviving Panthers were indicted on a total of thirty-one counts ranging from unlawful possession of firearms, through armed violence, to attempted murder. As he had anticipated, the grand jury had placed greater value on the testimony of the police and their experts than on the findings of the outside expert.

On the federal level, however, civil rights groups were exerting pressure on Attorney General John N. Mitchell and, within days of the formation of the aforementioned Cook County grand jury, Mitchell proclaimed the establishment of a federal grand jury to investigate the conduct of the raid. MacDonell testified before it less than two weeks after appearing before the Cook County jury. He was on the stand for two days and gave a careful analysis of the evidence he had studied, ending with the only conclusion that he believed could be drawn from it.

The federal grand jury admitted the value of his contribution to the solution of the mystery of what actually had taken place on West Monroe Street but proceeded to minimize his entire testimony by calling it "imaginative" and "defense oriented." MacDonell was furious, but he controlled his temper and replied in his best courtroom jargon.

"The references to 'defense oriented' . . . are stated very factually, when they could not possibly be more than opinion. This conclusion is unfounded and inaccurate. I was, am, and always shall be 'truth oriented.' "

He admitted that there was a degree of truth in the suggestion that his theory of the sequence of shots was "imaginative," but he thought that implied a greater degree of uncertainty than was warranted. His theory was based upon the science of mathematics, specifically geometry, but it also required two additional facts that had been established by the testimony of the officers conducting the raid: (1) the door was opening, (2) several shots were fired close together. He concluded:

"The grand jury did not listen, or did not comprehend, or did not desire to comprehend, when so simple a point could be overlooked."

It was not a total whitewash. The grand jury did find: "the performance of agencies of law enforcement, in this case at least, gives some reasonable basis for public doubt of their efficiency or even of their credibility." But it also issued a sharp reprimand to the Panthers, who "were more interested in the issue of police persecution than they are in obtaining justice. . . . Revolutionary groups simply do not want the system to work."

And because the federal grand jury did not find that the civil rights of the Panthers had been violated, no indictments were handed down against any of the officers or officials involved in the preparation and execution of the raid.

Meanwhile, a federal court order compelled the FBI to turn over the results of its own investigation of the firearms evidence to the office of the Cook County state's attorney. These agreed with MacDonell's conclusion that only one Panther bullet had been fired in the raid. Edward Hanrahan went into a Cook County courtroom on May 8, 1970, to obtain a dismissal of all charges against the surviving Black Panthers.

Although two grand juries had refused to recognize the value of his testimony, Herbert MacDonell's investigation was probably the largest single contribution to the Panther victory in the criminal case against them. It would take an additional twelve years to discover how well his conclusions would hold up in a civil action.

After the criminal charges against them were dropped, the surviving Panthers and the relatives of Clark and Hampton filed a $47.7 million civil suit against Edward V. Hanrahan and twenty-eight other city, county, and federal officials, charging that their civil rights had been violated in the raid.

It was not until November 1982 that an out-of-court settlement awarded $1.85 million in damages to the surviving Panthers and the relatives of Hampton and Clark. The Chicago city, Cook County, and federal governments had spent many more millions than that in attempting to cover up the liabilities of their respective law enforcement agencies.

From the beginning of his involvement in the case, MacDonell had no more sympathy for the aims and practices of the Black Panther Party than the FBI did, but there was one fundamental point on which he differed with the agency: What the evidence revealed must never be concealed no matter whom it vindicated.

Although the Black Panther case had established MacDonell's reputation as a nationally known criminalist, a certain natural prudence continued to govern his private life. It was not until almost three years after the event that he felt secure enough to resign his position as a research chemist with Corning Glass Works and devote all of his time to the practice and teaching of criminalistics.

4

PORTRAIT IN BLOOD

About the only times that Orange County hit the national newspapers were when a frost destroyed the citrus crop or a President visited Disney World. The county seat, Orlando, was the booming metropolis that Mickey Mouse had built, but Winter Garden better exemplified the other cities and towns in the landlocked county. It was a small Baptist town on the shores of Lake Apopka with no tourist attractions aside from some fresh-water fishing, and was more typically southern in look and feeling, a far cry from the high-living razzle-dazzle that had become associated with Florida by 1975. There was no drug problem to speak of and little crime of any significance. By and large, there was no racial tension, and it almost seemed as if the civil rights movement had skirted Winter Garden. Everybody knew just about everybody else and minded each other's business in the spirit of what they liked to think of as Christian charity.

The William Zeiglers, Jr. and Sr., were among the leading citizens of Winter Garden. They owned the big furniture store and were reputedly involved in many lucrative real-estate deals. They were a part of the small circle of successful merchants, judges, law enforcers, bankers, and local legislators who ran the town.

William, Jr., called Tommy, was a fastidious and well-regarded young man, a bit too thin, but wiry and deceptively strong from a daily routine of moving furniture and heavy appliances. His dark crew-cut hair crowned a face that, if not really handsome, was even-featured and pleasant and unmistakably American.

In his adolescence, Tommy had come as close to being a playboy as a young man could in Winter Garden. On one occasion, he had been charged with grand larceny and breaking and entering Smithy's Boats and Motors in Leesburg, in neighboring Lake County. He had pleaded guilty, but the judge had withheld adjudication and sentenced him to five years' probation. You didn't send a Zeigler to jail, not in those parts. He was only seventeen at the time, and the incident had almost been forgotten in the intervening twelve years. Tommy had simmered down and become a church-going, responsible citizen.

Tommy had always been a mama's boy and exhibited little interest in the town girls. People were surprised when he married Eunice Edwards, a nice young woman from Georgia. She was two or three years older than he, and she proved to be a steadying influence. He called her his "duchess" and wrote poetry about his feelings for her.

Some of Tommy's and Eunice's friends intimated that he wanted a baby and she did not, while others intimated the reverse. Eunice had kept temperature charts with indications of sexual intercourse. It was a way of determining when ovulation and, therefore, conception might occur.

They had been scrupulously written down in a notebook, but had stopped abruptly two weeks before Christmas of 1975. Somebody had ripped several pages out of the book.

Except for their immediate families, nobody knew that there was any trouble in young Zeigler's paradise. There was the usual appearance of togetherness between Tommy and Eunice during the preholiday festivities. Eunice's parents, Perry and Virginia Edwards, were down from their home in Moultrie, Georgia, to spend Christmas with the young couple, and seemed just as fond as ever of their son-in-law. Neither they nor their children let on that Eunice had invited them to Florida to take her back to Moultrie with them.

Tommy Zeigler arose early on the morning of Christmas Eve. He reached for his glasses on the night table. Without them, he could not see his way to the bathroom. After showering, he ran a comb through his short hair and shaved. In the spirit of the holiday, he donned a red shirt and green tie and made a mental note to remind his mother-in-law to wear the holly earrings that she had brought along with her.

Things would be rather slow at the store that day. Furniture and major appliances were not last-minute gifts but purchases thought about and ordered well in advance.

Tommy had done his Christmas shopping very early and was certain that he would be able to accomplish everything that remained to be done in time for Judge Van Deventer's party that evening. He gulped his coffee, longing for one of the cigarettes that Eunice and his mother had prevailed upon him to give up two years ago. He left the house and set off for work.

Tommy and his parents lived next door to each other in the best residential section, and it was only a short drive from there to the furniture store at 1010 South Dillard Street, opposite the Tri-City Shopping Center. Tri-City was a euphemism for the three towns of Winter Garden, Oakland, and Ocoee Hills, none of which could remotely be described as a city. Similar to many American towns, their centers had sunk into somnolence and decay as business had moved out to the new suburban shopping malls. A good driver could be through Winter Garden and out into the surrounding orange groves in a matter of minutes. The strange thing was that most of the inhabitants were actually proud to see progress passing them by. They boasted of the slow rhythms of life that did not seem to quicken from one generation to the next.

At 11:30 that morning, Charlie and Mattie Louise Mays came into the store. Charlie was an old customer and a rising leader in the black community of neighboring Oakland. He was a lusty young citrus crew boss and a deacon of his church. The night before, he had won $420 at jai alai, and the Mayses had come down to spend it on a grand finale to their Christmas shopping, something special for Mattie Louise and their four sons.

Tommy said, "I think I've got something you'll really go for. I can show it to you in the storeroom. Why don't you come on back with me and have a look?"

The two men went through a door that led to the storeroom in the rear while Mattie Louise ambled around the showroom.

The front of the store and the entire left side were used to display furniture. There was a wrapping and cash counter along the wall on the other side of the showroom. By the time Mattie Louise worked her way back there, the clock on the wall over the counter indicated that ten minutes had gone by. Charlie and Mr. Zeigler were probably striking a tough bargain. The stoves, refrigerators, and dishwashers were in the far corner behind the counter, with linoleum racks lining the rear walls. She was peeking into the door of the private kitchen that separated the appliances from the counter when the two men returned.

Charlie, who had hidden his big jai alai winnings at home, asked, "Mattie, you got ten bucks? I only have forty with me and I need fifty for a down payment on a real good buy Mr. Zeigler's givin' me on a fine color television set just like you and the boys have always been hankerin' after."

Tommy smiled. "Mattie, you've got a fine man here. He's too smart to let anybody put anything over on him. Not that I'd try. I gave him a good price, but he got a better one."

Mattie Louise cheerfully contributed her ten spot. It was going to be a grand Christmas. Mr. Zeigler was right. Her husband was a fine man.

Charlie said, "I'll get my money and be back to pick up the set."

Tommy replied, "Come at about seven-thirty tonight. I'll have it all packed and ready for you."

Tommy watched the couple leave the store. He adjusted his plans for that evening to include Charlie Mays. He was an unexpected but valuable addition. Tommy's salesman, Curtis Dunaway, remarked that he was looking mighty happy, and Tommy answered that it was turning out to be a profitable Christmas after all, stressing the point that Charlie Mays had made a purchase and was coming back to the store that evening to pick it up.

Curtis wished that he could feel a little more of the holiday spirit, but his car was acting up. Tommy said, "Use mine. I don't really need it. I'll be with Eunice. She'll bring me back to the store to let Charlie in. You can come by the house after we close and get the car."

Before lunch, Ed Williams stopped at the store. Williams worked part-time as a carpenter for Zeigler. He had been renovating an apartment in one of the buildings that Zeigler owned and had come to return the key. He was an ingratiating young man with a soft Bahamian lilt to his voice. Zeigler reminded him that he had promised to move some packages at the store. It was not convenient to do it at that moment, and Zeigler said, "The best time to do the job is after the store is closed. I'm lending my car to Mr. Dunaway, so suppose you come by and pick me up at my house at seven-thirty. We'll drive back here together."

Williams readily agreed, and Zeigler said, "Thank you, Edward."

Along with Mays, Williams would make two black men alone in the store with Zeigler after the closing hour. Winter Garden was a peaceful town with no real history of racial violence, but there were few white residents who would not have avoided this situation at that particular time. There was a gang of blacks who had been terrorizing the surrounding area. They were called "the ski-mask bandits," and their individual identities were unknown because of the masks. Their specialty was robbing and sometimes sexually assaulting whites.

Ed Williams left the store and went about his business. To most people, he was "Boy," or "Ed," or "Eddie," but to Mr. Tommy, he was usually a courtly "Edward," and the black man adored him for it. There was nothing he would not do for him. Hadn't he helped him to get those guns he asked for? Mr. Tommy had wanted a pair of .38s, no questions asked. There was such a ruckus being kicked up about gun control that he had not wanted them traced to him. It seemed strange, seeing as the police chief, Don Ficke, was the boss's best friend, but if that was what the boss wanted, that was what Edward Williams helped him to get. As he always was saying, "Mr. Tommy is like a father to me."

Williams had contacted his friend Frank Smith. Smith drove a cab for a living at that time, but Williams was sure he would know how to get the arms, and Smith came through. The cabbie bought them in an Orlando pawnshop, where he had been required to fill out a purchase form. That was okay. The guns could be traced to Smith but not to Mr. Tommy. Over a year had passed since the sale, and no questions had been asked.

It seemed to Williams that the man was accumulating a lot of guns, but that was strictly his own business. They were stashed all over the store, but he did not use them recklessly. All he did with them was get a little boy's kick out of strapping them around his waist or carrying one in a shoulder holster and playfully drawing on friends and employees.

Tommy Zeigler's mother, Beulah, had also arisen early on that morning. To some, the day might not have seemed long enough for all she had to do, but she was well known for her efficiency. She was a southern Baptist lady who had little patience with those who blamed God for the evils that befell them but neglected to thank Him for the blessings. The charm of the soft drawling voice did not quite deflect the listener from a recognition of the iron strength that reinforced it. She knew the value of her position in Winter Garden, who she was in that place, and there was a self-congratulatory pride when she spoke of "all our friends, all the better class of town."

The first order of business was arranging for somebody to look after her husband's needs during the day. William Zeigler, Sr., had suffered a stroke that year and, though there had been a corps of nurses and doctors, it had been

Beulah's determination that had seen him through the ordeal.

Beulah made it a practice not to leave her husband alone for too long, but that afternoon she still had some last-minute shopping to do. Eunice could come by and sit with Billy for a spell while she was gone. It was not as if it was a chore. She was right next door on affluent Temple Drive.

Eunice was a good girl, no beauty or heiress and, perhaps, a bit too old for Tommy, but she made him a good wife most of the time. Whatever problems the young couple had would be resolved if only she would produce a child. Eunice was still in her early thirties, and that was not too old. Beulah had been older when she had given birth to her only son, and he had turned out well. Tommy was a good boy, never profane, a keeper of all of the Commandments. She had raised him properly and, truth to tell, he was the light and blessing of her life.

That afternoon, Eunice and her parents, the Edwardses, went across the yard to sit with her father-in-law while Beulah went off to do her shopping. The old man had never fully recovered from his stroke, but he was sweet in his infirmity. He took out two crisp twenty-dollar-bills and put them in Eunice's hand. "This is for you. For your Christmas."

No matter what problems Eunice might be having with Tommy, she had a real affection for his father. She kissed him and said, "Thank you so much, darlin'. It's real generous of you."

Beulah returned and, as Eunice and her parents were preparing to leave, she reminded them that she was expecting to see them at 7:30 that evening, at the candlelight service at church. They promised that they would be there and went on their way.

Shortly after 7:00 Felton Thomas was walking along a street in the black section of Oakland. He was an itinerant laborer in the groves in which Charlie Mays was the crew boss. Charlie pulled up in his car and offered him a ride in exchange for his help carrying a television set that he was going to pick up at Zeigler's furniture store. Thomas considered for a moment. Riding somewhere was better than walking nowhere. Having something to do was better than having nothing to do. Helping Charlie might help him to get work in one of Charlie's crews.

Thomas got into the car, and Charlie started off in the direction of the store.

It was a happy time at the Spencer home, directly behind the Zeigler furniture store. At 7:10, their daughter, Barbara Spencer Tinsley, came over to wait with her parents for the arrival of her brother. About ten or fifteen minutes later, Mrs. Tinsley heard three or four noises that sounded like a car backfiring. Fifteen minutes later, there were six or seven similar noises.

The family paid no attention to the sounds beyond acknowledging their existence. Somebody was probably having trouble with a car in the parking lot of the shopping center just over the road. Either that, or it was some kids shooting off fireworks. After all, it was a holiday eve. There was no reason to connect the noises with anything that might be happening in the Zeigler store.

Beulah Zeigler had seen to her husband's comforts that evening before departing for church, where she greeted the friends and neighbors of a lifetime and looked in vain for her daughter-in-law and the Edwardses. She took a seat in the church and hoped they would not be late. The candlelight service was something special, and she was disappointed for them that they had not arrived by the time it began. At the midway point, she turned around and, when she still could not see them, her disappointment gave way to a slight vexation.

When she left the church at the end of the service, it was obvious that her relatives had never put in an appearance. She refused to become apprehensive. There could not have been a good reason for missing church but perhaps there was a valid one.

At 9:15, things were just warming up at the Christmas Eve party at the home of Theodore Van Deventer, a West Orange County judge, when the telephone rang. Van Deventer answered. The voice at the other end was extremely weak. "Ted, it's Tommy. Ted, I'm hurt. Let me speak to Don."

The judge summoned Police Chief Don Ficke to the phone. "It's Tommy Zeigler. I think there's trouble."

Ficke grabbed the receiver.

"Don, come quick. I'm at the store. I've been shot."

Ficke hung up and called to another guest, Robert Thompson, the Oakland police chief. "Tommy Zeigler's been shot over at his store. Let's get going."

It took only a few minutes to get to the store. Thompson was the first at the scene. He heard Zeigler shouting to him from within the darkened store. Somebody must have thrown the electrical switch out back. When Thompson reached him, the wounded man collapsed in his arms.

He carried Zeigler over to his police car and started for the nearest hospital. On the way, he noticed that Zeigler's face was spattered with blood and his clothing caked with brownish dried blood. He wondered how it could have dried and discolored that quickly.

When Zeigler came to again, Thompson asked, "Tommy, who shot you?"

"Charlie. Charlie Mays."

"Why?"

There was no response. Thompson tried again. "Was Charlie trying to rob you?"

Tommy nodded. "Yes."

Chief Don Ficke had stayed behind at the store, but he would rather have gone to the hospital. Tommy was his best friend, and he had a bullet in his stomach. There was a chance that he might not pull through. But Ficke had a job to do, and that job kept him at the store.

When his men arrived, he sent one of them around to the back of the store to check the electrical switch. A minute later, the lights came on. Ficke looked around. Even had he not been emotionally involved because of his friendship with the Zeiglers, the sight would have been enough to sicken him.

He had never seen so much blood. It was everywhere—floor, walls, ceiling. Four people had been brutally murdered in that place that night. If Tommy went, the total would rise to five. Four definitely, and of the four, three were good friends of his.

Eunice's mother, Virginia Edwards, was nearest the front of the store. Her body was separated from the others by almost the entire showroom. A shot had passed through her upper arm into her chest. Another pierced her right hand and entered her skull just above the ear, which wore a festive holly earring.

Eunice Zeigler seemed to have been entering the kitchen through the door from the appliance area, the same one into which Mattie Louise Mays had peeked on that very morning. Eunice had been shot in the back of the head and probably had never known what happened to her.

Near the linoleum racks that lined the rear wall of the appliance area, Eunice's father was lying facedown in a large pool of blood. Ficke thought that he could discern two bullet wounds in his head, but he could not be sure because the skull had been so badly battered by a blunt instrument.

Mattie Louise Mays's husband, Charlie, was lying on the floor near Edwards. He also had been bludgeoned and shot. His trousers had been clumsily hooked at the waist by bloodied hands not his own; there was no blood on his hands. The fly was open, exposing a portion of his muscular thigh.

Ficke could not figure out why Charlie Mays was there. He did not understand the reason for any of it. The motive was missing. Revenge seemed far-fetched. The Zeiglers were well liked by everybody. If the motive was robbery, why hadn't they taken any of the appliances that could so easily be fenced? Maybe they were only after cash, enough for a holiday spree.

Ficke walked behind the counter to look in the cash register. It was empty. He shook his head. All of this carnage for a few lousy bucks. He looked up at the clock over the counter. It had stopped at 7:24 and had not gone back on with the electricity. A closer investigation revealed that a bullet had entered from the kitchen side of the wall on which it hung. That was something—it just about pinned down the time of the murders. Still, there was something wrong. If the killings had taken place before 7:30, and Tommy had not called the Van Deventer house for help until 9:15, what in God's name had he been doing during the nearly two intervening hours?

Beulah Zeigler was back home, in her kitchen, preparing sweet potatoes for the next day's Christmas dinner, when the telephone call came. Tommy had been seriously

111

wounded in a hold-up attempt. Eunice had been killed. The Edwardses had been killed. All at the store. How? Why? None of it made any sense. Two of Tommy's friends, Lee Jones, a local banker, and Richard Smith, were coming by to take her to the hospital. It was not the right moment to tell her husband. She had to know more, find the moment when the shock would not endanger his health, as if such a moment would ever exist.

Jones and Smith did not know much more than she had already been told. On the way to the hospital, there seemed to be so little to say. Once there, she had to find out what Tommy knew about Eunice's death. He looked so frail, so ill, that it took all of her fortitude to ask the question instead of taking him in her arms.

"Where's Eunice?"

"I don't know, Mom."

They told him Eunice and her parents had been killed at the store, probably by the same person who had shot him. Tommy began to sob. As the tears rolled down his cheeks, he closed his eyes, unable to look at them or to control himself. Jones cradled him in his arms. He did not believe that his friend's grief was faked nor that he had told a lie. And Beulah, who knew and loved him better than anybody else, also believed him and went on believing him.

By shortly after 10:00 P.M., with the furniture store already jammed with policemen, crime-lab photographers, detectives, and whatever murder investigators a small town like Winter Garden could muster, the coroner arrived. Each of them had entered grumbling about having to work on Christmas Eve. A glance around stopped words in mid-sentence, though mouths remained agape. One tough old-timer gasped, "This has got to be the bloodiest, most

112

bizarre thing I've ever seen in all my years on the force."

The coroner said, "I've never seen so many bodies in one building outside of the morgue."

The sheriff of Orange County, Mel Coleman, and his detective, Don Frye, arrived at 10:30. Frye listened to the details and looked around the premises. By that time, the press had arrived, and one of the reporters asked him for some information. Frye was reluctant to say anything after so cursory an investigation.

"We think it was a robbery. There was definitely a shoot-out and quite a struggle here."

Meanwhile, the police were speculating among themselves. One said, "Could've been the ski-mask bandits."

"What about Mays? They don't shoot up their own kind."

A rookie volunteered eagerly, "Maybe he was one of them. Had his fly open ready to have a go at ole Eunice."

"Or Tommy," an older officer sneered, ending that round of speculation in raucous laughter.

Detective Frye kept nosing around the place and repeating to himself, "It doesn't add up. The whole thing doesn't add up."

Frye was trying to recall everything that he had ever learned from Herb MacDonell about bloodstain evidence.

After MacDonell published *Flight Characteristics and Stain Patterns of Human Blood* in 1971, requests for speeches began to pour in from law enforcement agencies and universities. He thought he needed to do more than talk. Nobody ever learned about blood without spilling some. And so he had founded the Bloodstain Institute (or, to give its more grandiloquent name, the Institute on the Physical Significance of Bloodstain Evidence) soon after resigning from Corning Glass Works in 1972. Using the most promising of his students as assistants, he traveled across the country setting up three- to five-day seminars at universities and in crime laboratories. They were attended by police officers, coroners, criminal attorneys, and private investigators. Under MacDonell's supervision, they conducted experiments utilizing real blood and learned how to catalogue and interpret their findings.

In 1974, Don Frye had attended a session that MacDonell gave at the University of Alabama. His fascination with the material was almost matched by his fascination with the man who was teaching it with such a unique blend of pedantry and gallows humor. After the last session, the class was invited up to MacDonell's hotel room for a farewell drink.

There was no booze in evidence anywhere in the room. When MacDonell reached into a carton clearly marked HUMAN BLOOD, Frye began to wonder what the hell kind of drink the eccentric professor had in mind. MacDonell brought forth an array of his favorite Canadian beers ("my survival kit"), Scotch, Irish whiskey, vodka, gin, mixers, and assorted snacks. He smiled at his students' astonishment. "It discourages thirsty chambermaids."

MacDonell was certainly eccentric, but he also had taught Frye everything that he knew about bloodstain evidence. As he examined the Zeigler store, he wished that the professor was there with him.

Felton Thomas stumbled into the Oakland police station. His brow glistened with perspiration, and the whites seemed to have taken over his eyes.

"You gotta do something! You gotta help me! They're gonna kill me. Just like they did poor Charlie."

If the officer on duty had looked, he would have seen fear, but he only listened and what he thought he heard was another black man who had had one too many. He told him to leave his name, that they would be in touch if they wanted to speak to him.

Thomas cried, "They're gonna kill me, I tell you. You gotta do something."

"I'll tell you what *you* gotta do, buddy boy. Go on home and sleep it off. They've done all the killing they're gonna do for one night."

Thomas left. The police were not going to help him. Nobody was going to help him.

Zeigler's wound was not as serious as had at first been assumed, and the next day he was able to make his statement to State's Attorney Robert Eagan, Sheriff Coleman, and Don Frye. After the lawmen expressed their sympathies and apologized for bothering him at such a time, Zeigler replied, "It's your duty. I'm sorry you guys have to be working on Christmas day."

He turned away, overcome for a moment, and then began to tell his story. On the night before, he closed the store somewhere between 6:30 and 6:40. He went home and exchanged cars with Curtis Dunaway. When he went into the kitchen, Eunice and his mother-in-law were preparing their contributions to the next day's family Christmas dinner. He murmured, "That would've been today."

He paused before going on. "They were fixing to go to the store to pick up a La-Z-Boy recliner for Mr. and Mrs. Edwards."

After the three of them departed, Zeigler went out to buy some liquor for a party. Ed Williams was waiting for him in the driveway when he got back, and the two of them drove to the store. It was shortly after 7:00 P.M. Zeigler unlocked the back door and went into the store, assuming that Williams was following him.

115

"I got hit over the head on the right side. I hit the floor. I lost my glasses. I can't see anything without them. I saw two blurs coming at me."

He was carrying a .22 in a waist holster and drew the weapon. It jammed and jammed again. He threw it at the blurs, but it did not stop them. The next thing he knew, he was flying through the air against walls and refrigerators. One of his assailants was bigger than he was and black, but he had no idea if they were all black. The fight continued into his office, behind the cash counter where he hit the desks and chairs. He snatched open one of the desk drawers, took out a .357 magnum, and then attempted to escape.

"I was scared to death. I tried to fire the weapon, but I'm not sure if it fired. I started swinging that magnum as hard as I could. I was thrown against the linoleum rack and, as I was trying to get off the floor, I was shot. It felt like someone slammed a hot poker all the way through. I heard voices. I don't know whose. 'Mays has been hit. Kill him.' "

Zeigler heard steps and thought that they had gone out through the back stockroom. He started crawling around the floor. He smiled bitterly. "There were Christmas bows everywhere."

He crawled over a body and eventually worked his way back to the office. He had to call somebody for help, but who? He presumed that his mother and wife and in-laws were in church by then. He could not call his father for fear that the shock would kill him. Before anything else, he had to be able to see again. There had to be another pair of glasses somewhere, and he started to grope around in one of the desk drawers.

Zeigler fell back against his pillows. There were some loose ends in his story, but it was obvious that he was too exhausted for them to question him. From his description, it looked as if the job had been done by the ski-mask bandits and that Charlie Mays and Ed Williams were members of the gang. They had better send out a call for the police to pick up Williams.

The three lawmen returned to Eagan's office. Before Williams could be brought in by the police, he voluntarily appeared before them. Fear underscored his melodic speech.

"If you please, sirs, I would very much like to be locked up."

At first, he was reluctant to tell his story. "Although Mr. Tommy's been like a father to me, I've got to tell the truth."

Tommy Zeigler had asked Williams to meet him at the Zeigler house at 7:30. Zeigler had told them that the meeting was at 7:00, and Frye recalled that the clock in the store had been stopped at 7:24 by a bullet, which seemed to pinpoint the time of the shootings. He asked if Williams was not mistaken about the time. The man insisted that he was right, and that he had checked it out.

"I drove up in the driveway. But the house was dark, and nobody was home. So I looked at my watch to see if I was late. It was seven twenty-eight. I looked at the back door, and there was a note. And it said, 'Edward, I'll be right back.' And it was signed 'Z.' "

Williams went back to his truck to wait. He reckoned that it must have been ten or twenty minutes, because he had time to finish the two beers he had brought along with him.

Zeigler returned accompanied by two black men. They were driving Curtis Dunaway's car. That was confusing. Williams knew Zeigler had given Dunaway his own car— that's why he'd asked Williams to pick him up, because Dunaway's car was in bad shape. And here he was driving around in it.

117

Zeigler got out and came over to Williams's pickup truck. "I'll be back in a few minutes. Wait here."

Zeigler then drove off with the other two. He returned alone about ten minutes later. Williams saw him go into the garage and wipe his hands with a towel before coming over to the truck. He climbed in and nodded in the direction of the store. "Let's go."

When they got to the store, Zeigler jumped out at the front door and told Williams to park in the rear and come in through the back. The lawmen exchanged looks. Zeigler had told them that they had both gone in through the back door and that, just inside it, he was attacked. One of them was obviously lying.

By the time Williams had parked behind the store, the beers were beginning to have their inevitable effect, and he stopped to take a leak against the fence. He heard Zeigler calling, "Ed, come on in."

Williams entered the back door. It led into a long narrow corridor that ran alongside the storage room and served as its auxiliary. It terminated in another door that opened into the appliance section in the rear of the store proper.

"When I got to the end of the hallway, I saw that he had a gun in his hand with a rag over it."

The gun was pointed directly at Ed Williams.

"He snapped it three times. Pop—pop—pop!"

Tommy had pulled the trigger, but the gun had jammed. It would not fire. Those were the loudest pops that Williams had ever heard. "I cried, 'Mr. Tommy, why do you want to kill me?' "

He did not wait for an answer but started to run with Zeigler pursuing him, shouting, "Wait! Wait! I didn't realize the man in the store was you."

Williams called back over his shoulder, "What do you mean? I work for you! I came over here with you!"

Tommy caught up with him outside the store and tried to sweet-talk him back in. He went so far as to proffer the pistol that had misfired. Williams thrust it back at him. He did not want any part of a gun, or Zeigler, or anything else that might be in that store that night. He just ran.

When Williams finished his story, his listeners were silent. It was only one man's word against another's, and Williams might be a very smart liar. He might have come forward only because he knew that Zeigler was still alive. It might be a ruse in anticipation of Zeigler's disclosure of his real activities on that night. Williams's request to be held in jail was granted, but that might also be only a clever trick to deceive the police.

After Williams was led away, Frye said he was certain the solution to their problem lay in the store, and that it could be found only by an expert in bloodstain evidence. He requested permission to call Herb MacDonell and ask him to come down and investigate.

Eagan asked, "Who's MacDonell?"

"The greatest expert on bloodstain evidence in the world. He wrote the book."

"Cool it. How much is this genius going to cost?"

"His expenses and a fee of—I don't know—I guess about a hundred a day."

The other two looked at each other and shrugged. "I suppose the county can scrape that much together. Get him on the phone and see if he can come down here. The sooner the better."

Frye was already dialing.

MacDonell said he would take the case but would not be able to get to Winter Garden before January 6.

Frye agreed reluctantly. It was a long time to wait. He hung up and asked Eagan to issue an order sealing the premises until midnight of January 7.

"That's two weeks! Zeigler's lawyers are going to scream the roof down."

"Tell them that MacDonell plays it square. He may even prove that Tommy's telling the truth."

During the rest of the week, more pieces began to fall into place. Barbara Spencer Tinsley called to tell of hearing what by then she knew were gunshots. The police obtained a statement from Mattie Louise Mays describing her visit to the store on the morning of the killings. The jai alai winnings were confirmed by two jai alai tickets and the cash found in Mays's pocket—along with a ring of keys to the store and the day's receipts. The latter two might have been planted on him after he was murdered.

Through Williams, they got to Frank Smith, the cab driver, who confirmed that he had sold the two .38s to Zeigler. The owner of Ray's Fish and Tackle Shop in Winter Garden reported selling Zeigler still another .38 two months before the shootings.

By Friday morning, December 26, the FBI report had come through. It confirmed that the bullets that had killed Zeigler's in-laws had come from one of the .38s he had purchased from Smith and that the other had been used to kill Eunice. Although Mays had been shot, the coroner reported the man had died from blunt trauma to the head caused by multiple fractures apparently sustained in eight separate blows with a blunt instrument.

All of the twenty bullets fired in the store that night, including those removed from the victims, the clock, and Zeigler, had come from the eight guns found there, all of which were traced to Zeigler. The .22 that had jammed, saving Ed Williams's life, had once belonged to Zeigler's pal, Police Chief Don Ficke.

In a meeting in the state's attorney's office on the afternoon of December 26, Eagan said, "It would appear that Mr. Zeigler is our prime suspect."

Ficke protested, "He can't be. He was shot, too."

Frye said, "He could've shot himself to try to make it look like he had nothing to do with the killings. The hospital report says that he only hit his side. He didn't hit anywhere near his gut. Even the most superficial knowledge of anatomy would've told him that he couldn't come to any great harm from that wound."

Ficke still could not believe it. "What about a motive? You don't kill four people for nothing."

Eagan removed a sheet of paper from beneath his desk blotter. "I've got a report here. I won't bother to read all of it to you. I'll just give you the salient point. Two months ago"—he turned to Ficke—"about the time your pal Tommy was buying a gun from Ray's Fish and Tackle, he took out two insurance policies on Eunice's life valued at five hundred twenty thousand dollars."

Frye smiled at Ficke. "I'd hardly call that nothing. It looks like we've got the weapons, the suspect, and the motive."

Eagan was more cautious. He was the one who was going to have to take the case to court. "Hold on. There's no law against a wealthy man—or a poor one, for that matter—taking out big insurance on his wife's life. The point is—does he really need the money?"

"Does anybody *not* need half a million bucks?"

"I've always thought that the Zeiglers were very well heeled. Maybe not. You'd better look into Junior's financial condition. As for the weapons, they could've been stolen from him."

Frye groaned.

Eagan went on. "We won't know much until we can

get another statement from Zeigler. At the moment, his lawyer isn't letting him make one."

"If he's so goddam innocent, why the hell's he got a lawyer buttoning him up?"

Ficke said, "He's still a citizen of this country. He's got the same constitutional rights as any other citizen."

"Oh, yeah," Frye challenged. "Well, I heard tell that there'd been a lot of problems between Eunice and him. What do you say to that?"

Before Ficke could say anything, the telephone rang. Eagan answered it and spoke a few terse words. When he hung up, he said, "Gentlemen, we've found Felton Thomas. The man whom Mays was seen picking up in his car just before the murders."

Felton Thomas was both relieved that his brief period of life on the run was over and fearful of what might happen to him next. "I didn't do anything," he told the police. "My friend told me—he said—'It's a good thing you didn't go into that store. There's four people killed up there.' "

He had gone straight to the police, but they had not wanted to hear what he had to say, and now he was afraid to say anything. His interrogators were patient and gentle. It was only after they finally convinced him that they were on his side that he began to talk.

Mays and Thomas pulled up at the rear of the store at about 7:30. Zeigler was waiting for them. He asked them to get into his car, said that he had a favor he wanted them to do for him. Charlie readily agreed for both of them. Zeigler was giving him such a good deal on the TV set, there was nothing Mays would not have done to keep on his good side.

Zeigler drove them out to a nearby, deserted orange grove. He pointed to a brown paper bag filled with guns that was lying on the seat beside him and asked them to test-fire them for him. It was a crazy notion, but Charlie persuaded Thomas to go along with it. The funny part was that Zeigler was in such an all-fired hurry that he would not let them take the time to get out of the car. Shooting from the window was good enough to satisfy him. They picked up the guns and fired them a couple of times, and then he drove them back to the store.

When they got there, Zeigler started asking them to do all kinds of peculiar things. He asked Thomas to throw some kind of electrical switch on the outside of the building. Then, he said that he had forgotten his keys and, if Charlie wanted that TV set for Christmas, they were going to have to help him break in. Thomas was not about to break into any white man's store, and he managed to stop the overeager Charlie from doing it by himself.

Zeigler agreed to go back to his house and pick up his keys, and they all drove over to this big house on Temple Drive. There was a black man waiting in a pickup truck, and Zeigler went over to speak to him. Thomas never did see him go into the house for the keys.

By the time they arrived back at the store, Thomas was thinking that there was something mighty wrong about the whole setup. Not Charlie—Charlie was only thinking about that TV. Zeigler invited them in, but Thomas backed off. He would wait in the car, thank you all the same, until Charlie came out with the set. The others went in and the more Thomas thought about it the less he liked it. He left the car and walked across the street to a convenience store. When Charlie did not reappear, he just kept on walking. To hell with the ride and all the crazy cats, black or white, in Winter Garden.

When he finished his story, they asked Thomas to show them exactly where they had test-fired the guns. He directed them to the grove. They found fragments of .38 slugs.

Frye summarized the case for Eagan. They had a time sequence for Zeigler's movements on the night of the killings, but that timing would be challenged. It would come down to the word of a prominent white man against that of two poor black laborers. They would need something stronger than that. What was missing was a scenario for what actually had happened in that store, the order in which each of the victims had been dispatched, the movements of the killer. Frye was counting on MacDonell to give it in a style so realistic that its veracity could not be questioned.

The state's attorney hoped that Frye's faith in the talents of his friend was justified because, on the strength of it, he issued an order for Zeigler's arrest on four counts of first-degree murder.

On Monday, December 29, Zeigler was arrested for murder and transferred from a private hospital to the detention facilities at Florida Hospital. The next day, his tiny hospital room was overcrowded with reporters, court clerks, and lawmen. Wan and listless, Tommy Zeigler lay beside a tray of uneaten food while Circuit Court Judge Peter M. de Manio stood at his bedside and read the charges. He then asked: "Do you understand the nature of these charges and your rights as the accused?"

Tommy was barely audible. "Yes."

"Each of the charges is punishable by death or imprisonment for life requiring that not less than twenty-five years of the sentence be served before you are eligible for parole. There is no bond set on any of these counts."

Zeigler did not move during the entire proceedings. His eyes never wandered from the face of Judge de Manio, and whatever emotions he might have been feeling were kept to himself.

Beulah Zeigler had been through the worst week of her life, but she knew that it was only the beginning of her ordeal. When it became apparent that her son was going to be charged with murder, she did not wait to consult anybody before hiring the best criminal attorney she could find, Edward R. Kirkland, to work along with Tommy's regular lawyers, Ralph Hadley III and Vernon Davids. She did not care what was necessary so long as they got her boy off.

Kirkland knew that the only motive the prosecution had was the $520,000 insurance that Zeigler had taken out on Eunice's life two months before the murders. He convinced his client to renounce all claims to the insurance money. If he willingly gave up any possibility of gain from his wife's death, it might dilute Eagan's case.

The next defense move was to have the older Zeiglers support their belief in their son's innocence by offering $1,000 for information leading to the apprehension and conviction of the real guilty parties. The sum was not as paltry as it sounded, when one took into account the income of black laborers in central Florida citrus groves.

Herb MacDonell entered Zeigler's furniture store for the first time at 10:30 on the morning of January 7. He was followed by a group of representatives of both the prosecution and the defense. He looked around, rubbed his hands together, and turned to his audience with a smile.

"What a bloody mess!"

At exactly 10:45, he started to work. MacDonell was in his element, up to his magnifying glass in enough blood drops, drips, smears, spots, and spatters to gladden the heart of any Jackson Pollock enthusiast. The picture revealed to him was as well composed and unalterable as any of that painter's masterpieces.

The blood sleuth put in a full eight-hour day, and by the time he was ready to leave the store the complete story had been uncovered by cross-referencing his findings on the premises with the detailed photographs of the bodies that had been provided by Don Frye.

Tommy and Eunice had arrived at the store in her car, parked it out back (where it was later found by the police), and had come through the rear door. They had walked down the storage corridor in which Tommy later attempted to shoot Ed Williams and had entered the showroom. From there, Eunice had started for the private kitchen. She had just entered it when she was shot in the back of the head by Tommy, who was standing behind her in the appliance area. She was found on the kitchen floor with her head haloed in blood and her feet extended out toward the door. Blood spatters from her wound on the door casing, threshold, and adjacent wall had pinpointed the shooting.

In total, Tommy would discharge twenty bullets before the evening was over. He apparently fired more than once at Eunice, because a stray bullet from the same .38 that had killed her had pierced the kitchen wall, stopping the clock on the other side of the wall at 7:24. MacDonell knew that this was the exact time of her murder because the bullets came from the same weapon, had parallel trajectories, and Zeigler had used another gun for the subsequent killings.

Doubtless, Eunice had been unaware that she was about to be shot. Her left hand had remained in her pocket holding a tissue. Had she known that she was in danger, she would have been doing something to protect herself rather than remaining in this relaxed posture. For the same reason, MacDonell deduced that she had been the first to be shot. She certainly would not have been so relaxed in her demeanor had she seen the bodies of her parents or

Mays. The electrical switch had not yet been thrown, and the lights were on, MacDonell knew, because the clock was still working, and Tommy had to have been able to see his victims in order to have been so accurate when shooting them.

The Edwardses were the next victims. Their car was found parked in front of the store. They must have seen the lights on the way to church and stopped to find out if anything was wrong. Because Tommy had closed the store almost an hour earlier, the double front doors were probably still locked. They knocked on them. Tommy must have let them in and locked up behind them. He certainly would not have wanted any more unexpected guests on that night.

From that part of the showroom, they could not have seen their daughter's body and, casually chatting with their son-in-law, started strolling toward the back. They could not be permitted to live to testify that Tommy had been in the store alone at that time. They got about ten feet inside to a spot slightly to the left of the cash counter. The spatters from the gunshot wounds told MacDonell that it was there that Zeigler shot them. They were not fatal wounds. Trails of blood leading to where the bodies were subsequently found proved that they had been able to move.

Perry Edwards was stronger than his wife and posed a greater threat to Zeigler. Leaving Virginia Edwards for the moment, Zeigler lunged at his father-in-law to finish him off. Had he gone after Mrs. Edwards first, her husband would surely have made some move to defend her. The trail of blood indicated that he had not done so, because he was too busy trying to ward off his killer.

Zeigler had rushed to the back, had grabbed the linoleum crank from its usual location between the racks, and then come after Edwards. Following the bloody route and analyzing the quality of the drops and spatters, MacDonell knew that Zeigler had pursued his victim past the counter

127

into the appliance area. The stains along the way proved that Edwards was continually being beaten on the head with the crank. He faltered for a moment, bracing himself against the kitchen door jamb, his head bent forward, dripping blood on his daughter's shoes as she lay on the kitchen floor, another proof that she was already dead when her father arrived.

Zeigler picked up a gun and shot Edwards twice in the head. He fell and was found lying facedown in a large pool of blood. During the struggle, Zeigler had administered fourteen blows to his head. It was then his mother-in-law's turn.

MacDonell returned to the spot where the Edwardses had been shot. Virginia's blood marked her route away from there like the red line indicating a road on a map. He followed it. While her husband was being bludgeoned, the frantic woman had obviously tried to escape. She went to the front door and tried it. No good. Zeigler had locked it and taken the keys with him.

MacDonell followed her path as she wandered up to the right, to the furniture display area. She "huddled down" beside a sofa in a vain attempt to hide from the killer. The photographs showed her lying on her left side with her left ear pressed against the floor, and her eyes were closed. Although her right hand was at her side, a flesh wound on her right index finger and powder burns on the hand indicated that she had been covering her ear.

MacDonell could imagine what she was feeling as she tried to shut out the terrible scene that was being enacted behind her, praying that she might be forgotten, disappear, awaken in another place at another time. There was no hope of that. Tommy was upon her. He fired, and the killing bullet struck her finger and entered her skull just above the ear.

The stage was now set for the entrances of Charlie

Mays and Ed Williams, who were cast in the roles of marauding ski-mask bandits. Tommy checked to see that there was no blood on his hands or clothing. He wiped his prints off the guns that he had just used and flung them into a paper bag, taking it with him when he went out to his car to wait for the guileless Charlie Mays to come by for his television set.

When Felton Thomas showed up with Charlie, Tommy probably thought that it would only improve the script. Three bandits were better than two. After Thomas eluded him, there was nothing to indicate that Tommy had second thoughts about killing Mays. It was too late for that. The first act had already been played.

Charlie Mays was shot twice, but he was actually killed by the severe beating that was administered after he fell to the floor. Zeigler had used the same linoleum crank with which he had battered Edwards. The many blood-stain patterns ascending like rays from the area of his head left no doubt in MacDonell's mind that the man was already down when the beating took place. Some of his blood was found on top of the swipe pattern stains already left by Perry Edwards as he staggered around trying to escape from his assailant.

Charlie's blood had not mixed with Perry's, which had dried. The fact that Perry's blood had dried before being covered by Charlie's proved to MacDonell that Charlie had been killed some time after Perry.

A shoulder holster had been found near Charlie's body. The investigators were supposed to assume that it had belonged to him. One look and MacDonell knew that it was a plant that had been placed there after the man had been beaten to death. The kind of mauling that Charlie had sustained would have produced a spray of medium-velocity bloodstains over its top surface. There were none on the holster. The area in which it had been found was bespattered with blood. None of it had transferred to the back of the holster, because the blood had dried before the holster was dropped in it. Bloodstains of the size that were on the floor required fifteen to twenty minutes to dry sufficiently so as not to transfer to an object, like the holster, dropped on them.

Zeigler had claimed that he was in the rear of the store when he was shot and had gone from there to the phone to call for help. Then he had gone to the front of the store to wait. Tommy's own blood told MacDonell that the man was a liar. It was true that the amount of blood on the phone indicated he was bleeding either immediately prior to or just after using it. The trail of blood from the phone to the front of the store also verified that part of the story. But Tommy was lying in the most important part of his story. He was nowhere near the rear of the store when he was allegedly shot by Charlie Mays, for the simple reason that there was no trail of blood from there to the phone. His bleeding began in the area of the phone, and he was clearly shot while in that area. The only person who was near the phone that night was Tommy, and so, it was Tommy who shot Tommy.

When MacDonell wrote his report, he concluded:

Undoubtedly, Mr. Mays entered the store after all three other victims were killed. To conclude otherwise would suggest that he was present while the other victims were being killed and did nothing to prevent their deaths. Had Mays been the perpetrator, his bloody sneaker prints would have been detected after he had beaten Mr. Edwards so badly. Instead, Mays was both beaten and shot, and another shoeprint pattern in blood is evident over most of the uncarpeted area. Most likely, this is the shoeprint of the perpetrator.

On July 2, 1976, William Thomas Zeigler, Jr., was found guilty of two counts of first-degree murder in the deaths of Eunice Zeigler and Charles Mays and two counts of second-degree murder in the deaths of Perry and Virginia Edwards. Herbert Leon MacDonell's vivid courtroom reconstruction of the slayings did much to convince the jury of its verdict.

The jury recommended a life sentence. Circuit Court Judge Maurice M. Paul sentenced Zeigler to death.

On June 12, 1981, the Florida Supreme Court upheld Zeigler's conviction. On March 22, 1982, the United States Supreme Court refused to hear his appeal. The governor of Florida has yet to sign the death warrant, because there is still recourse to federal courts.

Beulah Zeigler no longer goes to church regularly. Instead, her Sundays are devoted to visiting her son in the Florida State Prison. She recently said, "I thought the law was perfect, the FBI was lily-white. I had to wake up in later years to find they're black as black can be."

In January 1978, Tommy Zeigler said, "I think life in prison is much like life anywhere else. You make of it what you want. I try to make it as pleasant and acceptable as I can."

Four years later, after the United States Supreme Court had refused to hear his appeal, he said: "I'd just as soon be in the ground next to Eunice and my parents, when they die, and let that end it all."

He was still writing love poetry dedicated to his duchess.

It seems you're always there to lend a helping hand,
And with your beautiful smile to say you understand.

5

A SERPENT'S TOOTH

In 1881, Duluth, Minnesota, was a small village of less than five thousand inhabitants. With the opening of the rich iron mines and vast timber reserves of northern Minnesota, Duluth's great natural harbor on Lake Superior and the newly built railroads turned it into a boomtown, and by 1891 the population had swollen by thirty thousand new settlers. Rogues, outlaws, gamblers, immigrants, adventurers, clerks, peddlers—dreamers and schemers all—came to exploit the new land. Among them were Chester Congdon and his wife, Clara.

Congdon prospered. By the time his daughter, Elisabeth, was born in 1894, he was one of the most successful men in Duluth. Elisabeth was not the handsomest of the six Congdon children, but she was the brightest. Because there was little opportunity for a proper education in Duluth, her father shipped her east to an exclusive New England school for young ladies, Dana Hall, and from there to Vassar college to complete her schooling.

Chester Congdon died in 1915 shortly before his daughter was due to receive her college degree. During the little less than a quarter of a century that he had resided in Duluth, he had managed to become the richest man in Minnesota, leaving behind a vast fortune locked in a series of intricate trusts designed to keep the Congdons among the richest families in the state for generations to come.

Although Elisabeth Congdon suffered from the double handicap of being both plain and brilliant, she had the more than compensating asset of extreme wealth. Marriage proposals were forthcoming. In any of the five languages in which she had become fluent, the answer was the same: no. It took a certain amount of spirit to evade marriage in those days in Lutheran Minnesota, but she managed to do it.

She passed from her twenties through her thirties into her forties, surrounded by a large family of sisters, brothers, nephews, and nieces of which she was tacitly recognized as the head. She had discovered that a life devoted to bringing culture to Duluth and charity to the poor was not without its own rewards. She ruled in apparent contentment at Glensheen, the awesome estate that her father had built in 1905 on fourteen choice acres bordering Lake Superior. The thirty-nine-room red-brick-and-limestone mansion was replete with heavy, hand-hewn paneling, dark passages illumined by leaded windows, and fourteen great stone fireplaces. In addition to the big house, there were greenhouses, a caretaker's cottage, a gardener's cottage, and a boathouse and dock on the embankment.

In addition to this somber mansion, Elisabeth had a brighter summer lodge in Brule, Wisconsin, and a dazzling winter villa in Tucson, Arizona. Still, as she moved from residence to residence, solitude came with the luggage. In 1937, at the age of forty-three, she made a startling announcement to her lawyers. She intended to adopt not one but two little girls—she did not, she explained, approve of only children.

The lawyers protested that it was impossible for a maiden lady to adopt children, but Elisabeth knew that nothing was impossible when one was as rich as she was, and she prevailed. Marjorie and Jennifer Congdon were adopted when Jennifer was still in the toddler stage and Marjorie only three years older. To the criticism of her family and the Duluth community, she said, "I only want to help those less fortunate than myself. I shall give these poor children a good home and education."

She was more than true to that public statement. Marjorie and Jennifer were made equal participants in the family trusts and heiresses to her substantial private holdings.

From the beginning, there were marked differences in their personalities and temperaments. Jennifer was a sweet, obedient, orderly child to whom adults responded with praise and approval. Her sister, Marjorie, was an undersized tomboy, a hellion whose need to give and receive love was awesome. Temper tantrums alternated with wild excesses of generosity and physical affection. Only Elisabeth seemed to understand, reacting with a soothing, endless patience.

Marjorie became passionately devoted to horses. The Congdon relatives hoped that the animals' unqualified return of love would have a calming effect on the girl. They were disappointed. She still needed someone, a person who would love her without judging her. In 1950, at the age of sixteen, she thought that she had found that person. She married a young insurance broker by the name of Richard LeRoy. The LeRoys proceeded to have seven children in rapid succession.

Marjorie's children had to be perfect; they had to excel

at everything—and toward that end, there was nothing that was too good for them, nothing that would be denied them. Three thousand dollars a month went for figure skating lessons for her children and up to $4,500 for their horses and riding lessons. She was present at every lesson, at every contest, at every meet, at every activity in which the children participated. It was natural to her, for to Marjorie, the nature of love was to be always there, to know everything about the loved one, to be loved in return for this constant attention. It never occurred to her that it might seem to others that she was buying love. It never occurred to her that she might appear to her children to be overbearing and restrictive.

If Marjorie was a spendthrift, her extravagances were rarely for herself. Nobody could ever recall a shopping spree designed to satisfy her own caprices, but she was forever showering gifts on those less fortunate as well as on her friends, her mother, her children, her husband.

Finally, her husband had had enough, and he asked for a divorce after some twenty years of marriage. There was not enough love in the world to recompense for what Marjorie was spending to purchase it. Although she was heartbroken, her divorce did not curb her spending. As each child came of driving age, he or she received a new car. She bought a large tract of land near Stillwater, Minnesota, on which she built an extravagant horse farm with private living quarters for the children. They had the semblance of privacy without its reality, for Marjorie could not resist going through their mail and listening in on their telephone conversations. To her, it was part of love to know everything about the loved one. In 1973, when her oldest daughter, Suzanne, was eighteen, the girl could no longer stand this interference in her private life and, like her father, she left home. For the second time, the price that Marjorie was willing to pay for love was insufficient to obtain it.

The spending continued, and the Congdon trustees looked on aghast as Marjorie's bills mounted. Between 1967 and 1974, she had received nearly three million dollars from trusts set up for her by Elisabeth, and she was still over a million dollars in debt. It was compulsive buying on a scale that approached mania, but she was incapable of stopping.

Marjorie was desperate. She had speculated in real estate, and the Stillwater spread had cost a great deal more than she had anticipated. She needed money to cover some of her larger debts, or she would lose everything. The only person to whom she could turn was her mother, but she was extremely reluctant to do so, for Elisabeth had become an invalid.

In 1969, a stroke had rendered Elisabeth almost completely incapacitated, and she had to be under the care of round-the-clock nurses. Her mind remained sound most of the time, and her love for her daughter was undimmed. The aphasia manifested itself in a loss of the ability to recognize the written word; she would sign anything that was put in front of her. Marjorie was aware of the condition. But she also needed a bank loan of $345,000, and, to get it, she needed Elisabeth to co-sign. She may have rationalized that her mother would have done it anyway; she may have attempted to explain her predicament to the older woman. Nobody can know, for nobody else was present at the time Marjorie obtained the signature.

Marjorie defaulted on the loan. Litigation, which would be very disturbing to Elisabeth, was threatened. Marjorie consulted her attorney, David Arnold, about what she might do to forestall any distress to her mother. He advised her to sign a document admitting that she had tricked her mother into guaranteeing the loan. At first, she refused, denying that she had ever used false pretenses. After several weeks, she finally consented, realizing that she again had no alternative, still protesting her innocence.

Marjorie's financial problems did not abate, and for the second time she turned to her mother for help. On this occasion, she talked her into signing a $125,000 bank note. When the Congdon trustees discovered what they considered this most recent attempt to bilk money out of the helpless Elisabeth, they decided to take action. The invalid obviously needed a conservator, and her secretary, Vera Dunbar, was appointed to the position. Ms. Dunbar neither liked nor trusted Marjorie and would never again allow her to approach her mother for help.

Marjorie had gone through a considerable fortune seeking the impossible: total approval and unquestioning love. Now, she was on the brink of bankruptcy both financially and emotionally. Despite all her efforts to bind her children to her, only the youngest, Rick, remained in her care. In 1975, after discovering that the teenager was suffering from acute asthma, she decided to move to Colorado. Not only would it be good for his health, but it would also be a new start for her. She would need money to do it properly and, since she was barred from her mother by Dunbar, a loan from the trust against her future inheritance was the most expeditious source.

That year, there was a family reunion at Glensheen at which the partially paralyzed Elisabeth presided, guarded by her nurses and the wary Vera Dunbar. Marjorie's cousin, Thomas Congdon, was one of the trustees, and Marjorie approached him. Congdon lived in Denver, Colorado, and she mentioned how salubrious that area would be for Rick's condition, and said she was planning to relocate there. The problem was that a new home required furnishings and draperies made of special fabrics that would not aggravate the boy's illness. She wanted a loan of $200,000 to provide a setting that would be conducive to her son's well-being.

Congdon was shocked. "Ricky and you have no right to expect housing on such a grand scale."

Marjorie got furious. The frightening temper that she had sporadically displayed since childhood once again flared up. She screamed, "If my son dies as a result of this, you will be responsible for his death!"

From that moment, she began to believe that Thomas Congdon and Vera Dunbar, along with some of the other officers in the trust, were conspiring against her. It may have been paranoiac, but she assuredly could make it most unpleasant for all of them were she ever to gain control of her inheritance. In the management of a fortune the size of the Congdon trusts, there were always transactions that did not bear close scrutiny and decisions about which there might be some ambiguity.

That Marjorie could prove troublesome became immediately apparent. She began to order her personal accountant to make repeated audits of the trust. Thomas Congdon was president of a Colorado gas-and-oil-exploration company in which the family held a forty-two percent interest, and she was suspicious of all dealings involving Congdon funds. She said, "I don't trust them. They're making improper transactions."

Despite her financial problems, Marjorie and Rick moved to Colorado in 1975. If Thomas Congdon felt uncomfortable about having his cousin as a near neighbor, he nevertheless attempted to be as helpful to her as possible.

In 1976, Marjorie met Roger Caldwell. He was a man

who had made starts at many professions without conspicuous success in any of them. Mostly, he lived on hope and his wits. Caldwell saw beyond Marjorie's moodiness to her genuine charm and spontaneity and, at the beginning, seemed to give her the one thing for which she always had craved, total approval. They were married after dating for only two months.

The Caldwells shared a taste for impossible dreams that only plunged Marjorie deeper into debt. Credit cards, automobiles, and horses were repossessed. There was a serious problem about a bounced check used as a down payment on some property. Before long, his initial approval disappeared, and Roger began to complain, "That bitch! I run around trying to put out all her fires."

Roger demanded power of attorney as a fire-fighting weapon, and she gave it. To love meant withholding nothing. It meant accepting everything about the loved one including his faults. Even after discovering that Roger was an alcoholic, charming when sober and physically abusive when drunk, she stayed with him. He once beat her up so badly that a physician had to be called, and she still stayed with him, but from then on, she did take Rick and check into a motel whenever Roger had a few too many.

In January 1977, Rick was following the Caldwells home from a party at which his stepfather had become inebriated. He saw his mother reach over and turn off the ignition. They were having a violent quarrel in the front seat, and the boy pulled ahead of them, turning his car perpendicular to the shoulder of the road in front of their vehicle. When Rick tried to intervene, Roger grabbed a chain from the back seat and struck him twice. Rick leapt forward and started to retaliate, but Roger broke away, jumped into his own car, and drove off, leaving his weeping wife and her injured son at the side of the road. A

Colorado highway patrolman saw the incident and arrested Caldwell.

After Roger agreed to seek treatment for his alcoholism, the assault charges were dropped. The treatment failed, and he began to disappear on benders with ever-increasing frequency. Marjorie would rationalize his behavior by calling him "a regular Jekyll and Hyde." She grew adept at telling lies to cover for his absences, sometimes losing track and telling different stories to different people to conceal the same incident. Between lying for her husband and her mounting financial problems, the pressures on her were almost intolerable and she unthinkingly blurted out things that shocked even those who were closest to her. To her, they were only simple truths, but she did not pause to analyze how they sounded out of context.

To one friend, she confided, "The only way I'm going to get out of this financial mess is if my mother kicks the bucket."

To another, she said that her mother was "being kept alive" because a group of people were drawing handsome salaries working for her. Referring to Elisabeth's condition, she told Rick: "I'd never want to rely on a nurse twenty-four hours a day. I'd rather be dead."

By the spring of 1977, the Caldwells were in a desperate state both emotionally and financially. Marjorie longed for a place where they could all start over, where Rick could become well, where Roger could dry out, where she could be rewardingly occupied raising her beloved animals. The ranch of her dreams came on the market. The problem was that it carried a price tag of $750,000, which she did not have. If only she could borrow it, then all of their difficulties would disappear, and everybody could live happily ever after.

Marjorie knew better than to ask the trust for a loan.

Thomas Congdon and several of the other trustees had made it abundantly clear that they would have no more to do with her extravagant whims. She thought that Roger might fare better with the directors if only he would stay sober. It was worth a try. He was persuasive when he was sober.

In May, Roger went to Duluth to present his request to the trustees, arguing that ranch life was absolutely necessary if Rick was to recover his health. According to Thomas Congdon, he had even forged a letter from a physician that supported this claim. He was turned down. He had never met his mother-in-law and, before returning to Colorado, he went to Glensheen for the first time. The visit went well, but Elisabeth could not help the Caldwells. She no longer had any control over her own money.

Things between the Caldwells did not improve after Roger got back to Colorado. They had so little money that, in June, Thomas Congdon had to pay their bill at the Holland House Motel, in Golden, where they had been living for the previous three months. Roger became obsessed with Marjorie's debts. Because of the power of attorney that was his one control over her, he would become responsible for the debts should anything happen to her. They consulted her attorney, David Arnold, who suggested that Marjorie sign over a substantial portion of her inheritance to Roger, which he could then use to honor her obligations. It was only a sop. Arnold knew that no money would be forthcoming until after Elisabeth Congdon's death, and even then, it was likely that the trustees would tie up the estate for years. Roger nonetheless agreed that he would be satisfied with the arrangement; it was Marjorie who resisted. No matter what her relationship with them, her children remained her legitimate heirs. She was irresponsible with money, but not to the degree that she could simply leave it to an alcoholic to do the right thing after she was gone.

At a horse show in mid-June, the Caldwells had another violent argument in front of Rick. Roger was waving a document at his wife. He shouted, "You'd better sign this, or I'm walking out here and now."

Marjorie refused. She began to cry and ran off. Roger stormed after her. On June 24, she could resist no longer, and she signed the agreement that irrevocably assigned $2.5 million of her inheritance to her husband. A lifetime habit of buying love was not easily broken.

On the same Friday afternoon, June 24, Elisabeth Congdon was looking forward to spending the weekend at her summer place in Brule, Wisconsin. With Marjorie living in Colorado, and her other daughter, Jennifer, in Racine, her life had become increasingly solitary. Visitors were infrequent except for those who came on business or to beg for favors, and her only companions were her devoted servants and nurses. She also had a manager, Vera Dunbar, but she no longer had any real life to manage, and the title was a misnomer for a woman who functioned chiefly as a watchdog for Thomas Congdon and the other trustees. Elisabeth's pleasures were the occasional gin game, television, and the medication that eased her painlessly into sleep and back into consciousness.

In the warm months, Brule provided a break in the monotony of life at Glensheen. This weekend was particularly special to Elisabeth, because Marjorie's oldest son, Stephen, was going to spend it with her. One of her nurses, Mildred Klosowsky, packed her things for the weekend at Brule, and the chauffeur-houseman took them out to the car. Among the pieces were some wicker bags that neither of them remembered having seen before.

Later that evening, there was a person-to-person long-distance call at Glensheen, but Hilda Conger, the live-in maid, could not tell if the caller was a man or woman, nor did she know from where the call originated. The operator asked for Miss Congdon, and Hilda replied that she was in Brule and would not be returning until late Sunday afternoon. When she asked who was calling, the phone went dead. She was alone in the house, but the call did not make her apprehensive. There were three stout locks on the front door and so little fear of break-in that Miss Congdon had never installed a burglar alarm system.

Elisabeth and her staff arrived back at Glensheen at 4:00 on Sunday afternoon, June 26, 1977. Later that evening, she was taken up to her second-floor bedroom and prepared to retire. All of her jewelry was put away except for her sapphire ring and wristwatch, which she insisted on wearing to bed. She was being propped up with her pink satin pillows when the night nurse, Velma Pietila, arrived to take over for Miss Klosowsky, who left for home after having been on duty for the whole weekend.

Velma had retired the month before and was filling in for only that one night while the regular night nurse took her vacation. The day nurse had called and begged her to do it. Velma had replied, "I miss Miss Congdon, and so I'll do it. But just for this one night. You'll have to find somebody else for tomorrow."

Velma removed Elisabeth's hearing aid and placed the bell within easy reach of her good hand. The phone was turned off; the room was illumined by one dim night-light. Velma left the door slightly ajar as she left to cross the hall to the nurse's room.

Downstairs, Hilda Conger checked to see that the three

locks on the front door were secured and then went through the mansion to the back stairs, turning off lights along the way.

The Caldwells had dinner in the restaurant of their motel residence in Golden on that same Sunday evening. Marjorie was grateful for Colorado's blue laws. Her good nights were any during which Roger could not buy a drink. She had spent part of the weekend indulging in her favorite pastime: looking at properties that she could not afford to buy.

The next morning, Marjorie was the first customer at the local Laundromat, and it was in that unlikely setting that the longest nightmare of her life began. A long-distance telephone call from Duluth was relayed from the hotel. The Laundromat owner watched her agitation deepen to near hysteria as she listened to the message. When she hung up, she told him that her mother and her mother's nurse, Velma Pietila, had been brutally murdered during the early-morning hours of that day.

There apparently had been a break-in at Glensheen, for there were some indications of robbery. Nothing would be known for certain until they checked all of Elisabeth's possessions. Her mother had been smothered with her own pink satin pillow, while the maid lay bludgeoned to death on the landing of the mansion's grand center stairway.

Whatever Marjorie might have been feeling, she kept her counsel that morning. She had already spoken too volubly on the subject of Elisabeth Congdon's death, often expressing the opinion that the last few years of her mother's life had been wasted and pointlessly prolonged. Marjorie had attempted to build an illusory future on the foundation of promissory notes guaranteed by an inheritance that would be hers only at her mother's death.

She wandered around Golden, dropping in on friends and acquaintances. It might have been near hysteria, or the compulsive prevarication that had surfaced so often in the past, or something darker, but along the way, she told several contradictory stories concerning her husband's whereabouts that morning, including one that he had been at the Laundromat with her when she received the news. Some people thought she was once again attempting to cover up another of Roger's binges. She was distraught and trying to excuse his absence during this terrible moment in her life. Were she trying to alibi anything more sinister, they reasoned that her story would have been more consistent and less easily proven false.

As it happened, Roger actually was in Golden and sober that morning. His absence from Marjorie was caused by a misdemeanor committed by her son, Rick. The Golden (Colorado) State Bank had repossessed two of the Caldwells' cars with the proviso that they would be allowed to use them should it prove necessary. Earlier that morning, Rick was seen driving away from the bank parking lot in one of the cars without first obtaining permission. Roger was summoned to give a good reason for the boy's behavior. He appeared at the bank at 9:30 A.M. and looked "very normal" to the official to whom he spoke.

A short distance away, in his Denver home, Thomas Congdon received a telephone call from another trustee informing him of his aunt's murder. One of his first reactions was that Marjorie was somehow involved. It did not matter that the killings had been committed more than eight hundred miles and three states away. He later testified, "I felt the Caldwells were under some suspicion, and I felt that, either directly or indirectly, they could be considered dangerous. And they lived in a suburb of Denver."

Congdon called an acquaintance on the Denver police force and asked for the name of a private investigator. The officer recommended William Furman, who would seem a strange choice considering the low esteem in which the investigator was held by some members of the force. As Denver police officer Joel Humphrey would later testify, he believed Furman would "plant evidence or fabricate testimony if it suited his purposes." Humphrey would recall a Colorado murder case in which he claimed Furman had admitted to him he was "going to get fabricated evidence" if a new trial was ordered.

As far as anybody knew, Congdon had no way of knowing Furman's reputation at the time he contacted him. However, the personal security of his family and himself was not the only thing he discussed. Congdon later admitted that he also wanted the agent "to collect information relating to the murders."

Furman volunteered to "put some money on the streets" as a reward for any information about the murders and murderers. Congdon agreed to advance several hundred dollars for this purpose.

Congdon's most important instructions to the detective related to the Caldwells. He was to find out where they were going, whom they were seeing, and, if possible, what they were saying. To this end, Furman rented a room next to their quarters at the Holland House. He informed the management that he would be moving some sensitive equipment into it, and that he did not want the chambermaids or anybody else to be permitted access to it. Actually, he was going to use a bug that he had described to Congdon as "not a wiretap but a kind of device that enables you to hear conversations from a distance."

Congdon telephoned a Duluth police force contact, Detective John Greene, to report how pleased he was with Furman. He said, "I'm sure he's doing some things that you guys aren't allowed to do."

Greene knew that the call was being routinely taped by the police switchboard and replied: "Yes. But we won't talk about it."

By the following day, Marjorie had the distinct impression that she and Roger were being followed. The police had no reason to suspect them, but there were people closer to her who would enjoy making her life miserable. Her first reaction was retaliation, and she ordered another audit of the trust. Her accountant protested that it would look very cold-blooded if she had the books examined so soon after her mother's death. She did not give a damn how it looked. The trustees had shown that they were not her friends. There had already been some rumblings about adopted children being barred from sharing in the Congdon fortune. There was no telling to what lengths some of them might go to cheat her out of what she felt was rightfully hers. Marjorie had no more faith in them than they had in her. The lines of battle had been drawn long before the murders, and each side thought the other was capable of committing any act to gain control of Elisabeth's money.

On July 5, Roger Caldwell suffered a slight heart attack. After Elisabeth's funeral on June 30 in Duluth, he and Marjorie had gone down to Minneapolis, and he was admitted to St. Louis Park Methodist Hospital in that city. At 1:00 AM. on July 6, while still in the hospital, Caldwell was arrested and charged with the murders of his mother-in-law and Velma Pietila. According to the prosecution, the motive was greed. The Colorado police had opened his safe-deposit box and found Marjorie's power of attorney and the agreement, signed three days before the murder, irrevocably turning over a large portion of her inheritance to him.

After the arrest, the police reconstruction of the events that had taken place at Glensheen early on the morning of June 27 was made available to the defense.

At 2:00 A.M., a solitary figure had slipped through the front gates of the mansion grounds. He had a sheer black stocking pulled down over his face to hide his identity. The ground-floor windows and doors of the house were all locked. They might have been wired and, if there was any alternative, he did not want to chance breaking in. He circled the house beaming his flashlight over its lower façade. An enclosed concourse ran along the basement windows at the rear of the house. His light slowly followed it. He was in luck.

A pane of glass from one of the concourse windows had been removed by the gardener for repair. The intruder stepped through it onto a floor powdered with disintegrating plaster that had fallen from the ceiling. His light caught the row of basement windows at the far end of the enclosure. He approached them, leaving a trail of footprints in the plaster. They were locked, and he had to break the glass in one of the mullioned panes. It shattered with a crystal glissando on the floor of the room within. He paused to listen for anybody else who might have heard the sound. The night was as still and empty as before, and he continued on his mission. His arm could barely squeeze through the hole in the pane, but he managed to reach in to unlatch the lock and slide back the sash bolt.

He climbed into what had once been the children's playroom. A track of glass splinters and plaster marked his passage into the billiard room beyond, a relic of Chester Congdon's days, when men smoked their cigars and played their sporting games after dinner. Like the ghost of one of those long-dead men, he ascended to the paneled reception hall. A soft overhead light illumined the broad staircase with railings and newels heavily encrusted with intricate carving. It led to a spacious landing with three large leaded glass windows and an upholstered seat running below them. He tiptoed up the oriental runner toward the second floor. As he reached the top step, a woman in a white nurse's uniform emerged from one of the rooms. The beams of their flashlights crossed.

Velma Pietila tried to dash past the intruder but tripped on her shoelace. The shoe came off, but she continued toward the stairs. As she reached them, he retrieved the lost shoe and pounced, beating her head and raised arm with the heel. She tumbled down the flight to the landing.

He watched as she painfully hoisted herself onto the window seat. She was obviously too stunned to scream, which gave him time to look around for a sturdier weapon. A brass candlestick gleamed on a small hall table. As methodically as a butler about to start his polishing, he removed the candle and laid it on the table. He turned and started down the stairs.

He raised the candlestick and struck Velma in the face. Once he started, rage must have overcome him, and he brought the stick down again and again and again, ripping into her face and skull, tearing away the flesh and crushing the bone. Twenty-three times he swung that brass stick before letting the weapon fall from his hand.

He studied his victim. Did the tattered eyelid flutter, the hand tremble, or was it merely a trick of the moonlight streaming through the window behind her? He pulled the black stocking off his head and started to tie her wrists together with it, but they were lifeless to the touch, no trace of a pulse, and he did not bother to finish binding

149

them. The death of Velma Pietila had not been his purpose in coming to Glensheen. It was an unfortunate accident, how accidental he could not know, for she was there that one night only as a favor to an old woman.

He retraced his steps to the second floor. In the light spilling out of the nurse's room, he saw that his hands and clothes were smeared with blood. He went into the bathroom and cleansed himself as best he could before crossing back through the light of her room into the gloom of the corridor.

He tried one of the doors, but it was locked. Somewhere behind it, a dog began to yap. It was scratching at the other side of the door, which led to the servants' quarters. The cook had been awakened by the barking of her miniature French poodle. The dog had gone wild and raced out into the hallway. From her bed, she called, "Muffin! Muffin, come back here at once!"

The dog returned but would not quiet down. His mistress remonstrated, "Muffin, you must be quiet, or you'll wake up Miss Congdon."

The dog continued to howl.

On his side of the door, the stranger heard the dog retreat and was grateful that the mistress of the house sealed her servants off from her own quarters. He continued along the corridor. One door stood ajar, with a night-light within casting a path across the floor. It led to his destination.

What happened next had been subject to two police theories. The first had the old woman resting peacefully when the intruder entered. He went over to the vanity and rifled the drawers looking for her jewelry case. As he lifted it to the surface of the table, he caught sight of her reflection in the mirror. Her eyes were open, and she was watching him. She was unsuccessfully attempting to artic-

150

ulate something as her fingers sought the bell she thought would summon Mrs. Pietila. He crossed to her bed, picked up one of her pink satin pillows, and pressed it down over her face. As the life went out of his victim, the sapphire ring on Elisabeth Congdon's finger caught the glow of the light. He snatched off both the ring and her watch and added them to his cache of jewels. On his way out, his attention was arrested by an ancient Byzantine coin in a display of antiquities, and he slipped it into his pocket.

The theory on which the police settled had him entering Elisabeth's room for the purpose of murdering her. After smothering her, he took the jewels and coin to make it look as if robbery had been his motive.

He returned to the nurse's room and rifled Velma's purse for the keys to her car. He ran down the stairway, passing his first victim. He unlatched the two top door locks, opened the third with a turn of the handle, and went out into the driveway. Velma's brown Granada was parked in front of the house. He got in and started down the driveway. He did not turn on the headlights until he was some distance along Lincoln Road and heading toward Minneapolis.

For all of their conjecture, what the police never discovered was how he had gotten to Glensheen in the first place. A stranger going to that neighborhood at that time of night would certainly have been observed either by a taxi driver or in public transportation.

When Marjorie first heard the details of her mother's murder, it seemed incredible that the police would be foolish enough to attempt to link Roger with the killings. They were the work of a cold-blooded killer—it was all too calculated to have been done by a drunk and, everybody agreed, when sober her husband was incapable of that kind of violence. Beyond that, both Roger and she had been in Golden at the time the murders were being committed.

Her lawyer reminded her that she had told conflicting stories about Roger's whereabouts on the morning of June 27. She was very fortunate, he said, that she had not been indicted for conspiracy to commit murder. There was a chance that it might still happen. She did not reply.

The trial of Roger Caldwell opened on April 10, 1978. An ambitious young district attorney, John DeSanto, was pitted against Douglas Thomson, one of the ablest defense attorneys in the state. DeSanto had checked and re-checked all of the flights, both commercial and chartered, from Denver to Minneapolis that could have enabled Caldwell to reach the mansion in time to commit the murders. He also checked the flights that could have returned him to Denver. He could not place the accused on any of them. There were no fingerprints, or footprints, or anything else that placed Caldwell at Glensheen except some strands of hair that an expert could describe only as "similar" to his.

DeSanto did have some other things that he hoped would prove Roger's guilt. Nonetheless, the case remained so circumstantial that he indirectly apologized for it in his opening remarks to the jury. "No case is perfect," he said.

When cases are that flimsy, the lengths of the trials are generally extended as both sides attempt to overwhelm and confuse the jury with a plethora of witnesses. Caldwell's case was to be the longest, up to that point, in the history of Minnesota.

Velma Pietila's car, stolen at Glensheen, was found in the parking lot of the Minneapolis–St. Paul airport. A lot entrance ticket issued to it indicated that it had been brought in shortly after 6:30 A.M. on the morning of the murders. The ticket was found in a nearby trash can. DeSanto hammered away at the point that the murderer had driven directly from Duluth to the airport. Roger Caldwell had good reason to be in a hurry. He had to get back to Colorado to establish an alibi.

In his cross-examination, Thomson elicited the information that the ticket was not found in the plastic bag liner in the can, where it would have been disposed of with the rest of the trash. It was wedged between the bag and the frame of the can, where it would fall out separately from the rest of the garbage and be sure to be noticed. It took some effort to place the ticket in that position. The defense was asking if it seemed logical that a murderer on the run would make that effort, or was it more likely that somebody trying to frame an innocent man had made it?

At 6:45 that morning, a tan suede suit bag was purchased at the airport gift shop. The clerks testified that it was Roger Caldwell who made the purchase. Of the multitude of prosecution witnesses, they were the only people to place Caldwell in Minnesota on the day of the murder.

Under Thomson's questioning, the clerks admitted that, when first questioned on July 1, 1977, they had identified the man in the shop as weighing 185 to 195 pounds and having curly sandy-blond hair. Caldwell had straight grayish brown hair and weighed 20 pounds less. They also had been unable to recognize him from the photographs the police had shown them. Despite this, in court they pointed to Roger Caldwell and maintained that he was the man who had bought the bag. Thomson could not shake them on this point, although they did admit that they could identify him only after having seen newspaper accounts of the case that had carried his captioned picture. The prosecution relied on the visual impact of these guileless-looking women as they pointed out Roger Caldwell in the courtroom. It would surely remain with the jury long after the cross-examination had blurred with the countless thousands of words they were yet to hear.

Most of the evidence against Caldwell was damaging but not damning.The major portion of it was gathered in Duluth and Minneapolis hotel rooms occupied by the Caldwells during their visit to Minnesota for Elisabeth's funeral. A suede bag identical to the one sold in the gift shop was found, but Roger could have purchased it at any of a number of shops selling them. A receipt from the shop was uncovered in a trash basket. The price and date checked out, but it did not say what had been purchased. Roger claimed never to have seen the receipt before. If it was his, why would he have waited almost a week before disposing of it? The implication was that he was being framed, but nobody could identify the framer. Some jewelry identical to pieces stolen from Elisabeth Congdon was found in a night-table drawer. Marjorie claimed that her mother had given her these exact copies after she had admired the originals. The bulk of the missing jewelry was never found either on the Caldwells or on anyone else. There was much unresolved speculation about a wicker case missing from Elisabeth's closet. Elisabeth's nurse and chauffeur could not remember having seen it before the weekend of the murders. Marjorie swore that she had taken it while visiting Glensheen at the time of the funeral. It was not discovered missing until some time after the funeral.

One of the most important points concerning all of this evidence was that witnesses had placed Thomas Congdon's agent, William Furman, or one of Furman's known associates, on the scene each time something against the Caldwells was found on premises occupied by them. Douglas Thomson had to consider putting Furman on the stand. When he interviewed him, the detective was forthright. He freely admitted to having used a "military device" to eavesdrop on the Caldwells' conversations at the Holland House during the days immediately following the murders. He claimed to have overheard Marjorie say to Roger, "I hope we get away with this."

If the jury heard that remark, the results could be devastating to the defense case. Thomson decided that it was not worth the risk to put Furman on the stand. DeSanto certainly had no reason to call him. If Furman's reputation was ever revealed in court, it could place most of the prosecution's evidence in question.

By the end of Roger's trial, his fate could be said to hang on a metaphorical flip of the Byzantine coin stolen from Elisabeth's bedroom. It had been sealed in an envelope from the Duluth Radisson Hotel and mailed from that city, on the day of the murders, to Roger, at the Holland House, in Colorado. Whether or not they were acting on a tip from Furman, three police officers happened to be sitting in the lobby at the moment the envelope arrived three days later. The handwriting on it split the experts. The prosecution's qualified person identified it as Roger's, and the defense's person testified that Roger had not written it.

The most decisive evidence against Roger Caldwell was one small fingerprint on the envelope.

Three fingerprints were actually found but only one was identifiable. Steven Sedlacek, of the Colorado Bureau of Investigation, identified it as definitely having been made by Roger's right thumb. Seeking his own expert, Doug

Thomson took the print to Ronald W. Welbaum, a certified consultant fingerprint expert, in Minneapolis. Welbaum agreed with Sedlacek; in his opinion, there was no doubt that it was Roger's print. Thomson saw no reason to waste his client's money seeking somebody else who would challenge Sedlacek. Welbaum was a respected practitioner whose opinion was often sought in the area.

On July 8, 1978, Roger Caldwell was found guilty of two counts of murder. On July 10, he was sentenced to two life terms in Stillwater State Prison, not far from where Marjorie had tried her hand at horse ranching only five years before.

Some members of the jury later said that, more than any other piece of evidence, it was the fingerprint that had moved them to vote for conviction.

On July 11, Marjorie Caldwell was charged with two counts of murder and two of conspiracy to commit murder. Prosecuting attorney John DeSanto had been hinting that this would happen from the beginning. In his opening address at her husband's trial, he had referred to the agreement turning over part of her inheritance to Roger as "the carrot held out," implying that she was guaranteeing Roger a piece of the action in exchange for murdering her mother.

DeSanto had taken a chance. He obviously would not have been able to indict Marjorie had Roger been found not guilty, but he had not felt that he could afford to weaken his admittedly circumstantial case by trying them together.

From the moment of Roger's indictment, Marjorie Caldwell's attorneys had been trying to prevail upon her to get herself a criminal attorney. She had resisted, and it was not until well into Roger's trial that she finally took their advice and made an appointment to see Ronald Mesh-besher, in Minneapolis.

The firm of Meshbesher, Singer, and Spence Ltd. occupied a squat modern building set back from a quasi-residential street about a mile from downtown Minneapolis. Meshbesher's office was a spacious paneled chamber dominated by two pictures: a large surrealistic dreamscape by Salvador Dali and a somber depiction of the Sacco-Vanzetti trial by Ben Shahn. They may well have been selected because they epitomized the dual nature of the criminal lawyer: an appreciation of the surreal and a commitment to social justice. When Meshbesher rose to greet her, Marjorie saw that he was shorter than she had expected, and that put her at ease, for she was barely five feet tall. He wore a sport shirt, open at the neck, and chino trousers, another surprise, for the newspaper accounts stressed his courtroom elegance and his possession of one of Minnesota's most impressive arrays of custom-tailored suits. There was a humorous glint behind the horn-rimmed glasses and an expression on the bearded face that hovered between the extremes of Puck and satyr.

After listening to her story, he said, "Your husband's got a good man. If I were in trouble, I'd go to Doug Thomson. The best thing for you to do now is to keep a very low profile. Don't speak to anybody about the case—especially not to the press."

A few weeks later, Meshbesher opened his newspaper to find an interview with Marjorie in which she denounced everybody connected with the prosecution of her husband's case, especially John DeSanto. Meshbesher shook his head. That was one impulsive lady.

DeSanto would have been a fool not to indict Marjorie after Roger's conviction. His case against Roger would work even better in a conspiracy charge against Marjorie. First of all, he would not have to prove that she was anywhere near the scene of the crime. Second, given the stormy history of their marriage, there was no logical reason for her to have assigned irrevocably a large part of her inheritance except as payment for murder.

Despite his confidence in his case, DeSanto did offer to plea bargain later in the summer of Marjorie's indictment. Another lengthy trial would cost the state a great deal of money, and it was his duty as a public servant to attempt to avoid the expense.

Meshbesher described the deal to Marjorie as a "very big offer." He said: "You plead guilty only to conspiracy. That could mean a prison sentence of as little as two years. If you're convicted, like your husband, of two first-degree murder counts, you're likely to be imprisoned for at least thirty-four years. If I were you, I'd think seriously about accepting."

"No," she replied.

Meshbesher put his staff to work poring over every page of transcription from Roger's very long trial as well as every page of exculpatory evidence from the police investigation. They were looking for things that might have escaped the attention of Douglas Thomson in his preparation of Caldwell's defense. The exhausting hours, days, and weeks that this took must be measured in money, for to lawyers in Meshbesher's league, time truly was money. They charged by the minute. If he won, and the odds against that were the dream of every gambler who could not resist a long shot, he would be paid out of Marjorie's inheritance. If he lost, she would be barred from inheriting and unable to pay at all. There were only three types of lawyers who could afford to take a case like Marjorie

Caldwell's: those out to make a reputation at any price, those assigned to it by the court, and those successful enough to deduct the cost as a business loss. Although Meshbesher was in the last category, there actually could be no recompense for the expenditure of energy and intellect that would be involved.

Marjorie Caldwell's trial opened on April 2, 1979, almost nine months after her husband's conviction and a little short of two years after her mother's murder. The conviction of Roger Caldwell had been the biggest win in John DeSanto's career. Although he did not underestimate Meshbesher, he was certain that the same evidence that had served him so well with Roger would not fail him with Marjorie. It had been a circumstantial case but a good one, featuring the uncontestable piece of evidence of Roger's fingerprint on the envelope.

DeSanto began with a two-and-a-half-hour opening address to the jury. He characterized Marjorie Caldwell as "The woman behind the man who murdered Elisabeth Congdon . . . [she] dominated and was able to manipulate Roger Caldwell. . . . Marjorie Caldwell was a very demanding person of her mother. She was often insolent, often rude. She became a source of emotional upset to her mother because of her spendthrift propensities."

Those propensities, he claimed, had motivated her to plot the murder in order "to speed up her inheritance."

As Meshbesher would point out, there was a fallacy in this argument. Why would she plot to commit murder for money, when she already had agreed to give most of it away to an admittedly unstable husband who she could not be sure would remain with her once he was in possession of it? If the legacy was "a carrot" held in front of

159

Roger, its purpose surely was to keep him with her rather than to give him the means of independence.

Meshbesher looked at his client dispassionately and wondered how many members of the jury would believe that she was capable of the plot. Much of her problem was caused by her attempts to cover up for and shield her husband. To many, that was an admirable trait. She projected a motherly image and had once described herself as having roughly the dimensions of the Pillsbury Doughboy. She was accessible to those who approached her during the recesses, willing to chat amiably on any subject that might be initiated. She was a demure little figure, so slight of stature that her feet had to rest on two bricks in order to reach the courtroom floor.

The first two weeks of the trial were given over to witnesses and police officers who reconstructed the crime. Meshbesher did execute some of the fancy steps that had earned him his reputation, but his performance was not directed toward winning any new points for his client. His principal objective was to point out the sloppiness of the police investigation and the carelessness with which evidence had been handled.

A bloody palm print on the sink in the nurse's bathroom, at which the killer had washed the blood off his hands, had not been identified for over a year, and when it was, it belonged to chief investigator Gary Waller. Some of the photographs of the premises had been misdated; others were lost. Vital areas of Elisabeth Congdon's room had not been dusted for fingerprints until weeks after the murders. Meshbesher also led the jury to suspect the police of withholding evidence. By casting doubt on the quality of the investigation, he might be able to cast doubt on the prosecution's contention of who had committed the crimes. It was a remote possibility but worth the effort, for reasonable doubt would mandate an acquittal.

Meshbesher's performance during those first weeks was also directed, to no small degree, at amusing the jury. He knew that the jurors were reaching the point at which they learned what every judge and lawyer already knew. Only in drama and fiction was every moment of a trial enthralling. In truth, a trial was simply that—a trial. It was tedious and tried one's patience as much as it tried the accused. If there was one full hour of interesting testimony in a day, that was an unusually good day. The canny lawyer knew that a talent to amuse was often as important to his client as a knowledge of the law. One of Meshbesher's advantages in the Caldwell case was that DeSanto was essentially a conscientious but humorless young man.

The only way to prove that Marjorie was innocent was to prove that Roger was also innocent. Meshbesher was under no illusion that this could be done merely by punching holes in the police work. There were two things that had to be accomplished to exonerate the Caldwells: He had to point the finger of guilt in another direction, if only by inference, and he had to destroy the only piece of evidence that linked Roger Caldwell to the scene of the crime: the fingerprint on the envelope. He could accomplish the first by making shrewder use of Thomas Congdon and his detective, William Furman, than Doug Thomson had done in Roger's trial. For the second, he would need a reexamination of the fingerprint by an expert with sufficient qualifications to go against the Colorado Bureau of Investigation's man, Steven Sedlacek. Meshbesher thought of his old friend, Herb MacDonell.

Meshbesher first met MacDonell in 1970, at the annual meeting of the Trial Lawyers Association of America, where the criminalist was delivering a paper on the Robert Ferry case. The two men got to know each other. Both were on the brink of what would be extremely successful and controversial careers. The streetwise Meshbesher and the country-shrewd MacDonell sized each other up and found a fit for friendship, although each had confided to his respective mate that he found the other a very exotic bird.

Meshbesher now telephoned MacDonell: "Herb, I've got a fingerprint here that I'd like you to take a look at. I've got to tell you in advance that two experts have already agreed on the identification."

"And you're hoping they're wrong."

"How'd you guess?"

"Elementary, my dear Meshbesher. If you thought they were right, you wouldn't be calling me. Ron, why don't you save your client's money and my time. Forget it. In twenty-five years, I've only disagreed with the fingerprints experts once."

"Herb, do it as a personal favor. It can make the difference in not just one but two cases."

"Two for one? I'll have to double my fee."

"I assume you're joking."

"Okay, Ron. Send it along. We'll see what we can find."

Meshbesher sent photographs of the latent print on the envelope and of Roger's actual prints, so that a comparison could be made. An actual fingerprint is made when the finger is rolled in ink and then pressed down on a card or page, leaving behind a line-for-line impression of the original. Two prints of the same finger, made in this fashion, can always be identified as coming from the same source.

A latent or "hidden" print is outlined on an object in sweat, oily secretions, or other substances present on the finger. It is usually almost colorless and must be "developed" before it can be preserved or compared. MacDonell's invention of the MAGNA Brush had revolutionized the process of developing prints. A latent print was generally fragmentary or incomplete, which was what led to occasional disputes between identification experts. MacDonell's job was to find and count the numbers of points in the arches, loops, and whorls in which the actual and latent prints matched. There were three possibilities: The latent did not clearly show enough points to make any identification; there were sufficient points that matched to make a positive identification; there were so many differences that the prints could not possibly have been made by the same person.

While MacDonell was working on the fingerprint, Meshbesher turned his attention to preparing the jury for the appearance of William Furman. He had not repeated Thomson's decision in Roger's case and had subpoenaed the detective.

During the following week, DeSanto was able to establish that incriminating evidence had been found in the various hotel rooms occupied by the Caldwells. Meshbesher kept countering with the implication that it had all been planted by Furman working for Congdon.

When Thomas Congdon appeared for the prosecution, Meshbesher's cross-examination was surprisingly mild. This was a substantial citizen, and the weight of the establishment was in his favor. The lawyer was not going to risk antagonizing the jury by hounding him. He simply continued to register surprise that this man's first reaction to his aunt's death was to suspect his cousin of the murder, that he hired a detective to make the life of a mourning daughter more difficult.

Congdon admitted that Furman and his men had been watching the Caldwells in Duluth and Minneapolis as well as in Golden. Meshbesher again suggested that they were on the scene at every place where incriminating evidence had been uncovered. Congdon denied ever asking Furman or any of his associates to plant evidence. He had never asked them to do anything that was illegal.

Meshbesher asked how much had been paid for Furman's "legal" services. The reply was that the man had received between $13,000 and $14,000 for the investigation (the figure was actually in excess of $15,000).

The defense deferred the Furman-Congdon issue for a few days. The forthcoming appearance of Marjorie's daughter, Suzanne LeRoy, was a more immediate problem. When a daughter testifies against her mother in a murder trial, the implication has to be that the mother is some kind of monster.

Suzanne LeRoy was twenty-four, an ordinary-looking young woman. There was a certain sweetness about her, and she was visibly nervous when she took the witness stand. Her voice was so low that she had to be asked to repeat some of her answers. She began her testimony late on Friday afternoon, June 8, and it continued the following Monday morning. Her mother's eyes never left Suzanne's face.

DeSanto gently led her through her tale of a wildly extravagant mother who spent beyond her means on too many frocks, too many horses, too many cars, and too many residences for her family. To pay for these indulgences, Marjorie depended upon the generosity of Elisabeth and the borrowing power of her inheritance. She once told Suzanne to ask her grandmother for money, but the girl could not bring herself to do it. Of the countless skating costumes bought for her sister, Heather, and herself, she lamented, "She just kept buying more and more."

Suzanne LeRoy was only eighteen when she left home in anger at her mother's overprotectiveness. Like Marjorie, she depended upon Elisabeth and the Congdon inheritance to support the indulgence of her independence. Her grandmother had set up a special trust fund that paid all of the girl's expenses.

What emerged from Suzanne LeRoy's two days in court was the dual portrait of an obsessive mother and a willful daughter. Many spectators were saddened at the degree of vengeance demanded by that willfulness. A few speculated on just how rich the girl would be if her testimony helped to convict her mother. Marjorie's inheritance would then pass directly to her children. It would be intact. During his trial, Roger had renounced all claim to the benefits that were his by the agreement that allegedly had spurred him to murder.

After calling 102 witnesses, John DeSanto rested the case for the prosecution. He had taken eleven weeks to present what was essentially a restatement of his case against Roger Caldwell. It still hung on a fingerprint. That slight convolution of ridges and bifurcations had convicted Roger, and for all of Meshbesher's best efforts, it could also convict Marjorie. The prosecution expert, Steven Sedlacek, and Roger's defense expert, Ronald Welbaum, had concurred that it definitely was Roger's print. Two experts from the Minnesota Bureau of Apprehension, Walter Rhodes and John Douthit, had said that the print was too faint to make a positive identification from it. The scoreboard read: two for, two abstentions, and none against. To have a fighting chance, the least that Herb MacDonell's analysis would have to find was that it was unidentifiable.

The defense opened its case on June 27, 1979. Marjorie was ashen and dressed somberly. It was the second anniversary of her mother's death. In contrast to DeSanto's two-and-a-half-hour opening address, Meshbesher spoke for only fifteen minutes. The bulk of his speech dealt with William Furman and his unsavory character. He said that a Colorado police officer would testify that Furman had "a reputation for dishonesty and fabricating evidence." He implied that a man who could fabricate evidence could also plant it.

In summarizing the case that he would set forth, he mentioned a handwriting expert who would swear that the writing on the envelope did not belong to Roger. DeSanto had already presented one who had sworn that it did. Meshbesher did not mention another fingerprint expert. That was one piece of evidence that he gave the impression of not wanting to handle.

MacDonell arrived in Minneapolis on July 5. When John DeSanto heard that Meshbesher was going to put him on the stand, he requested a meeting between his expert, Sedlacek, and MacDonell. It was scheduled for later that afternoon in Meshbesher's office. Meshbesher and MacDonell were there early. The lawyer said, "It's going to be your word against Sedlacek's. He's highly regarded by the Colorado Bureau of Investigation."

MacDonell sighed. "Maybe it's the altitude out there. That guy didn't even identify the correct finger. He says it's the thumb. In holding the envelope, there is no way that the thumb could get up in that position. It has to be the ring finger."

"Let's forget that part. We've got enough to do without muddying the waters."

"No matter which finger that latent print comes from, it doesn't belong to Roger Caldwell."

Meshbesher shrugged. "He's a certified latent-finger-print examiner of the International Association for Identification. That's more than you are."

MacDonell knew he was being baited. He said, "I'm a member of the association. It would be easy enough to be 'grandfathered in' for certification. A lot of them are. I don't *choose* to be. I don't agree with some of their standards of certification. When Sedlacek made this identification, he proved my point."

Meshbesher looked at him with a twinkle in his eyes. "There's nothing like humility, is there, Herb?"

"You should know, Ron."

Sedlacek arrived with DeSanto, and MacDonell presented his case. There were blowups of the latent print from the envelope and of Roger's prints taken after he was arrested. MacDonell pointed to the latent. "See that? It's a scar, isn't it? There are no scars on any of Roger's prints. Look at the variations in the ridges in both pictures. There is no way that the print on the envelope could have been made by Roger Caldwell."

Sedlacek studied the photographs.

MacDonell urged him. "Prove that I'm wrong. I'm a reasonable man. You just prove it to me."

Sedlacek rose. "You have your opinion, and I have mine."

DeSanto smiled. "We'll see you in court."

MacDonell watched them leave and said, "Nice fellows."

Meshbesher shook his head. "It's a one-to-one fight. And Sedlacek's credentials are awfully good."

"Except for one small point. He's wrong."

Meshbesher got up and headed for the door. "Come along with me. Maybe we can improve the odds."

Walter Rhodes had recently retired from the Minnesota Bureau of Criminal Apprehension. He had already testified for the prosecution, one of the two men who had said that the print on the envelope was unidentifiable. He had also examined a partial fingerprint found on the brass candlestick used to bludgeon Velma Pietila. He had testified that that print also did not have sufficient characteristics to make a positive identification. Then he had added something that had elated Meshbesher. The candlestick print *did* have enough characteristics to determine who had *not* made it. He concluded, "And Roger Caldwell did not make that print."

Meshbesher took MacDonell over to see Rhodes to explain his position on the envelope print to him. After studying the pictures again, Rhodes said, "I always knew that it was a chickenshit print. What the hell's going on down there? We'd never have gone to trial on something like this. There is no way this is that guy's print."

Meshbesher asked, "Are you willing to come back into court for the defense and back up Herb?"

"You bet your ass I am."

MacDonell was put on the stand on the following day, July 6. In three hours of cross-examination by DeSanto, he did not budge from his position. He reiterated his analysis, pointing out what he called "the gross unexplained discrepancies." He concluded, "I have no question about it."

DeSanto told the jury that his expert had interviewed MacDonell on the previous day and remained convinced that his original analysis was the correct one. He stuck to that story even after Walter Rhodes supported MacDonell in his testimony.

When William Furman walked into court on Monday, July 10, Ron Meshbesher could not believe his eyes. The man looked as if he had been sent over by Central Casting to play the role of a sleazy detective. Wearing dark glasses, his right arm in a cast from an accident, a potbelly un-concealed by an ill-fitting jacket, he was accompanied by a young Colorado attorney. Furman had unsuccessfully fought a defense subpoena in Colorado, and his lawyer wanted to stand next to the witness to advise him on his responses. Meshbesher objected. "It's improper."

The judge compromised by permitting the lawyer to sit at the head of the court dock. In the course of his testimony, Furman took the Fifth Amendment against self-incrimination fifty-nine times in reply to questions from both the defense and the prosecution. His constant re-frain, "I'll take the Fifth on that, sir," was repeated so often that the spectators began to mouth it along with him. His young lawyer was so openly signaling to him when to take the Fifth that the jury was looking back and forth between them like fans at a tennis match.

Among the questions on which Furman took the Fifth were those regarding statements he had made to the po-lice, reporters, and defense investigators; the activities of his associates, Gary Fick and Daniel Dolan; his surveil-lance of the Caldwells; his putting $700 "on the street" for information about the Caldwells; his tip to the police about a box of "valuable papers" (old letters of no con-sequence to the case) that could be found at the Caldwells' residence in Golden; the possible fraudulence of his report to Thomas Congdon.

Furman did not take the Fifth when Meshbesher asked him if Thomas Congdon had ever said that Marjorie Cald-well did not deserve her inheritance. He replied, "There was a statement to that effect, yes."

Several police officers had already testified that it had been their impression that Furman was shadowing the Caldwells twenty-four hours a day, and that he had been present in both Duluth and Minneapolis when crucial pieces of evidence had been found in their hotel rooms. Furman testified that he had been in Minnesota for only one night, and that was two months after the murders and two days before submitting his five-page report to Congdon, but he already had taken the Fifth on the activities of his associates.

A short time after handing in his report, Furman was fired by the Congdon trust attorney, Joseph Johnson, because he suspected that the investigator had obtained most of his information from the newspapers. Congdon and Johnson both alleged that Furman was a liar and a cheat who was trying to bilk the Congdons out of money without ever having taken the specified trips to Minnesota. Nevertheless, when the detective submitted a bill for $15,171 for six weeks of work, Congdon paid it without a murmur. Meshbesher pointed out that the trustee could have brought suit to get his money back if he felt that he was being swindled. He never did. Of course, it was not his money; it belonged to the trust and, indirectly, to the heirs, including Marjorie Caldwell.

Before completing his testimony, Furman added gratuitously that he had once thought that Thomas Congdon was somehow involved in the murders.

DeSanto was becoming extremely uneasy. The trial was not going according to expectations. He had anticipated a replay of the Roger Caldwell trial, in which he had so adroitly put the accused behind bars for life. He had to do something, and quickly. The fingerprint was his only hope. He had to find somebody who could totally wipe out MacDonell's testimony.

DeSanto called on George Bonebrake, the former head of the FBI fingerprint division. He was also chairman of the certification board of the International Association for

Identification. Bonebrake studied the print and, in short order, said that MacDonell was right. Instead of testifying for the prosecution against MacDonell, he testified for the defense in support of him.

After opening the trial with loud protestations about the incontrovertibility of this scientifically proven piece of evidence, DeSanto was forced to withdraw the fingerprint from evidence and apologize to the jury. The jury deliberated for less than nine hours before finding Marjorie Caldwell innocent of all charges.

Douglas Thomson returned to the judge who had presided over Roger's trial and made a motion for a new trial, largely based on the disproven fingerprint. The judge turned him down. In essence, he said that there was no new evidence. Thomson simply had not used the evidence that always had been at his disposal. The lawyer decided to appeal to the Minnesota Supreme Court, but his client would have to remain in jail while he prepared the long and intricate brief necessary to make that appeal.

In the meantime, Marjorie was having problems of her own. After their mother's acquittal, Suzanne LeRoy, her sisters, and one of her brothers joined to bring a civil action against Marjorie seeking to have Elisabeth Congdon's will set aside, so that she would be disinherited and her share of the estate would come directly to them. The other three LeRoy boys refused to have anything to do with the action.

The estate was tied up by this litigation, and Marjorie had yet to see a dime of her inheritance. Alienated from most of her family and lonely, she began a relationship with an old friend, Wallace Hagen, who was twenty-three years her senior. A marriage license was issued to them on August 7, 1981, in Valley City, North Dakota. She gave her name as Marjorie C. LeRoy and attached the 1971 divorce degree obtained from her first husband. She later claimed that she did this to avoid the publicity that would have ensued had she used the name of Caldwell. After the wedding, the Hagens returned to Minnesota, where Marjorie took up the fight to have her children's civil action put aside.

She took her case to the Minnesota Supreme Court, and she lost. It was the court's decision that even if a person was acquitted of murder in a criminal proceeding, he or she could be prevented from inheriting the estate of the victim, if it was proven in a civil proceeding, by a preponderance of the evidence, that he or she was responsible for the murder.

There are two essential differences between a civil and a criminal trial. In a civil action, the accuser need only establish a wrong by the bulk of the evidence and not, as in a criminal case, beyond a reasonable doubt, and there is no presumption of innocence.

Despite the legal jargon of the court, Ron Meshbesher felt that Marjorie was actually going to be tried twice for the same crime. The justices declared that this did not constitute double jeopardy, because she could not be sent to jail. The most that could happen to her would be the loss of her inheritance.

Under the conditions laid down by the court, a case could be made. Marjorie had signed an agreement giving Roger a substantial share in her future wealth and another giving him power of attorney. Items stolen from the scene of the crime were found in their possession, and it was never proven that they had been planted on them. Marjorie had lied about Roger's whereabouts at the time of the murder. Roger had been convicted of, and was still serving time for, the murder. Probably more important than that to Marjorie's attorney was the fact that in a civil suit, she would be forced to take the stand and submit to examination under oath. She was too outspoken and volatile to make a good witness for herself and had not been put on the stand at her own trial. If she wished to avoid this ordeal, the only option open to her was to settle out of court with her children. Marjorie did not have to make up her mind about that for some time, as the civil action was not due to be heard until mid-1983.

Roger Caldwell's appeal finally went up to the Minnesota Supreme Court and, on August 2, 1982, four years after his conviction largely based on a faulty piece of evidence, he was granted a new trial. In its decision, the court said:

> Under the unusual circumstances of this case, where the uncontroverted testimony of the state's expert [Sedlacek] substantially proves to be incorrect, and the testimony was the basis of the only circumstantial evidence tending to establish that the appellant was in Duluth on the date of the murders, appellant is entitled to a new trial. Although Sedlacek never "recanted" his own testimony, there appears to be no doubt that the fingerprint was misidentified.*

Soon after the supreme court decision, Caldwell was released in his recognizance to await a new trial. It was said he might never face trial again on the murder charge.

*On the subject of the fingerprint experts in the Caldwell trials, the three who confirmed that it was Roger Caldwell's print, Steven Sedlacek, his Colorado superior, Claude Cook, and Ronald Welbaum, all had their certification revoked by the International Association of Identification. It was on the basis of Herbert MacDonell's work, and MacDonell remained obdurate in never even applying for his own certification.

DeSanto indicated he doubted there would be any purpose in trying to get another conviction. Five years had passed since the crime, and the case was cold.

In January 1983, Marjorie Caldwell Hagen hit the headlines again, and it had nothing to do with her children's civil action against her. She was arrested and charged with second-degree arson and insurance fraud in connection with a fire in an unoccupied house that had occurred on September 15, 1982.

On January 19, 1983, North Dakota officials began a bigamy investigation against Marjorie. Although she had married Wallace Hagen in 1981, there was no proof she had ever divorced Roger Caldwell. Roger refused to discuss the matter, but his brother, acting as his spokesman, said Caldwell had never been served with divorce papers and that, as far as he knew, Marjorie and he were still married.

North Dakota officially charged Marjorie with bigamy in April. Because of the expense, the state decided not to ask for extradition. The charge would stand and if ever Marjorie set foot in North Dakota, she would be arrested. Meshbesher tended to dismiss the whole thing as meaning no more than that his client was exiled from North Dakota. There were worse fates.

After Roger was released from prison pending a new trial, he was offered a plea bargain. If he would confess to the murders of Elisabeth Congdon and Velma Pietila, he would never have to spend another day in prison. The prosecuting attorney had said the case was cold and there would probably be no new trial. But the element of possibility remained, and Roger was terrified by it. While Roger was still in prison, Roy Larson, a fellow prisoner, had observed that Caldwell was doing "bad time." He was not adjusting to his situation, was losing weight, and was not making any friends.

He might be vindicated by a new trial, but it was a gamble. He had won his appeal, and Marjorie had been acquitted, largely because MacDonell had destroyed the validity of the fingerprint evidence. In a new trial, the prosecutor would not introduce the envelope with the invalidated fingerprint into evidence. It would be as if it did not exist. He would be retried on the strength of the other evidence and testimony. It was a gamble, because some of his original jurors had later said the fingerprint had not weighed as heavily as the rest of the prosecutor's case in their decision to convict him.

Roger was financially broke and broken as a man. He was in no state to take risks. He accepted the offer and confessed to the murders. This action gave the decided advantage to Marjorie's children in their civil suit against their mother. Marjorie needed money, and she needed it quickly. Her legal fees were approaching the half-million-dollar mark and would mount with the coming new trial on the arson and fraud charges. She decided to settle out of court with her children with what was reputed to be a fifty-fifty settlement.

Marjorie Caldwell Hagen's trial opened on December 13, 1983, and on Friday, January 13, 1984, she was found guilty of arson. On February 9, she was sentenced to two and a half years and fined $10,000. The sentence imposed was considerably harsher than that recommended by the Minnesota sentencing guidelines, which suggest one and three-quarters years and no fine. Meshbesher filed an appeal, and Marjorie will remain free on bail pending a decision.

Whether Roger Caldwell actually committed the murders or was simply taking the expedient way out by confessing, only he really knows. If he did not commit them, the real killer or killers will probably never be found. The case is not only "cold," it is closed.

Meshbesher and MacDonell saved Marjorie from a murder conviction. They could not save her from herself. In the course of pursuing her reckless profligacy, she lost a loving mother and three lovingly overindulged daughters. Shakespeare wrote, "How sharper than a serpent's tooth it is to have a thankless child."

Whether that observation is truer of Marjorie in relation to her mother or of her daughters in relation to her must be left for them to answer. It can be said only with some degree of accuracy that her later ordeals, and those still before her, would have been far easier to face had she retained the love of her children.

6

A CORPUS DELICTI IS NOT A CORPSE

It was a bleak November evening in 1975. As it always did in that part of northern Oregon, the winter had come early, and the man pulled his stocking cap down so all that could be seen on his face were the thick, curly sideburns and the Fu Manchu mustache. He was slight and of medium height, but he used his body shrewdly to maximize its strength.

He looked up and down the street to make certain that nobody was astir and then climbed the steps to the porch of the modest house. He knew that Vicki Brown had stashed her kid with her mother for the night, and that she was out screwing around. Doing it with someone. Anyone. Everyone. Everyone but him, although he was better to Vicki than anyone else. Didn't he fix the stovepipe for her right in this house just a little while back? And didn't she promise to return the favor any way she could? He should have taken her right then and there, but instead he had played the little gentleman.

The next day, he had asked her how the stove was working—twice he had asked her, in case she hadn't heard the first time. And what did she do? She didn't even answer. Looked right through him like he wasn't there. Like a piece of shit.

He laughed. Well, he reckoned that he'd shown her. That was when she started getting them dirty notes. He had a good time writing them and then watching her reaction. She began whining that she was scared somebody was going to break in on her. Somebody was. He laughed again. He was. And he was going to get away with it, too. People were just too dumb to know what was happening right under their noses.

He jimmied open the window. It was child's play. Nobody did much about security in Rainier. Oh, they talked about fear of break-in, but they didn't do anything. There were only two thousand people in the whole town, and very few of them thought that they had enough to steal worth the price of a high-tech lock.

In a minute he was inside. Vicki would not be back for hours, and he thought that he might as well make himself at home. He took a beer from the refrigerator and wandered around the house. His heart began to palpitate when he saw her bed. The linen was not fresh. She had to have slept in it. In the raw. She was not the type to wear a nightie. Not her. Not that whore. The sheets had touched her all over. Maybe she'd even screwed in them. Her and some guy.

He flung himself upon the bed and started to roll around. Oh, God! It felt good. He could smell her in the linen. Rolling around. Feeling good, until his hand hugging the pillow came upon a book under it. A small black book. He took it over to the night-light and read. It contained a list of men's names. He knew most of them. There were stars crudely drawn next to each name and a sum of money beside some of them. The bitch! The stars were for fucks and the money—what they gave her for them. The whore! He wanted to tear the book to shreds but, instead, he flung it on the rumpled bed. Let her know that somebody had seen the filthy thing. Somebody knew her for the whore she was.

He rummaged through a chest of drawers, coming upon a stack of her undies. Cute little strawberries printed on one pair of panties. Such dainty bikini bras and panties. They didn't seem large enough to cover her amply round ass and breasts. He could see her spilling over in them, his hands running over her. He went into the bathroom and undid his pants with one hand while rubbing the undies over his face with the other.

No good. It was no good. They were freshly laundered, and there was no scent of her in them, no feel of her. Damn! He angrily hurled the beer bottle into the toilet bowl and stuffed the underwear into his black vinyl motorcycle jacket. At least, she'd know that somebody had been handling all of her private possessions, that somebody had taken some of them away with him. She'd know that, and she'd be more scared than ever. He giggled. That was something. Her fear.

When he got home, he considered giving the underwear to his wife but decided against it. She was a good girl. She wouldn't get the joke. The following night, he tossed the stolen lingerie to the woman with whom he was having an affair. "I got an early Christmas present for you. They belong to Vicki Brown. But they're clean and like new."

He boasted of his revenge on Vicki, all the time hoping that the woman would put on the undies, that he could look at her in them and see Vicki, and then tear them off and make love to her. Better love than they had ever made before.

She stared at him for a moment and then folded the things up and put them in her purse.

"Thanks. A girl can always use some undies."

After they parted, he hoped the next time they met she would be wearing the panties with the little strawberries on them, and he could tear them off and make love to her. Better love than they had ever made before.

Like all northern Oregon winter mornings, the morning of February 9 began in cold darkness. The clock radio went on with a voice repulsively cheerful for 6:45, as it gave the dreary forecast for another dreary day. Vicki stretched out her long shapely arms, silken with a sheen of fine golden hair. She turned on the bed lamp and reached under her pillow for the little black book. It had become hateful to her after the break-in but, bookkeeping being bookkeeping, she made another entry of another sum and drew another crude star. They were loans, that was all, and someday she would pay them back. God knew, she had paid the interest in advance.

Monday morning, she thought, and wondered how she would make it through Friday. Her thoughts had darkened since the robbery. What kind of sex fiend would only take one pair of panties and two lousy bras? She had pondered and pondered over who it might be. For a little town, Rainier had more than its share of oversexed jerks, and— her luck—she seemed to know them all. But which one? She drove a school bus, and it could have been any of the guys at the bus barn, more like a stable the way they acted. It might have been one of the high school kids. She wouldn't put that kind of prank past any of them. From fourteen on, they used any excuse to rub their little peckers against her as they got on and off the bus.

He had left a beer bottle in the toilet bowl like some kind of weirdo phallic symbol pointing up at her. That must have been some scene! Whacking off into her underwear. She was grateful that she hadn't found any of his you know what in the bowl. The bottle and the forced window were all that she had reported to the police. The missing underwear and her little book and the messy bed were her own business. She was not about to have the cops prying into her relationships with men. In a place like Rainier, there were things that were better kept to herself. She was not about to get a reputation as the local pump that her daughter would only have to live down.

Kristina was the best thing in her life, and she was going to grow up good and straight and make Vicki a young grandmother. It could happen in ten years. Kristina would be going on nineteen then, and she'd be thirty-five. Wouldn't they be cute together! Or instead, the kid could become a movie star, or a Gloria Steinem, or one of those names you hear on television. Why should she be tied down to a man? Vicki had tried that. Knocked up and married at sixteen. The only good things to come out of it were the baby and a trip to Germany, when Robin Brown was in the army and stationed in Nuremberg.

Maybe it was Robin who broke in. Didn't he come around after they were separated, when she was rooming with Shirley Ogada, and demand money and push her around and force her to have sex with him? Shirley could tell a few things about that, if she wanted to. Rape, that was what it was. Even if he was her husband, if she didn't want to do it, it was rape. She had read that somewhere.

The dirty light of morning was turning the window shade gray. She smiled grimly. Enough of these lovely thoughts. It was time to rise and face the day. She threw some wood in the stove and reminded herself to be nicer to the guy who had mended it. He was always wanting to do her favors, and her car radio needed mending. He would do it for a smile. Why did he make her skin crawl? Except for the mustache, he wasn't bad-looking, she had known worse, but he was so icky. You didn't want to touch him or have him touch you. Well, she could handle him. He was such a puny thing, and she was a big, strong, strapping girl.

She pulled on her jeans and washed. As she was putting on her makeup, she studied her face. The broad unlined planes, the clear blue eyes, the natural blond hair (always a pleasant surprise to her lovers) all attested to her Finnish ancestry. Still pretty, but she wouldn't be forever. She was twenty-five and had better start getting her act together. She slapped her rump. For starters, ten pounds off there wouldn't hurt.

Fear brought tears to her eyes. A big rear end might be the least of her problems. The previous Wednesday, she had crossed the bridge over the Columbia River into Washington State to go to the Cowlitz County Health Center, in Longview. She had also gone over the Wednesday before. Two Pap tests, both with the same result: "abnormal finding."

The nurse had said, "You'd better follow up on this and see a specialist."

"You don't mean it could be cancer, do you?"

"I think you'd better find out just what the problem is." The woman bit her lip. "It may be anything. But your concern is justifiable as far as we can see."

That was why she had left the kid with the Olmsteads for the weekend. She had intended to go to Portland to consult a specialist. But then she'd met this guy—real

182

cute—well, she'd decided that she needed a few laughs before hearing what that doctor might have to say.

She smiled. Mustn't let Stanley Olmstead know about that. Stanley made her life possible. He was the head man at the school bus barn, and his brother was the district transportation supervisor. Her bus-driving job was part-time and paid only $5.36 an hour. Stanley saw to it that she got the choice runs and extra work. The other women drivers resented it and got bitchy. To hell with them, she thought. She was the one who was spreading her legs for Stanley. If they wanted similar treatment from him, they should give him similar treatment. Equal pay for equal work. Did that make her a liberated woman or a sex symbol, or could she be both? Have her cake and eat it, too. Maybe the saying should be changed. Equal lay for equal pay. She laughed. It could be that she'd make it through the day, after all.

Vicki wondered if Selma Olmstead knew about Stanley and her. She doubted it. If she did, she sure as hell wouldn't be taking care of Kristina when Vicki went off for a weekend, or worked late, or was screwing Selma's husband, or was screwing somebody else's husband.

Stanley was a strange duck. Five years of being her lover, and most of the time so guilty that he couldn't even get it up. But he was good to her and not only at work. The money he had given her had helped her to survive. Five thousand bucks to date. She had checked the figure out in her black book on Friday, when he'd left after another no score. Oh yeah, he had to have his innings of trying. That was the price for Kristina's lodgings for the weekend.

Nice guy, Stanley, but, sometimes, he got too possessive. He acted as if he had the right to be mad if she was giving somebody else a good time. Like the time he found out that she was doing it with that student and screamed bloody murder that he wasn't given her money to take out other guys. Hell, that boy had accumulated more sexual know-how in his sixteen years than most of the others had in double that time. She could always handle Stanley by letting him give her butt an extra pat when most of the other drivers could see him do it, and make him feel like super stud.

Buttoning on a blue-and-green flannel shirt, she headed for the kitchen. Maybe she'd be able to get over to see the doctor in Portland today. No, she couldn't do that, she was working late, and she needed the extra money. After that, she had promised Krissie that she would bring her home and spend the evening with her. That was sacred. She pulled some meat out of the freezer for their dinner and put it on the counter to thaw. No matter what else they might say of her, and she knew that some of the women said plenty, they had to admit that she was a good mother. The kid was the only good thing that had ever happened to her. She was so bored with life in Rainier. It was a nothing life in a nowhere place. A nowhere place and nowhere men. If her health checked out, she was going to take the kid and move on. Come spring, she would head north to Seattle or south to Portland, or farther down the coast to San Francisco or L.A., maybe, where there was a lot of action, and it was always warm. She laughed at the thought. She enjoyed laughing and having a good time, but there had not been much of that lately. She would get out and be happy, if only nothing bad was happening to her. She had to see a good doctor and soon.

When Vicki got into the garage that morning, she threw Stanley a big smile and walked past him to her bus. The creep, Steve, was waiting for her. He sidled up and asked, "Been getting any more of those hot notes?"

She forced herself to smile and made a wisecrack about not having received any fan mail lately. She added, "How'd you like to do me a big favor? My car radio is on the fritz. Maybe you can fix it after we finish the morning run."

"What's in it for me?"

"If you turn it on, maybe you can turn me on, too."

"When?"

"You can't tell in advance when a thing like that's going to grab you."

"Tonight."

"What's the rush? Half the fun is in getting there."

"Tonight."

She smiled, thinking that she had the situation under control. She was working the late run. He would be gone by the time that she pulled her bus back into the barn.

Steve Heflin, the second mechanic at the Rainier Union High School bus barn, did a last check on the vehicle and smiled at his pal Harry Withers. "She's a-one okay. You're ready to go."

Harry was setting off on a long haul. The bus drivers vied for the long trips because they meant earning more money. Usually, the best of them went to Vicki Brown, and everybody knew why or thought they did. Steve asked, "When do you think you'll be getting back?"

"Not until after eight. Why?"

"Nothing. I just thought we might get together for a beer."

"I'll give you a ring, if I'm not too tired."

Harry pulled out. Although Steve was only three years older, he thought of Harry as a kid. It was not only that Harry was simple and easily rattled and had a funny look of startled adolescence that made him seem young even for twenty-one; the age difference could be counted in terms of the Vietnam War experience. Steve had been in the Marine Corps and had been honorably discharged in 1973 with a Good Conduct medal. If he thought that giving the time to his country merited some greater reward than becoming a second mechanic in a school garage, he did not speak of it. Nobody had a great deal in Rainier. It was not the kind of place in which people became millionaires, but the hunting and fishing were fine, and the erose wooden countryside had a rugged beauty. Steve was always exploring and had discovered many secret places that nobody else knew about.

At 5:00 that afternoon, Steve was getting ready to leave for the day when Selma Olmstead arrived to pick up Stanley. They mentioned something about stopping for some groceries on the way home, where Vicki Brown's daughter was waiting for them. Quite a cozy little group, Steve thought. He doubted that Selma knew just how cozy Vicki and her husband were. Maybe she did. Maybe that was how she got off. In a place like Rainier, there wasn't much choice, and you had to get off as best you could.

By the time Steve and Olmstead closed up the barn, the school was coming back to life. The day students had left, and the night students were arriving. They could hear the whirr from the woodworking shop next door. On the auditorium fire escape, which overlooked the barn, some of the cast were already gathering for a rehearsal of the school play, *Just Another Western*. One of the boys pulled out a prop gun and pointed it at another: "Bang-bang! You're dead!"

The kids began to laugh and tussle for the weapon. Below them, a skinny lad well over six feet tall dribbled an imaginary ball and feinted his way into the building. He was unmistakably a basketball player arriving early for one of the two games scheduled for that evening. Steve's wife, Kathy, was working the swing shift at a market over in Longview, and he had considered staying for one of them, but that was before Vicki Brown had asked him to fix her radio. His plans were further complicated when his mother called to say that she had a load of Presto logs she was willing to share with him. He had to pick them up that afternoon. He had learned that Vicki was on the late shift. There was time to do everything but perhaps he would stand her up. That would show her that he did not think enough of her to let her mess around with him.

Steve got into his 1951 Chevrolet pickup truck, an ancient heap that he kept in excellent condition and felt lucky to own. It had been school property and, when the district had decided to buy a new one a few weeks earlier, he had gotten a good deal on it. When he started on the five-mile drive to his parents' house in Alston's Corners, it was already dark. After he finished loading the logs into his truck with the help of his nineteen-year-old brother, his mother asked him to stay for supper.

He looked up at the sky. Rain was threatening, and he said, "I'd better get these logs home as quick as I can. Kathy's left some chili on the stove for me to heat up. I'll have a couple of beers and look at TV."

It was only 5:30. He still had plenty of time to get home, unload the logs, and get back to the bus barn— that is, if he decided to keep his date. He stopped for a six-pack of beer and two dollars' worth of gasoline at the Fern Hill grocery store and gas station. He might share the beer with Vicki in the barn; then again, he might stay home and polish it off alone, or invite Harry Withers over after he returned from his run. He paid and went out to pump his own gas. He overran by a penny and dashed back into the store with the coin.

The clerk remembered the incident for a long time. It

was not the kind of honesty that he would have expected from a hippie-looking type with long sideburns and a drooping mustache, driving a beat-up old Chevy pickup truck. So many customers did not bother. They just skipped out on a few cents overrun, and that could add up by the end of the day.

At 6:30, a high-school senior was dashing past the bus barn when he saw Vicki Brown pulling in. They exchanged waves, but he did not stop to talk to the pretty driver for fear of being late for rehearsal of the play in which he had a role.

Fifteen minutes later, a former student, Marty Allerdings, and a friend drove up in his van looking for a parking space. They were going to the basketball game and wanted to get as close to the building as possible because of the rain forecast. They pulled up behind a Chevy pickup truck that was backed up to the door of the first bay of the bus barn. Marty's friend asked, "You think it's okay to block that truck? The owner might want to get out."

Marty replied, "That old wreck belongs to the school. I can remember it from when I was a freshman. Nobody's going to be using it until morning."

As the two boys entered the building, a young actress in the play sneaked out to the fire escape, thinking none of the teachers would catch her smoking out there in the dark. She heard scuffling noises coming from the barn. She lit her cigarette, dismissing the sounds as only a couple of kids horsing around.

A night-school teacher was pulling into the circular driveway between the barn and the school. She parked near the bus gas tanks and, as she was locking her car door, she distinctly heard a scream and a shot. She looked around, wondering where the sounds could be coming from, and then remembered that the students were rehearsing a Western. Smiling, she glanced up toward the auditorium, where the glow of a cigarette extinguished her smile.

"Snuff out that cigarette!"

The teacher was late for her class and could not spare the time to get the student's name. "Young lady, get back into the auditorium this minute!"

Inside the building, the teacher looked at a school clock and realized that her own watch was fast. It was only 6:48. She had plenty of time and regretted not having taken the girl's name.

Outside, another student trotted toward the school, fearing that he might miss the start of the game. He stopped short when he saw the van of his pal Marty Allerdings rolling very slowly down the driveway without its lights on. He wondered if it had slipped its brake until he caught sight of a driver. It was not Marty but a complete stranger wearing a shiny dark jacket and stocking cap, sporting a Fu Manchu mustache and curly sideburns.

About an hour later, at 7:50, Stanley Olmstead's brother Phil pulled into the space in which Marty Allerdings had been parked. He left his car and went into the barn, ostensibly to pick up a few quarts of oil for a bus that was stationed in the country. He was a meticulous transportation boss and looked around to make certain that everything was in order. Vicki Brown's bus was pulled into its regular space, but Harry Withers had yet to return from his run. Everything seemed shipshape.

As Phil Olmstead was emerging from the barn, he saw a distraught young man standing beside his car, shouting, "Where's my van? I parked it right here before the game."

Marty Allerdings had become bored with what had

turned out to be a dull basketball game and left the gymnasium. He looked for his van in the space where he had parked it but, instead, found Phil's car. He was justifiably upset until he caught sight of his vehicle pulled up at the curb at the bottom of the drive. He bolted toward it, crying, "There it is! How the hell did it get down there?"

Olmstead shrugged and took off to deliver the oil. He did not notice that Vicki's little green Mazda was parked next to the barn, in front of the woodworking shop.

When Allerdings reached his van, the wing mirror was broken, and his first thought was that he had been robbed. He flung open the door and searched frantically, but nothing was missing. There was a strange substance that looked like dried blood on the gear shift and steering wheel and more of it smeared on the outside of the driver's door. It made no sense, but he was too relieved at not having been robbed to look for explanations. The only thing on his mind was to rid his truck of the foul-looking stuff. He drove to the nearest service station and washed it off with a paper towel. As he started for home, he tossed the soiled towel into the street.

Shortly before Allerdings left the game, Lois Heflin had received a telephone call from her son. Steve had wanted to know what time it was. It was a strange question. She had looked at her watch. "Seven-thirty. Why do you want to know?"

"How much do I owe you for the logs?"

She had answered and asked again why he wanted to know the time.

"I unloaded the truck as soon as I got home from your place. While I was carrying some logs in, I must've knocked over my clock and stopped it."

He told her he had been watching TV. Reruns of "Bewitched" and "Adam-12". She had thought that it was very peculiar. How could anybody have been watching television and not know what time it was?

Harry Withers returned from his run at 8:15. All of the doors to the barn were blocked by students' cars, and he went into the school to get the owners to move their vehicles. While he was waiting, he made a telephone call to Steve Heflin. There was no answer.

When Harry finally pulled into his space in the barn, he saw that there was only one light on in the garage, which was unusual but not alarming. He swept out the interior of his bus and did a hasty check of the garage doors. The door to Vicki's bay was open a crack. He closed it and left for home.

At 8:30, Steve Heflin called his mother's house again. This time, there was a note of urgency in his voice. He asked, "Is the kid home?"

Mrs. Heflin put her younger son, Gus, on the phone. The boys spoke for a minute or two and, when Gus hung up, he headed for his bedroom to get a 12-gauge shotgun.

"Somebody's messing around with Steve. There's some kind of trouble. I'm going out there."

Steve and Kathy lived in a trailer parked on a lonely road next to a Christmas tree farm. He had often complained that people were hassling him in the isolated part of the woods in which he lived. By the time Gus arrived, there was no sign of trouble. His brother was certainly acting strangely that night. First, he had to get home to a can of chili instead of eating his ma's home-cooked meal. He could have thrown a tarp over the logs and they would have kept dry in any weather. Next, he had to call for the time in the middle of watching television. Finally, he had asked for help when he did not seem to need it. All of this checking-in was weird coming from a guy who was only sitting home by the TV.

Steve was in a highly agitated state. When Gus challenged him on his behavior, he said, "I've got this funny feeling that things aren't right."

Steve insisted that they get into Gus's car and check around. They drove to Harry Withers's place but there was nobody home, and they went on to the bus barn. There was nothing out of order. Harry's bus was back. They must have passed him on the road, and Steve wanted to go back to Harry's place to see him. Steve's edginess had not abated and, on the way down the school drive, he turned to look back in the direction of the barn. He cried, "Is that Vicki Brown's car? Did you see it? A little green Mazda?"

They got to Harry's home shortly before 9:00, and Steve ran from the car, leaving his brother in it.

Harry was already undressing for bed when Steve came in asking if he had seen Vicki's car down at the garage. Harry replied, "I don't think so."

"I thought I saw it." Steve's voice was steady, but there was something disquieting beneath his tone, and Harry could not figure out if his friend was calm or disturbed. He rattled on for a half hour despite the fact that his brother was waiting outside.

After Steve finally left, Harry went to bed, but he could not sleep. Something that Steve had said continued to rattle him. He had never known Vicki Brown to leave without her wheels. He got up and tossed on some clothes and returned to the barn. Sure enough, the green Mazda was there.

When he got back home, he called Steve. "You're right. Vicki's car is there."

"Oh, God, I wonder what it means."
"It sure as hell ain't like her."

When Vicki had not turned up at his house by 7:30 that evening, Stanley Olmstead had decided to take little Kristina Brown over to Vicki's mother's house. He and his wife had taken care of the child for the whole weekend. Enough was enough. Vicki probably had picked up some guy and was off having a high old time with nary a thought for anything else. That was just like her. He sighed. It was not like her—not where her kid was concerned. Whatever else Vicki might be called, she was a good mother. Nobody ever had denied that. But if she was such a good mother, where was she?

Stanley would never have admitted to being jealous. It was only that he was irritated by his mistress's lack of any sense of responsibility to her daughter, to her lover, or to *his* wife. That good woman had enough to do looking after her own family without taking in strays.

Olmstead deposited the little girl at the home of her grandmother. He said that he was going right back home to go to bed. He did not know about other people, but he needed his rest. He had to be on the job at 6:30 in the morning. He worked for his living and could not be expected to wait up while Vicki took her own sweet time about getting around to doing the right thing.

Vicki's mother closed the door and told her granddaughter to prepare for bed. She shook her head. Olmstead's litany had not been necessary in front of the child. The man would be less of a problem if only he did not seem to love Vicki almost to the point of obsession, to the point where the girl sometimes complained that he frightened her.

As the hours passed, she grew increasingly uneasy.

She had seen Vicki that morning, and nothing had been said about the possibility of leaving Kris with her that night. Whenever Vicki had a late date, she always made arrangements for somebody to look after the child well in advance. Olmstead was wrong. Vicki did not run off irresponsibly. The woman had to admit that it was not entirely unlike her daughter to have found a date at the last minute, but she always called to make certain that Kris was taken care of. Why hadn't she called?

At 6:15 the next morning, Selma Olmstead dropped her husband off for work. As usual, he was the first to arrive and was surprised when Steve Heflin walked in a short time later. It was much earlier than he usually checked in, and Steve explained, "I thought maybe one of the drivers would be out, and you'd want me to take the run."

That sounded fairly feeble, unless the guy suddenly had become some kind of screwball psychic. Instead of getting down to work, Steve wandered off and started pacing back and forth, kicking pebbles along the gravel drive that led to the barn.

A while later, the other drivers began to drift in. One of the women, Melanie Donner, saw Steve go over to his tool box in the barn office and take out a .44 magnum revolver and strap it to his waist. When the hour for departure arrived, another woman driver, Gail Bennett, asked Steve to back out her bus. He reached for the brake lever with his right hand. She noticed that he did not have enough strength in the hand to set it and had to switch to his left. He showed her the right palm, which had a big black-and-blue mark near the thumb and said, "See what a giant Presto log did to me last night."

Stanley Olmstead shouted, "Hey, Steve, it looks like

you were right. You'll be driving twenty-one. Vicki hasn't shown up yet."

Harry Withers got excited. "And her car's right over there. Did you see it? Been there all night."

It was only after the drivers returned from the morning run that Stanley Olmstead noticed a strange-looking substance on the bus barn wall and on the back of the bus that was parked next to Vicki's in the last stall. He pointed it out to Steve. "It looks like blood."

"That's paint."

Olmstead shook his head. "No, that looks like blood."

"No. That's oil."

Olmstead had too much to do to stand around arguing. Steve was not acting like himself that morning. He supposed that everybody was entitled to a bad day once in a while. Steve was usually a good worker. Not a bad mark against him. He was always helpful, and not only on the job. Just the day before, he had fixed Vicki's car radio and before that, he had gone over to her place to mend a stovepipe.

By then, Vicki's mother had called to find out if she had come to work. The drivers were commenting about her absence. Some wondered if she had gotten into trouble the night before, but others dismissed it as just Vicki's way. Gail Bennett said, "Wouldn't it be nice to come and go as Vicki does?"

A little before 10:00, Steve told Olmstead that he and Harry Withers were going up to the administration office to report that Vicki was missing.

Early that afternoon, Gail Bennett returned from a trip to Portland to find Steve edgier than ever. He said, "I wish they'd find Vicki. She's giving me an ulcer."

As Gail was climbing back into her bus to make her last trip of the day, she saw a big stain on the gravel drive outside the repair shop at the near end of the barn. There were also some spots on the inside wall. The first thing that popped into her head was blood, but that was plain crazy. This Vicki business was getting to her, too. But while she drove her short run, the mental picture of the stains stayed with her and, by the time she got back, she was convinced that they actually were blood. She hopped down the bus steps and ran to Phil Olmstead's office. She said, "You'd better come on out to the barn with me. There's blood all over the place."

"Are you nuts?"

"Phil, I'm telling you—there's blood."

"This whole joint's turning upside down just because some babe took a powder."

"You come along with me and take a look-see for yourself."

He sighed and followed her. When he examined the big stain on the ground, damned if it didn't look like blood. Everybody gathered around him. Phil said, "It sure as hell is blood."

His brother turned to Steve. "Didn't I tell you—on the bus and walls this morning? Blood, that's what it is."

Steve replied, "And I'm telling you, it's oil. Transmission oil, which is just as red as dried blood."

Phil said, "This stuff is clotted. Transmission oil don't clot."

Steve said, "I'm telling you—"

"We can settle this easy enough." Phil sent his brother to get a can of transmission oil. He poured some of it on the ground a little distance away from the stain in question. The oil was absorbed down into the gravel. It did not clot.

Phil got up. "It's blood. And I'm calling in the police. I suggest that all of you stick around."

They all began to talk at the same time.

"Can't deny it's blood."

"It's gotta be Vicki's blood."

"What do you think happened here last night?"

"Rape, assault, robbery. Take your pick."

Somebody gulped loudly. "Murder."

As they circled away from the bloody spot, as if it were quicksand that could suck them down into it, eyes involuntarily sought Stan Olmstead. He looked away and then rushed off after his brother.

A school bus from another district pulled up to the gas pumps. Steve ran out to it. "I'll take care of him."

As he was filling the tank, he struck up a conversation with the driver. "Have you heard about Vicki Brown?"

"No. What about her?"

"She's disappeared. It looks like somebody's snatched her."

"Is that a fact?"

"It's these kids, you know. The drugs and stuff."

"What's the world comin' to?"

"You're full up."

"Thanks, pal." He drove off and Steve returned to the barn, which was becoming bloodier by the moment, as new stains and spatters were discovered on the walls, floors, and vehicles. The police were on their way. Steve's hand slid over his holster. He hastily removed the gun and thrust it into his tool box.

Criminal Inspector Dean Renfrow, of the Oregon state police, and Martin Sells, the district attorney of Columbia County, took charge of the investigation. The quantity of blood, combined with the disappearance of Hilda Victoria Brown, suggested homicide. The drivers and mechanics were interviewed one at a time, while the police fanned out through the school looking for people who had been there the night before and might know something relevant to the case.

Steve Heflin particularly interested Renfrow. His nervous reactions were far beyond the investigator's experience of the often idiosyncratic behavior of innocent people when having to face police interrogation about a serious crime. He approached Heflin and asked offhandedly, "Don't you find it warm in here?"

"Not particularly."

"You don't?"

"No. Why?"

"You're doing a hell of a lot of sweating."

He walked away, leaving Heflin more unstrung than ever. When one of the drivers suggested that they band together and search the area around the barn and athletic field, Heflin was among the first to volunteer his services.

They had found nothing by the time the sky dimmed into early twilight. The driver who had organized the search suggested that they quit, but Heflin said that he was going to take a look in the sapling forest beyond the field. Within five minutes, he came bolting back holding a woman's sodden and dripping handbag at the end of a stick.

"It's Vicki's! I poked the stick in just far enough to see her wallet with her name in it. It was floating in the little pond back there."

That clinched it for the police. The presence of her car and her purse so close to the barn made them positive that the young woman had not voluntarily left the premises. She had been murdered or very seriously injured, and her body had been removed by her assailant.

Renfrow's interest in Heflin was renewed by his discovery of the purse. The guy was quite a little detective. He wondered if he might be able to find Vicki with equal facility. If Heflin actually was involved, the detective's first order of business was to find the motive. He wondered if Vicki had any close friends among the women drivers with whom she might have exchanged confidences about her relationships with the men. He rounded them up for questioning and, under their tutelage, Renfrow and Sells received a quick course in the sexual behavior of the Rainier Union High School bus crew.

By universal accord, Vicki Brown had been the sexual star of the barn. They thought that it would be terrible if anything had happened to her but that one had to face the facts. She had been asking for trouble for as long as any of them had known her. She had been asking for trouble ever since she first came to work there. There was even talk about her having sex with one of the students, and that should have been against the law. It was certainly against the rules.

But mostly, there was Stanley Olmstead. They had been having an affair for years. Vicki had been playing him for a fool, and it had paid off for her. The best runs. Food. Money. Even baby-sitting. He knew that she had been two-timing him, but what could he do about it? He was a married man. He could not be blamed if he got a little jealous.

Renfrow asked, "How jealous?"

"Not *that* jealous. Nobody's pointing a finger at good old Stan. He's a nice guy."

Nevertheless, Stan Olmstead had a very good motive, and he was rapidly becoming the prime suspect. But the investigation is still in its early stages, Renfrow thought. He could not get the other man out of his mind, and he asked, "What about Steven Heflin?"

Heflin was married to a sweet little thing named Kathy, and it seemed as if it was a very good marriage. One of the women smirked. "Of course, that didn't stop him from having an affair with another woman. Grace Talmadge."

"Is Miss Talmadge around?"

"*Mrs*. Talmadge. She moved to Georgia about two months ago."

They were using the garage office for the interrogations, and Renfrow glanced through the doorway. Outside, Heflin was pacing nervously. He was still sweating. The detective jerked his head toward him, so that Heflin could see that he was being talked about. "What about him and Vicki?"

He would not have minded, but there was nothing. He had a thing for her. They all did. She was pretty, and she was available. Heflin would do special favors for her. She never actually encouraged him, but she kept on letting him do them. Actually, Steve seemed to be the one man in whom she did not seem to have sexual interest. It was strange, because he was really no worse than any of the others and, in some ways, a better person than most. He was always ready to help when any of the drivers had trouble with a bus.

At that moment, one of Renfrow's men came in. They had found a young man who had been to the basketball game the night before. He had seen an old gray-green Chevy pickup truck parked in the first bay but was certain it belonged to the school.

One of the women interrupted. "That's Steve's truck. It used to belong to the school." She pointed to it. "That's it over there."

Renfrow went out to speak to Heflin. "Do you mind if I have a look at your truck?"

"What do you want to do that for? You won't find anything in it."

"Routine. We're checking all of the vehicles. Of course, you do have the right to refuse to let us."

"How would it look if I did?"

"Not good."

Steve hesitated for a moment and then gave his permission. Renfrow examined the truck quickly but did not find anything of significance. By the time he was finished, Heflin was wringing wet, and the detective had to consider the possibility that it might be a disease rather than nerves.

The police cordoned off the garage and dismissed most of the drivers, asking only a few of the men, including Heflin and Stan Olmstead, to remain. By 9:00 P.M., more witnesses had come forward, and they had a fairly accurate account of the events relating to the crime except what actually had taken place in the bus barn. At 6:30, Vicki Brown had been seen pulling into the barn. Fifteen minutes later, Steve Heflin's pickup truck was parked in the first bay. A few minutes after, scuffling sounds were heard in the barn followed by a scream and a shot. Almost immediately thereafter, a man resembling Heflin was seen backing away another vehicle that had been parked in front of his pickup truck.

What they did not know was exactly what had taken place in the barn. They did not know how many people were involved or which crime they were investigating: murder, assault, rape, robbery, or any combination of them. They did not know if Vicki Brown was alive or dead or if the blood splashed around the barn belonged to her.

Sells said, "We've got to start somewhere. Let's presume that whatever happened here happened to the missing girl."

One of the officers said, "Not necessarily. It could also be that she committed whatever it is, and that she's hiding out. She was a big, strong girl—five foot ten inches. One hundred forty pounds."

"We know that whatever happened occurred between

six-thirty and seven. We know Steve Heflin's truck was there during a portion of that time and was gone by seven-thirty, when Allerdings came out of the game. According to Phil Olmstead, the garage was empty at that time, and there was no sign of anything out of the ordinary."

"But he might be covering for his brother."

Sells sighed. "Let's forget Vicki as perpetrator. What have we got in the way of suspects?"

Stanley Olmstead had the best motive for killing her, but he had a wonderful alibi. He was at home with Vicki's kid. Heflin had no known motive, but he was at the scene of the crime at the time that it was committed. The ex-husband and the other drivers all had alibis that checked out. It was Heflin, Olmstead, or a person or persons unknown.

Renfrow got up and headed back into the barn. "Come on. Let's have another look at Heflin's truck. I may have missed something."

Renfrow had missed quite a bit on that first examination. The second and more thorough search turned up a "red mucuslike substance" in the bed of the pickup as well as dark stains on its plywood cover. There were dark blond hairs caught in the tailgate. In the cab, Renfrow found suspicious dark stains on the bench seat and a pair of gloves on the floor that had specks that might be blood.

Renfrow and Sells asked Heflin to get into a police car. Heflin cried, "Where are you taking me?"

"Nowhere. We just want to ask you a few questions where we can't be overheard." They squeezed the mechanic into the back seat between them. The stench of his perspiration was overwhelming.

"What do you know about those stains in your truck?"

"What stains?"

"The ones that look like blood."

"You don't know they're blood."

"We'll find out. We're impounding your truck for investigation."

"Is that legal?"

"We'll make it legal. How did they get there?"

"What's this all about?"

"We have reason to believe that there's been a murder here. And it looks as if you're one of the prime suspects."

"Murder! You don't even know if there's a corpse."

"Do you?"

Heflin's clothes were sticking to his body. He peered at Renfrow and said, "I don't know what you're talking about. Can I go now?"

"One more thing. We'd like your permission to come up to your place tomorrow and have a look around."

"I'll have to ask my wife."

"Things'll go easier with you if you cooperate."

"Yeah?" Heflin laughed. "Like with the truck?" He climbed over Sells and got out of the car. "I'll let you know tomorrow."

They watched him go into the office and sit down. He opened his tool box and withdrew something. Renfrow shouted, "The gun!"

He jumped from the car and raced toward the office with his men following after. Heflin was staring vacantly at the gun that lay on the desk before him. He made no protest when Renfrow roughly seized the weapon and examined it thoroughly. There was no blood on it, and it looked as if it had not been fired for some time. The gun was clean. Heflin's .44 magnum was not the murder weapon.

When he got home, Heflin told his wife that he was considered one of the chief suspects in the murder of Vicki Brown. She asked, "Did you have anything to do with it?"

He protested his innocence. Nobody even knew if Vicki

had been killed. "If anything happened to her, it had to be an accident. That's all."

They needed a fall guy, and they were trying to pin it on him. They wanted to search the trailer.

She asked if there was anything that they could find, and he could not answer. She said, "You'd better get yourself some legal advice."

Early the next morning, Wednesday, February 11, Heflin telephoned a Rainier attorney, Robert Lucas. He explained the situation and said that the police had asked for permission to come around and search his place. He wanted to know what he should do.

Lucas said, "If you've committed a crime, don't give your consent. If you haven't committed one, then let them make their search. It should clear things up."

Heflin hung up on the attorney. He thought for a moment and then dialed Renfrow's office. He said, "You can come ahead."

Heflin was right in one respect. Renfrow and Sells were convinced that no matter what crime had been committed in the barn, he was their man. Proving it would be something else. On the remote possibility that Hilda Victoria Brown was still alive, her description was put on an alert broadcast throughout Oregon and its neighboring states. Investigators fanned out from the high school to search the surrounding woods. Even before Heflin had given permission for them to come to the trailer, the experts had been summoned.

Two criminalists from the Oregon state police crime laboratory were already examining Heflin's truck in the Rainier police garage. They doubted that the gloves that Renfrow had found would yield any significant bloodstain evidence. The stains inside the truck were another matter. They were indeed blood. More human hair was found in the pickup bed. A police officer was dispatched to Vicki's house to get her hair brush and curlers, so that microscopic comparisons could be made between the hair found in the truck and the woman's own hair.

The criminalists moved on to the cordoned-off bus barn. After the police photographers had taken copious pictures, the scientists took blood samples from the walls, floor, doors, and buses. Word came that permission had been granted for them to examine Heflin's trailer just as they were completing their work in the barn.

Lieutenant George Winterfield, of the state police, drove Renfrow and his experts out to a remote part of Fern Hill Road, where a modest mobile home was ensconced on the edge of a picturesque evergreen farm. The meager surrounding grounds had been cleared and showed signs of having been cultivated during the warmer months. The snow-crowned mountains in the distance were as remote and indifferent as glacial beauties at a dull party.

Heflin waited at the door, his fingers tapping a dissonant tattoo against the jamb. Inside, Kathy Heflin tried to be cordial and helpful despite the circumstances. Her husband had proclaimed his innocence, and she believed him. They had nothing to fear or hide, and the sooner they got through this ordeal, the sooner they could return to their uneventful private lives.

Some attempt had been made to tidy up the trailer, but not even the most pristine conditions could dispel the shabby, cramped, claustrophobic atmosphere in which the young couple lived. The investigators did not mind, for a spartan area would have offered less opportunity for concealment. Although lawmen have great pessimism about the ability of judge and jury to find a verdict and dole out the sentence obviously merited, they are eternal optimists about their own ability to nose out incriminating evidence. They opened a closet door and half expected Vicki's body to fall into their arms. They were disappointed. There was no sign of a corpse anywhere on the premises.

One of the criminalists, Bonita Garthus, noticed some fresh blood on Heflin's thumb. She asked about it, and he replied that his nose was bleeding. She asked if she minded if she took a sample. He held out his hand, and she took a swab. While she had his arm, she drew some blood from his vein. "We'll need this to make some comparisons."

Renfrow took note of the perspiration again appearing on the suspect's brow, but it could have been attributed to the taking of blood. Killers who wallowed in the blood of their victims were often quite squeamish about their own.

The criminalists wanted to see the bedroom. As Kathy Heflin led the way, they passed a rather messy room, and she smiled embarrassedly. "That's our junk room."

In the bedroom, they found a pair of blood-spattered dress boots and a small knife with traces of blood on it. Nearby, an empty holster with a built-in knife scabbard also had blood on it. Ms. Garthus asked, "Where's the gun?"

Kathy took them to the kitchen, explaining, "It's out here. We've kept it here for about two weeks. Steve is going to use it to get some stray cats that have been messing around in our garbage. He knows that I'd shoot to miss, and that would only scare them away for a while."

She opened a small plastic box on the counter near the sink and took out a .22 Ruger revolver. Winterfield grabbed it out of her hands. The gun was empty, but the grip was covered with a sticky substance that looked like blood. As Garthus took charge of it, her partner noticed Steve Heflin steal into the "junk room." He was stuffing what looked like articles of clothing down behind a game table. The criminalist shouted, "What's that? What are you trying to hide in there?"

They were upon him, and Heflin handed over a black vinyl motorcycle jacket and a pair of leather gloves. They were sopping wet from a recent washing, but no amount of scrubbing could remove all traces of blood that had soaked through and through.

Ms. Garthus asked, "Who do these things belong to?"

Kathy said, "The jacket is Steve's."

Heflin interrupted, "Not the gloves. They belong to my brother, Gus. All my things have name tags sewn inside. You see—there's no tag in these gloves."

Kathy corroborated, "That's right. There's no tag in them. Those gloves can't belong to Steve."

Gus Heflin later denied ever having owned the gloves.

As they were driving back to town, Ms. Garthus said, "We'll need to know Vicki Brown's blood type."

Winterfield said, "That's routine stuff. I'll have it for you in a couple of hours."

He was wrong.

The day after the discovery of the blood (and for several more weeks), the men had to roll the buses out for the women drivers. They would not enter the barn, nor would they be alone with any of the men. They had known these guys for years, or thought that they had known them, and suddenly one of them might be a rapist or a killer. A Jack the Ripper. The risqué laughs in the barn had a hollow ring. Stan Olmstead's teenage daughter was more intrepid than the older women and, one afternoon, decided to play Nancy Drew. Snooping around the barn, feeling safe because her father was nearby, she found a broken dental bridge and some strands of crushed fair hair.

Dr. Richard Edmiston was a respected Rainier dentist. The moment that the police showed him the bridge, he said, "The last time that I saw that, it was in Vicki Brown's mouth."

"Will you testify to that?"

"Oh, yes. I have X rays to back it up. You see, it's a cantilevered bridge. Until Mrs. Brown came to see me, I hadn't seen one in ten years. We don't use them anymore. They weaken the adjacent teeth. I had to remove it to fill a cavity and then put it back again."

He pointed to some tabs with a dental pick. "I attached these to take the strain off the other teeth. Mrs. Brown had a congenital birth defect. She never grew the two teeth on either side of her front teeth."

That eliminated the theory that Vicki Brown had gone off on a date. A pretty girl was not going to let a man see her with a hole in the middle of her face. She had been assaulted in that barn. Her assailant had struck her, knocking out her bridge.

On the same day that the police interviewed the dentist, a shovel with blood on the handle was found in a shed near Heflin's trailer.

The report came down from the Oregon state police crime laboratory. It was a mixed bag as far as furthering the district attorney's case was concerned, but it did not mitigate Sells's and Renfrow's conviction that Heflin was their man.

Using the crime lab's special microscope, Sergeant Charles Baughn had determined that there were thirty points of similarity between the hair from Vicki's brush and the hair found in Heflin's truck. Unfortunately, hair, unlike fingerprints, was not accepted in court as positive identification. Under oath, the most that Baughn could say was that it was extremely unlikely that two or more people with the same type of hair as Vicki would have been in the barn, in Heflin's pickup truck, and also have left three strands lodged three inches down the inside of the left glove found in Heflin's home.

The investigation hinged on an analysis of the blood. If blood on something belonging to Heflin and blood in the barn were both the same type as Vicki's and different from Heflin's, it would make compelling circumstantial evidence, for it would establish that Heflin had been in contact with her blood. The only logical way for that to have happened was if he had injured or killed her in the barn.

The analysis disclosed that Heflin's blood was human type O with a positive Rh factor. Approximately eighty-five percent of the population have a positive Rh factor, and forty-five percent have type O blood. All of the blood in evidence was of this type. However, one splotch found in the barn and the blood on the shovel found in Heflin's shed contained a relatively minor factor, called small "c." This factor was missing from Heflin's blood. If Vicki's blood was also type O positive but contained the missing "c" factor, it would provide the link between the splotch in the barn and Heflin's shovel. Sells was encouraged and prodded Lieutenant Winterfield to get on with the job of finding the missing girl's blood type.

In the meantime, somebody had painted "Heflin is the killer" in front of the bus barn. Heflin spray-painted it out. He also sprayed a whole wall on which blood had been discovered. He was too late. A vital section of board from that wall, along with the .22 Ruger found in his kitchen, was locked away in the district attorney's office.

Winterfield called Sells and blew away any hope of a blood tie. The Seattle hospital in which Vicki Brown had been born was out of business and no record of her blood type had been retained. Her daughter had been born in St. John's Hospital, in Longview. Their records only showed that Mrs. Brown had a positive Rh factor. The lieutenant had checked all of the doctors who had ever treated her, her insurance agent, and the board of education. Nobody had made any notation of her blood type. The only way to find her type was to find the body.

The search intensified, coordinated by Captain Bruce Oester of the Columbia County sheriff's office. His men, along with the Oregon state police, had made up the original search party. The area was riddled with hiding places—forests, hills, caves, ravines, abandoned (as well as functioning) wells, and the Columbia River, which marked the border between the states of Washington and Oregon. The original party was augmented by 200 local volunteers, 100 members of the Oregon National Guard, the Cowlitz County Sheriff's Cadets, 25 members of the Civil Air Patrol, and Explorer Scouts. Dogs and mounted searchers were flown down from the Seattle Search and Rescue Dogs Association. Some ponds were drained, others were probed by the Argonauts, a St. Helens scuba diving club. Coast Guard helicopters waited for the appropriate temperature to start photo reconnaissance. A decomposing body gives off heat that can be detected by infrared film. They had to wait for several weeks because extremes of temperature slow decomposition, and they were still in the middle of the severe northwestern winter. The search covered an area of 130 square miles and consumed more than 7,000 man-hours spread over a period of better than two months.

The body of Hilda Victoria Brown could not be found.

Martin Sells deliberated for almost two months before seeking an indictment. Did he dare to bring the case to court without a corpse? The last Oregon murder conviction in which the body was never recovered had been in 1904. The case against Steven Heflin was also weakened by lack of a compelling motive.

A telephone conversation with Grace Talmadge, in Georgia, changed everything.

Grace had been Heflin's mistress in November 1975. He had boasted to her of having broken into Vicki's house and had expressed a desire to get even with Vicki for not having given him the time of day. He had been convinced that everybody was making out with her except him. The line between hate and lust had blurred, and the more Vicki had rejected him, the more he had to have her.

Grace said, "That time he broke into Vicki's house, he stole some of her undies. A pair of panties and two bras. And he gave them to me."

Sells all but shouted, "What! Do you still have them?"

"Yeah. They're around somewhere. I feel funny about wearing them after—you know."

"Send them up here to me as fast as possible."

The district attorney hung up. Eureka! At last, he had his motive. Sexual obsession. There were a lot of men in Columbia County who were obsessed with sex, but Steve Heflin was the one guy with a sexual obsession. There was a big difference between the two, and that difference was called murder.

When Martin Sells showed the panties with the little strawberry pattern to Kristina Brown, the child cried, "You've found my mommy!"

Steven Heflin was arrested on April 6, 1976, and charged

211

with the crime of murder. Sells's indictment was necessarily ambiguous.

"On or about February 9, he did unlawfully and intentionally cause the death of Hilda Victoria Brown by means unknown, contrary to Oregon law."

The Oregon state police crime laboratory had done a splendid job but, to clinch the case, Sells needed more. Had Heflin shot or beaten Vicki to death? If he had shot her, in what part of the body was she hit? His .22 Ruger was unloaded. There was no way of telling whether it had been fired on that specific night. The blood on it could have come from beating Vicki. A beating would seriously weaken the case for murder. At most, the charge would be manslaughter. Furthermore, a jury might believe that a beating was not necessarily fatal and, without a corpse to prove that she was actually dead, they could bring in a verdict of not guilty. A defense attorney could hypothesize that she had developed amnesia after the beating and wandered off somewhere, having lost all memory of who she was and where she had come from. A jury might buy that. The lawyer could plea bargain for a reduction of the charge to assault in exchange for a guilty plea.

The question of the missing body was also complicated by the fact that no death certificate had been signed for Hilda Victoria Brown. Dr. William Brady, the Oregon state medical examiner, was an inflexible man. Although he had the power to issue certificates for missing persons, he had three criteria that had to be met in a murder case: (1) The event must unquestionably have occurred; (2) I must be satisfied that the missing person is the one in question; (3) I must be satisfied that the person could not have survived.

Sells knew that he could not fully satisfy any of these

criteria. The case against Heflin was circumstantial in the extreme, and only in Sells's mind was it *unquestionably* a case of murder. He did not know if he could prove that Vicki Brown was the missing person in question. Without knowing her blood type, he could not positively link her to the copious amount of bloodstain evidence on which so much of his case rested. If Vicki had been beaten or raped only, who was to say beyond doubt that she had not survived?

Sells's case might be thrown out of court. He could become a laughingstock or, worst still, gain a name for being the kind of D.A. who tried to railroad innocent men. He had put his reputation on the line largely on the strength of a gut reaction. He asked one of the criminalists at the crime lab: "Can any of you really prove that Vicki was shot in that garage, and shot by Heflin's .22?"

There was no response. Sells cried, "Don't you know somebody who might be able to?"

"The only one who comes to mind is Herb Mac-Donell."

"Where do I find him?"

"Corning."

"Where the hell is that?"

"Upstate New York. First, you change planes. Then, you change planes again."

"I'll telephone."

In May 1976, as Herbert MacDonell was preparing to chair a four-day seminar on death investigation, due to begin on May 24, he received a call from Martin Sells. Sells introduced himself as the district attorney of Columbia County, Oregon, and said: "I've got a case up here, in the town of Rainier, that I think might interest you."

"What kind of case?"

"A very special murder case."

213

"All murder is special."

"Oh—but this one is super special. You see, we don't have the corpse. I've got a murder indictment against a fellow named Steven Heflin and a fairly good circumstantial case—that could possibly become solid with your help."

"I can't get up to Oregon. At the end of this month, I'm chairing a seminar here in Corning. Then, in June, I'm doing a bloodstain seminar in Philadelphia. From there, I'm off to testify in the Zeigler case at the diametrically opposite end of the country from you, in Florida. After that, I have to be back in Elmira for another institute in July. Then, my direction is due north to the fishing camps of Canada."

"All of the evidence is bloodstain. If you could find some time—"

MacDonell heard the desperation in his voice and said, "All right. Suppose you tell me what you've got."

Sells replied that they had the blood-soaked jacket and gloves that Heflin was wearing during the alleged attack on Vicki Brown. They also had blood spots in his pickup truck and all around the school bus barn where the attack had taken place. The problem was that it was all type O with a positive Rh factor. Heflin was type O with a positive Rh factor. The only blood that differed was a splotch in the barn and some on the handle of a shovel found on Heflin's property. These were also O positive, but they had a small "c" factor missing from the other evidence and not found in Heflin's blood.

MacDonell said, "I take it this factor is present in Vicki Brown's blood."

Sells admitted that there was another problem. They did not know Brown's blood type. What he needed from MacDonell was a scenario for what had happened in the barn that would be convincing enough to convict Heflin despite the fact that they had neither the victim's body nor her blood type. He concluded, "What I'd like to send you is what we think is the weapon. We obviously don't have the fatal bullet either. And a board from the bloodiest part of the scene of the crime."

No body, no blood type in a case in which the bulk of the evidence was bloodstain, no bullet; the challenge was irresistible, and MacDonell said, "Get the board and gun off to me immediately. I'll take a look at them. When you get a chance, I'd also like a complete set of the police photographs of the barn and a floor plan."

MacDonell went upstairs to the kitchen humming to himself. His wife looked at him warily. He asked, "Phyllis, do you know one of the most common mistakes in those detective stories you're so fond of? It's assuming that the corpus delicti is the corpse. It can be, but it isn't necessarily. The corpus delicti is the body of the crime—all of the evidence—and not just the body of the victim in a murder case. In arson, a match can be part of the corpus delicti. Now, wouldn't that be dandy in a crossword puzzle?"

She nodded. "Shall I forget about the fishing trip? You're about to take a case of murder without a body."

MacDonell received a bulky package containing Heflin's .22 revolver and a board from the end stall of the Rainier Union High School bus barn. It measured two inches by six inches by twenty-eight inches, and had been removed from the bloodiest part of the barn before Heflin had attempted to erase the evidence in that area with spray paint.

After untying the package, MacDonell rubbed his hands together. With only these two pieces of evidence, he was going to prove either that the Oregon law enforcers had made jackasses of themselves, or that a murder had been committed even though the body had never been recovered. Whatever the outcome, he was going to have a bloody good time. What a remarkable word—*bloody*—and only the British seemed to appreciate that it was epithet as well as adjective.

Putting aside the board, he concentrated on discovering what the gun had to say. There were blood spatters in the muzzle, along the barrel, and in the empty cylinders. The blood on the barrel and in the cylinders was the result of back spatter. The bullet had hit its target, and the blood from the wound had spattered back over the gun. Did that mean that the lethal bullet had been fired from this gun? Probably, but not necessarily. It meant only that the gun was so positioned in relation to the source of blood that the spatter had hit it. The blood in the muzzle was much more telling.

There were instances in which blood in the muzzle was also the result of back spatter. The spatter could occur at a range of up to one to two feet, but that was most unlikely in a muzzle as tight as that of Heflin's .22. The blood in this gun was proof that it was the murder weapon. It had been drawn back into the muzzle by suction. Expanding hot gases are produced by the progressive burning of the gunpowder. They cool and immediately contract, causing a sucking back into the muzzle. The suction drawing in this blood could only have happened when the bullet struck bare skin at very close range.

Before receiving the Heflin evidence, MacDonell and his students had been conducting experiments on the suction properties of close-range firing at bare skin. For a long time, he had suspected that a very good index of the distance from the gun to the target could be developed by measuring how far down the muzzle the blood was sucked.

To conduct the experiments, Herb MacDonell and his students had made synthetic heads out of styrofoam, filled them with real blood, and covered them with a leather that simulated skin. They had fired at distances ranging from point-blank to one foot and used guns ranging from .22s to 12-gauge shotguns. The results were excellent and compared favorably with the data obtained from actual case histories, but MacDonell was not satisfied. They had not been able to approximate the bony structure of the human skull. There was excessive spatter from their softer styrofoam heads. If his index was to be used in cases in which a defendant was on trial for murder, it had to be based on scientific tests that more closely approximated the real conditions. The defendant's life might hang in the balance.

A few weeks after these experiments, MacDonell heard about a group of large, ill, and abandoned dogs that were scheduled for execution by the ASPCA. They had the cranial formation that he was seeking, and he asked that they be turned over to him. His manner of execution would be no less humane than the society's, and the result might save an innocent man or punish a killer.

The heads of the animals were shaved so that no hair could interfere with the release of blood from the bullet wound. Prior to being shot, they were injected with sodium phenobarbital, so that they were already dying before the experiment took place. By the time it was over, MacDonell was satisfied with the index that he was about to use on Heflin's gun.

The blood had been drawn roughly a third of an inch down into the muzzle. By consulting his index, MacDonell knew that it was impossible for the muzzle of the .22 to have been more than three inches from the victim's head and, more likely it was only one inch away, possibly even in contact with it.

MacDonell studied the floor plan of the bus barn and the photographs taken within twenty-four hours of the murder. Using the information he had learned from the board and gun sent to him by Sells, and all the details Sells had provided, MacDonell was able to reconstruct exactly what had taken place.

The killer was waiting for Vicki Brown in the bus barn. He had backed his pickup truck into the space in front of the first bay. It had been one of those rare times when the place was deserted, and he had been able to enter the barn unobserved. He was wearing a vinyl motorcycle jacket and a pair of leather gloves so new that he had not had time to sew in a name tag. In his pocket, he carried a .22. He did not have long to wait.

The doors of the next to the last stall opened automatically, and Bus 21 was driven into its space. The doors closed behind it with a muted thud. He threw the light switch, plunging the barn into darkness. Vicki would not be alarmed. Power failures were not infrequent during the severe winters.

He watched her start to descend from the bus and, moving catlike in the dark, he threw himself upon her, tearing at her clothes, pawing her body, moaning huskily. She pushed him off and started to run, getting around the rear of the bus before he caught up with her.

She put up a good fight. They were the same height and only thirty pounds separated them in weight. If she could only get by him, it was ten feet to the door at the far end of the barn—ten feet to freedom. He could not let her get away. He whipped her across the face with the butt of the gun. A tooth flew out, tearing some of the hair that had fallen over her face along with it. And still, she fought on, stretching toward the door, pulling him along with her, marking their progress with her blood.

Finally, he was able to pin her against the far wall of the barn just above the section of board that was later removed and, ultimately, sent to MacDonell. The killer knew that it was too late to let her go. He raised the gun to her head and pulled the trigger. The shot, the deafening eruption of sound, the hot gun in his hand, the viscous blood sticking to his glove. He drew away from her and watched her slide down the wall, slowly, slowly, a figure in slow motion, her head finally falling over making a pool of her own blood on the floor.

He would hide her, bury her where nobody would ever find her. Only he would know where she was. He reached for her body. She was heavy, and he half-pulled, half-dragged her across the entire length of the garage. Her long dark blond hair was streaked with shimmering fresh blood as if sprayed with glitter. It swung freely, leaving swipes of blood on the stall doors and walls, a glistening trail.

He opened the door of the first stall. His luck was holding. There was nobody in sight as he backed the pickup truck up to the first stall. He let down the tailgate of his truck and pulled out the plywood cover of the bed, angling it against the tailgate to form a ramp. He dropped her body on it. Her blood, trapped between plywood and head, left a single, slightly askew horizontal streak on the wall. The makeshift ramp collapsed under her weight. As her body fell to the ground, she left another, straighter streak just beneath the first one. He finally pushed and pulled and hauled her into the bed and covered her with the plywood.

He closed the tailgate and looked down the drive. A van was blocking his way. He broke into it, released the brake, and rolled it a distance down the driveway. He returned to the barn, closed the stall door, and then drove out into the dark forest and beyond.

The board had told MacDonell about the moment of death. The sizes and distribution of the bloodstains could only

219

have been the result of somebody having been hit with a high-velocity impact and at very close range. Using his index on the gun had told him how close: three inches or less.

The blood spray on the board told him something else. The bullet had struck bare skin. If it had struck an area of the body covered by clothing, the blood would have been absorbed into the fabric, and could not have spewed forth. In the cold of winter, the two parts of the body one was likely to find exposed were the head and hands. Because of the anatomical structures of the hand and the cranium, this enormous quantity of spatter could have only come from a head wound.

There is an old legal saw: If you have a good case, waive the jury and let the judge make the decision. Steven Heflin's lawyers thought that they had a good case. There was no corpse. Martin Sells's evidence was circumstantial. They waived the jury, and the trial opened on September 8, 1976, in St. Helens, Oregon, with Circuit Court Judge Donald L. Kalberer presiding.

Herbert Leon MacDonell testified on the morning of September 17. On September 23, Judge Kalberer did not retire to deliberate after the final arguments. The counsels finished, and he immediately found Heflin guilty of the murder of Hilda Victoria Brown. In setting forth the reasons for his verdict, he quoted from MacDonell's expert testimony.

On September 28, Kalberer sentenced Heflin to life imprisonment. On August 28, 1977, the Oregon Court of Appeals upheld his conviction.

7

THE PIPER PAYS

Mr. and Mrs. Harry Piper, Jr., were among the most respected citizens of Minneapolis. He was the president of Piper, Jaffray, Inc., the parent company of Piper, Jaffray & Hopwood, one of the city's largest investment firms, founded by his family in 1895. It was assumed that Piper was a man of substantial means, but only a very few insiders knew how extremely wealthy he was. There was nothing ostentatious in the way the Pipers lived—comfortable, upper-middle-class, never showy. They were simply not that sort of people. Mrs. Piper was president of the board of directors of the Northwest Hospital and a member of the Hennepin County Republican Women's Club. Her taste in clothes tended toward the sedate and elegant Adolfo look. She was a trim, handsome, silver-haired woman of indeterminate middle age with an attractive throaty voice that suggested a fondness for cigarettes and martinis. She had three sons ranging in age

221

from eighteen to twenty-eight and could take for granted the inevitable compliment that she did not look old enough to have children of those ages.

Their home was in the exclusive residential section of Orono, a gray-and-white colonial house looking down across a rolling lawn to a small lake. The well-to-do of Minneapolis tended to cluster around the city's myriad lakes.

On the afternoon of July 27, 1972, Virginia Piper was in her garden picking dead blooms off the pansies when a church clock struck one. The Pipers' regular servants were off, and she was alone except for two cleaning women who always came on Thursdays. One of them came running out of the house shouting, "Oh, those men!"

Mrs. Piper looked beyond the terrified woman to see two black-clad men with hoods over their heads coming after her. They carried guns and motioned both women into the house with them. Mrs. Piper automatically tugged at her dark cotton blazer, adjusting it neatly over her crisp light trousers as she walked toward the door. She was cool and collected and would remain so throughout most of the long ordeal that was only just beginning.

As they were entering from the garden, the other cleaning woman made a dash for the front door but was quickly apprehended. Both domestics were gagged and tied to dining-room chairs. One of the men asked, "Where's your safe?"

"We don't have one. If it's jewelry you're after, there's none in the house except for three small pieces upstairs in my bedroom."

It was not jewelry that they were after, and they did not bother to take the time to check. "Where's your old man?"

"My husband is at his office."

Her inquisitor turned to the other man. "That dumb Cheeno screwed up again. He said that Piper'd be here."

She was struck by that. Her husband frequently took Thursdays off to attend classes at a seminary or to fly to New York City for meetings at the stock exchange, but she thought only those business associates who knew his work habits could be aware of that.

The questioner shoved his gun toward her. "Okay, Mrs. Piper, you're coming with us. Behave yourself, and you won't be hurt."

He had handcuffed her and was marching her toward the door when his accomplice cried, "The notes! We forgot the notes!"

"You keep her covered. I'll get them." He ran out to their car, while his partner kept muttering something about fuck-up after fuck-up.

The ransom notes were left in the house, and they departed with one last instruction for the maids. "If you get free, you mustn't use the phones in the house, or things will get tough for your boss."

When the women finally did manage to loosen their bonds, a sense of order preceded all else. The first things they did were put away the vacuum cleaner and take some food out of the oven. It was only then that they trooped over to a neighbor's house to ask if they could use the phone. There was nobody home. One of the women asked, "Do you think we should go over to Mrs. Piper's son's house and tell him what's happened?"

"That's a thought."

They got into a car and drove around looking for the son's house, but they could not find it. After getting a little lost, they decided to go over to the home of John Morrison, a Piper in-law, and it was from there that Harry Piper and the police were finally notified of the kidnaping.

A pillowcase was slipped down over her head, and Virginia Piper was forced to lie on the back seat of a green

1972 Chevrolet Monte Carlo. It was a long drive and, robbed of sight, she tried to memorize the turns and stops and changes in the quality of the road surface. She was distracted from this effort when her abductors compelled her to tape-record a message to her husband giving preliminary instructions for the delivery of the ransom. For her safe return, they were asking for one million dollars in unmarked twenty-dollar bills.

She was doubled over in a cramped position, attempting to remember the details of the route, listening for any helpful hints in the laconic exchanges between her captors; the drive was a long nightmare in which each new memory cloaked recollection of the one that had preceded it. When they finally removed her from the car, the ability to stretch her legs again was almost as sweet as freedom. They slipped the pillowcase off her head and taped her eyes closed before marching her through woods and tall grass.

It had started to rain by the time they reached their destination. They stretched a polyethylene sheet on the ground near a stunted tree. Her eyes were uncovered, and she was told to sit on the sheet. She was grateful for her blazer and slacks, for it would have been very cold without them. Both men had stockings pulled down over their faces. One of them departed almost immediately, and she was to spend most of the next thirty hours in the company of the other. She was chained to the tree only when he left her alone for short periods and then immediately freed on his return except for the handcuffs.

They spoke like polite strangers enduring a hardship equally trying to both of them. All during that time, she attempted to preserve in her mind the details of their conversations, the quality of his voice—gruff, illiterate, southern or rural, possibly black. He fed her hunks of cheese and Fritos and 7-Ups out of a Piggly Wiggly supermarket brown paper bag. He lit mentholated cigarettes and passed them to her. There was an awkward gentleness in the way he refrained from touching her, from doing anything that might be construed as sexually suggestive or menacing.

She was admonished not to look at him but, using peripheral vision, she was able to observe that he often rubbed his leg either to keep warm or because of an arthritic condition. She complained of the cold and damp, and he gave her a pair of olive brown trousers that were too small to fit over her own pants and a sweatshirt with a St. Olaf school insignia on it. Unlocking her handcuffs, he helped her to slip her arms into the sweatshirt. She pulled it down over her jacket and, as the manacles were replaced, she asked, "Where are we?"

He laughed. "Wouldn't you like to know? I'll tell you this much. We're still in Minnesota. We didn't cross no state lines. In case we get caught—God forbid—I ain't going to take no federal rap."

They were silent for a while. It was he who started to speak again. He told her that he would not have become involved in the kidnaping had he known that it was a woman that they were going to take. He had been told that they were going after her husband. She expressed surprise that they had known that he was often at home on Thursdays.

"Aah—everything was planned down to the last detail. We didn't want no slipups. We'd been casing your place. And we had all the dope on Piper."

She had a sense of revulsion that their private lives had been spied upon, invaded without their knowing it, but she contained it. She wanted as much information as possible. She said, "You mean—you and your partner?"

225

He told her that he barely knew the other man. They were only acquaintances who frequented the same bar and had become part of an operation involving a man he called Cheeno and others.

"A gang?"

"You're asking too many questions." They remained silent for a few minutes, and then he said, "I don't belong to no gang. I'm a construction worker. Just in this for—you know—the dough."

He nodded as if he had scored a point and then was quiet again. After a few minutes, he lit another cigarette and passed it over to her. "You can call me Alabama."

"You're from the south?"

"Everybody calls me Alabama, on account of I'm always talking about Governor Wallace."

The conversation meandered over the weather and sports. Basketball was the only sport that he really liked. He said, "Recently, I'm into reading. You read much?"

She could not believe her ears. Was he actually asking her if she had read any good books lately? He started to tell her about a book he had just read about criminal psychology and then interrupted himself to ask if she had ever heard of St. Cloud Reformatory. It was a terrible place. They treated the young inmates like animals and provided next to no rehabilitation programs.

"You've been there?"

"When we let you free, the cops are going to show you a lot of mug shots, you know? Well, you ain't going to find my face among them."

His face, she wondered. What was his face like beneath that nylon stocking? Did she dare to try to sneak a look at him? The Friday dawn was grayly brightening the sky. She asked for another cigarette. As he passed it to her, she glanced up for a second. The stocking was sheer and had a run over his left eye. His skin was swarthy, might be mulatto, but how peculiar that eye was. She had never seen anything like it before. The iris had a white ring encircling it and a red streak going through it. She was too timid to look closer for fear that he might catch her at it.

The day passed slowly, and the dark of another night covered them. He chained her to the tree and said that soon they would take her to a place where she would be found by her husband and the police, and then he departed. The promise of rescue made it seem as if he was gone for hours. What if he was only taunting her? What if there were no plans to take her anywhere ever? A new struggle began. It was to keep her fear from turning to hysteria. She heard somebody approaching and screamed, "Help! Please! I'm over here!"

A man emerged from the woods. Although she could discern his white shirt, she could not see his face. He asked, "Is everything all right? Where's Tom?"

Tom—Tom had to be Alabama's real name. "He's gone. He's been gone for a long time."

"I'll be back." She understood nothing. It was like one of those plays by Pinter or Beckett. If their aim was to torture her, they were succeeding. At length, the man in the white shirt returned.

"Everything's all right. It went according to plan. Your husband delivered the ransom without trying any funny tricks. You're going to be rescued."

She cried, "When?"

"Soon."

"Here?"

"Safe and sound."

He departed and soon after, she saw two headlights coming toward her and then retreating. She heard two

227

short honks of the horn. As the car drove away, a strange voice jeered, "Grandma, Grandma, we're going now."

And then, nothing. She could not give up the fight, or she would truly be lost. It was her second cold, sleepless night in the forest, and the fear was overwhelming, but she had to fight. She dug frantically at the roots of the tree to which she was chained, hoping—she was not sure what—to upend the tree, to break off a piece for food.

She slumped back against the trunk. It was hopeless. The sounds of the forest, to which she had grown accustomed the night before, again grew alien. It would never end. She would never be found. In the dark, she dared not think of death. Another day sidled slyly into the sky. A thin layer of clouds masked the sun like a sheer stocking. How many days did this make? How long had she been there? She counted back to find her sanity.

Thursday in the garden picking dead flowers—and the clock struck one. That was when it began. Friday—and now, it was Saturday. The date. What was the date? The last newspaper she saw—more interested in the sales than the news—July 27. July 28. It was July 29.

Dear God, where was she? Did nobody ever come this way? She began to scream until the burning hoarseness in her voice was doused by tears. Steady, she told herself. Save your energy. Remember every detail. Wasn't that what prisoners always did? Over and over again, she reconstructed the journey and every word that her captors had said. She was being so good and still, but nobody came. Where was she? It did not matter, for she would never be found. She would die in this unmarked place. No! Harry would not let that happen. Harry loved her and had followed their instructions. She would be rescued. Safe and sound. That was the last thing that had been said to her. No, no, the last thing was: "Grandma, Grandma, we're going now."

It was getting hot. She had on that dreadful sweatshirt and could not get out of it. St. Olaf. Who in God's name went to St. Olaf's? How much time had passed? If only she would twist around and see her wristwatch. What difference did it make? She was doomed.

Then, faintly, she heard something. A car in the distance, coming nearer. She began to scream. Not words. Just screams. Animal sounds. She saw the men approaching.

"There, there, Mrs. Piper. You're safe now. We've come to take you home."

It was 1:00 P.M. on Saturday when the members of the rescue party found her chained to a tree in Jay Cooke State Park, just north of Duluth. As far as Virginia Piper was concerned, she had spent forty-eight hours in hell.

The FBI wanted to enter the case. The bureau felt that with its vast facilities, it had a much better chance of cracking the case than the local authorities. If the kidnapers had crossed no state lines, it would remain under the jurisdiction of Minnesota. Alabama had told Mrs. Piper that they had not done this, but the FBI was determined to prove that he was lying.

There were several routes that could have been taken from Minneapolis to Jay Cooke State Park, but only one of them passed through two thousand feet of Wisconsin. The G-men took Mrs. Piper back over it, and she claimed to recognize several landmarks, although she had been unable to see throughout the original trip. They did not test her memory by taking her over any of the other routes that might have been similar "landmarks" and were both more direct and less well traveled. They were satisfied with that single journey because it established that this was a federal case and came under their authority.

During the rest of the summer of 1972 and well into

229

the following year, the FBI worked diligently, methodically following up on every lead in the Piper case. Their sole purpose was to apprehend the kidnapers and see that justice was done. They started by reviewing the few clues and pieces of evidence at their disposal. The ransom and instruction notes were typewritten, quite literately phrased, and yielded no fingerprints. Tracing the chain and handcuffs used to bind Mrs. Piper led nowhere. They sifted the ground around the location at which she was held and came up only with some cigarette butts with no identifiable fingerprints on them. Later, they found an empty Kools cigarette wrapper of negligible value. She had been given mentholated cigarettes but some time had passed between the abduction and the find, during which hundreds of sightseers had passed through to look at the site of her captivity and any of them could have dropped it. They kept the wrapper on file. It might prove useful if a future suspect was a Kools smoker.

A Piggly Wiggly bag proved to be the only significant piece of evidence found near the spot where Mrs. Piper had been held prisoner. She identified it as probably being the one that carried the food she had shared with her abductor. A piece of the top had been torn away.

Mrs. Piper had described the green 1972 Chevrolet Monte Carlo used by the kidnapers. A few days after her rescue, an abandoned car fitting that description was found in Minneapolis. It had been stolen two days before her abduction. On the floor, they found the missing piece torn away from the Piggly Wiggly bag. There were fingerprints on the piece of brown paper and in the car. None of them matched the prints of known criminals on file with the Minnesota police or the FBI. The investigators believed that the print on the paper would prove to be the most significant evidence. In all probability, it had been torn away by the kidnaper who had carried the groceries.

Although the twenty-dollar-bills in the ransom money had not been marked, the serial numbers had been retained. The list had been sent all over the country, and the hundreds of men assigned to the case were waiting hopefully for them to be passed. In the meantime, those most immediately involved in the Minneapolis area were following up on the leads provided by Mrs. Piper from her memory of conversations with her guard. The man had an accent that was southern or rural or black. Judging from his disdain of St. Cloud Reformatory, he probably had been an inmate. From what she could discern of his complexion under the stocking mask, he was swarthy. Her most significant recollection was her description of the condition of his left eye. A white circle around the iris with a red streak running through it.

She was taken to a professor of ophthalmology who showed her a photograph of an eye that she identified as being exactly like the one she remembered seeing. The eye was afflicted with arcus senilis, an irreversible condition that almost always occurred only in older persons. If her captor had suffered from the disease at the time that she was with him, then he still had it and always would. There was a chance that her observation was incorrect. She had seen the eye only through the screen of a ladder in a nylon stocking.

In building their portrait of her kidnaper, they put aside the possible fallibility of her information. The man was called Alabama, although his real name may have been Tom. He had a swarthy complexion and spoke with an accent that was southern or rural or black. He smoked mentholated cigarettes. By trade, he was a construction worker, and the only sport he favored was basketball. He did not really know the other man who actually had committed the kidnaping with him and, although Alabama was not a member of a gang, the crime had been planned by a group probably under the leadership of a man called Cheeno. Alabama was probably middle-aged or old and afflicted with arcus senilis.

Although Alabama had boasted that Mrs. Piper would not find his photograph among the mug shots of known criminals, if, as suspected, he once had been incarcerated in St. Cloud Reformatory, an early picture of him would probably be on file. Mrs. Piper spent hour after hour looking at mug shots. It was to no avail, for she had never seen the man without a mask. The only real identifying mark that she had was the eye disease, and that did not turn up in any of the pictures.

The search for a suspect continued. There was a roundup of every man with a criminal record living in the Minneapolis area. Among those brought in for questioning were two small-time criminals with long histories of nonviolent crime, Donald Larson and Kenneth Callahan. They were jailhouse buddies who, along with another ex-con, Harold Combs, had opened a custom-cabinet shop.

Larson was a fair Nordic type with clear blue eyes that hinted at mischief and a sense of humor. He came from sturdy Minnesota farm stock, but somehow the stiff Lutheran work ethic had gone awry, and all of the energy that his people usually reserved for hard work had been displaced into mischief. He had had his first brush with the law when he was nine years old and, starting at the age of twelve, in 1939, he was to spend most of the rest of his life in Minnesota penal institutions. In 1959, he was sentenced to life on a first-degree larceny charge. All of the guards agreed that he served "good time," and he was out again by 1970.

His wife had become fed up with him and run off with one of his best friends. He could not really blame her, but this time he was determined to stay clean. He had spent well over half of his forty-two years behind bars, and that was enough. There had to be a better life than the one he had known.

Things seemed to break for him. He met Ruth Powell, a lusty young divorcée some fourteen years his junior. Despite the age difference, he thought that she went for him the same way that he went for her. They got married and, in 1971, she gave birth to a boy. Little Mark became the center of his father's life. With this child he was determined to make up for his failures with his first family.

Early in 1972, he went into partnership with two other ex-convicts, Kenneth Callahan and Harold Combs, in the cabinet business. Larson knew nothing about carpentry except for some woodworking that he had learned in the pen, but Callahan was a master craftsman and taught him the trade. His relationship with Combs was casual, but Kenny had always been his special pal.

Unlike Larson, who had never gotten beyond the eighth grade, Callahan was well-spoken and quick-witted. There did not seem to be much of anything that he could not do (he even flew his own plane), except keep out of trouble or make a big score. By the time he linked up with his two partners, he was as ready for the straight world as they were. Of course, they did not go completely straight; one had to ease into that lest one suffer a severe case of culture shock. In addition to ordinary carpentry, they ran a little fence for stolen goods on the side, nothing that was going to make them rich, but it was enough to keep their hands in. The boys occasionally daydreamed about the big caper, like the Piper kidnaping that pushed everything else off the front pages during that summer of 1972.

When the FBI pulled the three ex-cons in for questioning about the case, it was strictly routine. Nothing about any of the three matched Mrs. Piper's description beyond the facts that Larson had served time at St. Cloud and Callahan smoked mentholated cigarettes. They all had healthy eyes, the wrong accents, the wrong coloring, and, most important of all, none of their prints matched the one found on the piece torn from the Piggly Wiggly bag.

Larson, Callahan, and Combs were scratched off the possible suspect list and excused from further questioning. Their alibis had been verified, and not one shred of evidence linked them to the kidnaping. The same was to prove true of all of the ex-cons and hoodlums brought in at that time by the investigators.

The investigation proceeded. New leads came to light. They found the shop where the St. Olaf sweatshirt had been purchased shortly before the kidnaping. The owner's description of the men who had bought it led to no new suspects. Some of the twenty-dollar-bills from the ransom money began to turn up as far afield as Philadelphia, Pennsylvania, but the people who reported these offered very little help about those who had passed them. The total was $4,000, but the bulk of the money never surfaced.

In 1973, one of the hoods originally questioned by the FBI, Robert Billstrom, was killed in a shoot-out. Billstrom had started as a promising suspect. He had been a member of a gang that met at a bar not unlike the one described to Mrs. Piper by Alabama. The gang was one known to the police as having a potential for violent crime. He was released after an alibi was provided by his common-law wife, Lynda Lee Billstrom. She said that the couple had checked into a motel in Prescott, Wisconsin, on the day of the kidnaping. The motel records proved that she was telling the truth.

In 1974, Mrs. Billstrom was serving time in prison for aggravated robbery. Word came back to the bureau that she had confided to another inmate that Billstrom had been in on the Piper kidnaping and that the alibi she had provided had been a setup. The investigators took her out of prison for questioning. There was some indication that her cooperation could buy an easier time in jail as well as earn some money. A story began to emerge that directly implicated the Billstrom gang. She was naming names, dates, and places. Suddenly, she stopped in mid-interview and asked for permission to telephone her attorney. The lawyer told her, "You'd better clam up. You're getting yourself involved in a possible conspiracy charge."

No amount of threats could move her to say another word. The FBI attempted to track down the leads that she had already given, but her story had been too incomplete. The matter was dropped as interest in the case began to wane. It had already cost the government many millions more than the ransom, and they had gotten nowhere. They could not afford to spend any additional time or money on it, and the still-open case was ignored except for some diehards in the St. Paul–Minneapolis office of the FBI.

By the time the FBI caught up with Lynda Lee Billstrom, three of the original possible suspects were no longer partners. Harold Combs had decided to pull out of the carpentry business, and Donald Larson and Kenneth Callahan had closed the shop. Larson had discovered that he had a bad heart and decided to return to farming, which he had not done since he was a boy. He borrowed $16,000 and bought an eighty-acre spread in a small farming community some eighty miles north of Minneapolis. It would have been a good life were it not for his wife, Ruth, who was always taunting him about not being man enough to satisfy her sexually.

A neighboring farmer, Jim Falch, was a virile young

fellow who did not take his own or anybody else's marriage as an obstacle to seduction. Ruth was there, and she made it apparent that she was more than available. It was not long before Larson caught them in flagrante delicto. Ruth and Jim promised that it would never happen again, and Larson forgave them. Jim's wife was not so forgiving. She walked out, leaving their children behind.

When Ruth heard that Falch's wife was gone, it was as if all restraints were off, all promises made only to be broken. She told Larson that she was leaving him to go to live with Falch. He begged her not to do it, to think of their son and of her two boys from a previous marriage who were living with them.

She said, "Don't you see—I've got to be with Jim. There ain't no other way for me."

Larson looked at her for a moment. "I wonder what hurts most. Love or hate."

On April 24, 1976, Larson returned from visiting his heart specialist in Minneapolis. He was carrying two loaded pistols. He went into the kitchen of his house to find Falch and Ruth packing up the power tools that he had bought while still in the cabinet business with Callahan and Combs. They were *his* power tools, worth thousands of dollars. First his wife and now his property. It was too much. He roared, "What the hell do you think you're doing?"

Ruth replied that they were taking the tools over to Jim's place. She giggled. "You ain't strong enough to use any tool. We'll keep them safe and well oiled. I've got plenty of use for a big power tool."

She was laughing at him. So was Falch. Larson pulled out his guns and started shooting. By the time the guns were empty, Ruth and Jim were dead. So was one of her older sons, Falch's son, and Larson's baby, Mark.

236

The criminal in Larson took charge, and he fled the scene of the crime, disposing of the guns and his bloodied clothes in the Mississippi River. He checked into a cheap motel in Minneapolis with enough drugs and alcohol to kill himself. Before oblivion, he wrote letters to a friend and relatives attempting to justify what he had done.

"I didn't want to hurt nobody. I just wish somebody would shoot me."

Larson was found on the day of his wife's funeral. He had overdosed on the drugs and alcohol and was unconscious. When he came to in a hospital two days after his capture, he said, "I died when I saw my little son die."

Ronald Meshbesher took the case for the defense. He announced that his case would be based on the fact that all of the shootings were without premeditation, and he would build his pleas on the results of psychiatric testing.

The judge instructed the jury that they could consider a verdict of manslaughter. While they were out, the jury sent back for a definition of "heat of passion." The judge replied: "A state of mind resulting from such emotions as rage, anger, fright, or passion."

After deliberating for two days, the jury returned on November 3, 1976. They found Larson guilty of the first-degree murder of Jim Falch, the second-degree murders of Ruth Larson and Falch's son, and the third-degree murder of his own son. He was acquitted of the murder of Ruth's older son on the grounds of mental illness. His life sentences were to be served concurrently, which would make him eligible for parole in 1993. With his heart condition, it was doubtful that he would live that long.

During the Larson murder trial, a photograph of him appeared in the newspapers. It was a 1963 mug shot. From that picture, a young schoolteacher who had been a gas station attendant at the time of Virginia Piper's kidnaping four years before identified Larson as the driver of the kidnap car.

The federal statute of limitations on kidnaping cases was five years. The Piper case was the largest unsolved kidnaping in the FBI's history, and its expiration would come up on July 27, 1977. They had spent over ten million dollars unsuccessfully trying to break the case, and it was a source of great embarrassment to them. They might have let it slide into oblivion were it not for the schoolteacher's identification of Larson, from a bad photograph almost fourteen years old, as a man he had seen only once on a night four years earlier.

The Minneapolis–St. Paul FBI branch was the only office still working on the case, and it had long been their dream to crack it. The identification was admittedly questionable, but they decided it was worth having another look at Larson.

Two weeks after Larson was sentenced for the killings, two FBI agents visited him in Stillwater Prison and asked if he minded if they took his fingerprints again. He knew that something was wrong when they put them on a blank sheet of paper instead of a record card.

Larson later told how the FBI came after him. It might well have been a "prison story," a con doing his thing, except that so much of what he told was later verified in testimony. They started coming up to see him. They told him that they knew that he was guilty of kidnaping Virginia Piper.

What follows is Larson's own description of what happened.

They says: "Now the best thing is—if you want—we're gonna make a deal with you. You cop out. You get ten years. You know you don't belong up here on no murder rap. We'll get it cut down to manslaughter, second degree."

So I says: "Will you put that in writing?"

They wouldn't do it. I knew they were lying to me. So, I figure—you want to play games with me, I'll play a few games with you. So, I told 'em: "No. I ain't gonna do it."

They kept on coming back to see me. I never seen such a nice, wonderful bunch of boys. They were going to do everything they could to help me. When they talk about making a deal, I ask what I'm supposed to have done with all that money. They say: "Just tell them you lost it up in Las Vegas. Don't you be interested in that."

That wouldn't have been bad at all. If they would've put it in writing—we'll get you ten years, and we'll get your murder knocked down to manslaughter—I would've done just like they said. I would've took the beef. I would've said what they told me. I lost all the money gambling, and young girls took it away from me. I would've got on the stand and said—you know, I was out there gambling, and these prostitutes knew I was just a farm boy from Minnesota, and they took me for it.

They didn't care what happened to the money. They spent a million on the Hoffa case, about eight or nine million looking for Patricia Hearst. And they said—this was the most expensive case. All they wanted was to get the case solved. I would've took the deal. I didn't have anything to lose, but I wouldn't have fingered anybody.

But the FBI wouldn't even put it down in writing. They lied so many times. I seen it in here, where they promise guys deals. . . . And the dumb bastards go in there with nothing but the cop's word. And when the cop gets what he wants—then he'll deny it. Honest to God. I wouldn't take the deal, because they wouldn't let me talk to my lawyer or put anything in writing.

Now, it's getting down to about thirty days before the statute of limitations. Then, they says: "Okay. We're gonna nail Kenneth Callahan."

I knew him all my life. They knew they had to get somebody else. What the hell, they thought, Larson's only got an eighth-grade education. He couldn't mastermind this thing. He couldn't type those ransom notes. They were long and detailed. They knew I couldn't have done it—so they had to get somebody who could. So, they said—Callahan worked with him in the custom cabinets. He smokes Kools cigarettes. Now, the Kools come up, because maybe forty-five days after Mrs. Piper was held there, they found these butts at the scene. Maybe, a hundred thousand people went through there in those forty-five days. Not only your normal tourist traffic, but mobs coming to gawk at the site of the famous kidnaping. But they find these Kools after all that time, and this is brought in as verified, bona fide evidence that it had to be Callahan. You know—he was on a lineup. Mrs. Piper saw him— talked to him for a half-hour. She couldn't identify him. But the butts did it.

And me. They checked my fingerprints four times. Three times, positive this is not Larson or Callahan. The fourth time, positively, it was mine.

Here's an FBI agent. He's no friend of mine. I don't care. I don't mind making a deal. I'll get up there and say—hey, I'm guilty as hell. And they would solve this crime. But you gotta have them put everything in writing—your FBI—because they're treacherous.

The identification of Larson by a reputable high-school teacher was the first real break the FBI had had since the Lynda Lee Billstrom story turned cold after she refused to cooperate. They may well have tried to work out a deal with Larson to save the additional expense of further investigation and a lengthy trial. It was not very different from plea bargaining. Whatever the motive, they saw a possible solution to a case that had already given them a black eye at a time when their activities in civil rights investigations had brought the bureau to the point of lowest repute in its history. The statute of limitations was running out, and it was either act then or allow the case to remain forever unsolved on their books.

The FBI decided to make an all-out effort. They moved one of their kidnaping experts from the Chicago office to Minneapolis–St. Paul to take charge of the investigation. He had no doubt that Larson was his man. A statement by the prosecuting attorney who had put Larson away for the murders was the first thing that the public saw after the Chicago man came on the scene and began building his case. In it, the prosecutor told a reporter that he had been certain Larson was guilty because the FBI had told him that the man had killed his wife and her lover when he found them searching for the hidden ransom money. The FBI based this leak on a report from a prison informer who told them a friend of Larson's claimed the money was buried on the farm.

The next bureau step was to conduct its own search of Larson's place. Agents scoured the farm buildings for the money. Floorboards were torn up. Walls were hacked open. Bulldozers were moved in to dig up every inch of ground. They did not find a dime, let alone one million dollars in twenty-dollar-bills.

The photograph of the latent fingerprint on the piece of grocery bag was resubmitted to the FBI fingerprint expert, despite the fact he had twice denied that it was Larson's. Along with this submission, they sent the copy of Larson's prints that had been taken in prison on a blank sheet of paper. The expert reported that he apparently had been mistaken in his previous analyses. The latent print did indeed belong to Larson.

They may not have had the ransom money, but they did have an identification and a fingerprint. That was enough for the investigators to build a case against Larson. All that remained was to find an accomplice. Some of Larson's fellow inmates at Stillwater told him that the FBI had come in and offered them deals to "take the beef." In one case, the prisoner's alibi was unshakable. Another had refused to "finger" an innocent man, and Larson had been protesting his innocence to anybody who would listen. It was then that the investigators settled on Kenneth Callahan on little more evidence than a Kools wrapper.

After closing the shop he had run with Larson and Combs, Callahan and his family had relocated to Cumberland, Wisconsin, where he continued to work as a custom-cabinet maker. He was respected and well liked in the community and had not been in trouble with the law since 1971. He seemed to be enjoying his life as a husband and father in the straight world when, in the late spring of 1977, every move he made started coming under federal scrutiny. Where had he obtained the money to buy his house? How could he afford to keep a small plane? How did he pay for his vacations? None of his expenses indicated that he might be a man with a million dollars stashed away, but the way the investigators framed their questions and used his answers made it seem to many that he was living the high life.

In June, the FBI summoned Callahan to Minneapolis to appear in a police lineup before Mrs. Piper, the two maids who had been on duty on the day of the abduction, and several other witnesses who claimed to have seen the kidnapers. All of the men in the lineup wore stocking masks. They turned one profile to their audience, then the other, and, finally, full face.

The majority of the witnesses, including Mrs. Piper, selected the second man in the row. He was a Minneapolis police officer. None of them selected Callahan. On a voice test, only one maid selected Callahan's voice as similar to that of the kidnaper. Mrs. Piper again chose the policeman.

A strand of hair had been found in the abandoned kidnap car. It was sent to the FBI crime lab along with a strand of Callahan's hair. The expert said that they were similar, although he had to admit that the texture of hair changed chemically with time, and a long time had elapsed since the hair in the car had been found.

The FBI had one voice identification, a strand of hair, and an empty cigarette wrapper found in Jay Cooke Park a month and a half after the kidnaping. It was enough for them to build their scenario.

Callahan had written the ransom notes and had planned the kidnaping. Larson was his accomplice. The two of them had abducted Mrs. Piper. Larson was the driver, because the gas station attendant had identified him at the wheel. Callahan had stayed with Mrs. Piper, because he smoked Kools cigarettes. Larson had fetched the groceries, because he tore an edge off the bag. To make matters worse for the suspects, their original alibis had turned cold during the passage of five years.

A grand jury was convened during the week of July 10, 1977. It was then or never. They had to hand down indictments against Larson and Callahan before the statute ran out on July 27. On July 11, the indictments were made, and the trial was set for September 7. At first, Ronald Meshbesher was going to handle the case for both defendants but when he learned that, although they would be tried together, they had been charged separately, he decided that this would lead to a conflict of interest. He called on his good friend and colleague Bruce Hartigan and asked him to take over the admittedly more difficult defense of Larson. Hartigan was an urbane fellow whose style more closely approached that of the eastern establishment. Although he was as capable as Meshbesher of going for a witness's jugular, his manner was disarmingly affable.

The attorneys knew what the FBI had, and set about evaluating what they did not have. Nobody had found the ransom money or traced it definitely to either of the men charged. Neither of them had arcus senilis, the eye disease that Mrs. Piper had discerned through the mask of her captor. The prosecution was claiming that it was Callahan who had spent almost thirty hours with Mrs. Piper, but nothing about him resembled her recollections of the man who had been with her. Nobody had ever known him by the sobriquet of Alabama nor was he called Tom. His accent was devoid of regionalism, and he used the language well. He had never been in St. Cloud Reformatory (although Larson had). He was not a construction worker and knew very well that his face could be found in police mug shots. If he could be said to have a favorite sport, it was fishing and not basketball. Most important of all, Mrs. Piper had not been able to identify him in a police lineup, or from a voice test, mug shots, or a simulated police drawing.

Meshbesher and Hartigan made a request for all of the exculpatory evidence. Rather than cull the mass of documentation, the prosecutor gave them the entire FBI report, which ran to sixty-six volumes containing over sixteen thousand pages. It would take time to get through all this material, and the lawyers were determined to read every line. They would need all the help that they could find for, shaky as the prosecution case might seem, the most telling piece of evidence, the fingerprint, was alleged to have been left by a defendant that the jury could not escape knowing was serving time on four convictions of murder, including those of his wife and son. They asked for a postponement, and the trial did not actually start until October 11.

Virginia Piper testified on the second day. There was not a hair out of place in her immaculately groomed silver-tinted coiffure. The fastidiousness of the woman, in a smart burgundy dress with matching jacket, only underscored the ordeal she had suffered during those forty-eight hours in the wilderness.

Meshbesher reminded the court that she had selected a policeman rather than her captor from a police lineup. Mrs. Piper protested, "I only said that he was similar. I used the words—most familiar."

Mrs. Piper also testified that the man had an eye disease that was subsequently identified as arcus senilis, and that it was irreversible and worsened with age. Hartigan asked the two defendants to approach the witness stand, and she had to admit that neither of them had the ailment.

The prosecution called a series of witnesses with criminal records. Some were serving time at the time that they testified. All of them had been questioned in the roundup of petty hoods soon after the kidnaping. At that time, none had mentioned the incidents about which they were about to testify. They apparently had not recalled them until they were approached by the FBI five years later and immediately prior to the grand jury hearing.

Harold Combs, who had been the defendants' business partner at the time of the kidnaping, was among the first called. His police record made him susceptible to FBI suggestion and, on October 17, he told the court that in May or June of 1972, Callahan had shown him a pair of handcuffs in their shop that was similar to to the pair used to bind Mrs. Piper.

Meshbesher confronted him with the testimony that he had given to the grand jury, in which he had said that he saw the handcuffs in the basement of Callahan's house. Whatever the locale, he had not mentioned the cuffs during his questioning in 1972, when the incident would have been much fresher in his mind. Perhaps that was because the boys were his partners and friends at that time; perhaps it was because he had not been subjected to the FBI powers of suggestion at that time.

Combs also admitted that Callahan had helped him to move his girlfriend's furniture at 7:30 on the morning of July 29, the day the FBI found Mrs. Piper in Jay Cooke State Park. She had already testified that her abductors had left her very late the night before. Presumably, Callahan had been up all night. He had driven the almost two hundred miles from Duluth to Minneapolis, had picked up the ransom money and hidden it, and then had come to move heavy furniture. Yet Combs admitted that Callahan had not looked or acted tired.

One witness had several felony convictions against him. At the time of the trial, he was serving a forty-five-year sentence at Stillwater. He testified that he saw both Callahan and Larson handling handcuffs before the kidnaping. He also claimed that Larson had asked him if he had ever heard of Harry Piper. Meshbesher got him to admit that the FBI had promised to get him out if he testified.

The man's forty-five-year sentence was later reduced to three years in one of "the country clubs," as the minimum security prisons were called by the cons. To start a new life, he was also given a $5,000 reward for the return of some silver that he had been accused of stealing.

The next witness sworn in by the prosecution was a six-time loser and sexual offender. He was also a drug addict who admitted on the stand that he had needed a fix before he could appear in court. He told the jury that Callahan had asked him how to "launder money." He also claimed to have seen Larson wearing the St. Olaf sweatshirt when he visited the prison shortly before the kidnaping. Lawyer Hartigan played incredulity to the hilt. He exclaimed, "It was a hot, sticky summer day in July, and Larson was walking around wearing a sweatshirt!"

Two other convicts testified for the defense that this man had boasted of "putting a story on the feds to help him get out of prison." His sentence was commuted shortly after the trial, and he received the first parole in his long prison career.

It certainly seemed as if Larson had been singularly lacking in trust to have asked the FBI to put the deal in writing. Bruce Hartigan said of these witnesses' payoffs: "The currency was not money. It was much more valuable than gold. The currency was freedom."

The case was drawing to a close. Having destroyed the credibility of many of the prosecution witnesses and put into question the reliability of the memories of most of the others, Hartigan and Meshbesher knew that the fingerprint evidence probably would swing the verdict. The FBI had gathered seventy-three latent fingerprints at the time of the crime. They had been compared with the prints of all the people involved, including the Pipers. Only the print of the torn piece of brown paper ultimately came up with a match.

Hartigan took this latent to the local fingerprint expert, Ronald Welbaum, who found that there was no doubt that it was Larson's. It was disheartening news, but Hartigan had no reason not to accept the word of this accredited expert.

Shortly before resting their cases, the lawyers found the name of Lynda Lee Billstrom buried in the sixteen thousand pages of FBI documentation. They read about her interview with the investigators in 1974, in which she admitted to having arranged an alibi for her husband, Robert Billstrom, for the day of the kidnaping, and of how she had come close to implicating Billstrom and his gang as the kidnapers. They located her in Alderson Prison, in Virginia. She had not consented to cooperate in 1974 after her lawyer warned her that she could be held for conspiracy. She was no longer liable to the charge, because the statute had run out. With nothing to fear anymore, she agreed to help the accused by telling what she knew in court. She had arranged an alibi for Billstrom, but it was phony. He smoked Kools cigarettes. He had mentioned knowing a man called Alabama. She had overheard the members of his gang mention the name Piper. They hung around the Sportsman's Bar, which was where Mr. Piper had dropped off the ransom. She had gone to a victory party held on the night after the ransom was delivered.

By the time they secured Mrs. Billstrom's cooperation, the defense lawyers had rested their cases but had not yet delivered their final addresses. Hartigan and Meshbesher went to the judge and requested permission to re-open in order to put her on the stand. He turned them down.

Hartigan became indignant and began to press. Mesh-besher muttered, "Cool it. In case things go against the boys, this is our ticket to a new trial."

The jury retired. Their first vote was ten to two for acquittal. They hung ten to two for three days. There was one extremely strong juror who was convinced of their guilt. By the fifth day, he had turned the jury around, and they brought in a conviction.

After the trial, Meshbesher and Hartigan brought in Lynda Lee Billstrom to tell her story to the judge. They asked for a new trial on the basis of it. The judge denied the motion, ruling that "her statement would have been of little, if any, worth to the defendants' case."

The lawyers went to the court of appeals. On January 27, 1979, the convictions were overturned, and a new trial was ordered "in the interests of justice."

The new trial was set for October 15, 1979. Two things about the case continued to rankle the defense attorneys. The jury might not believe Lynda Lee Billstrom. She was a convicted felon who had been interviewed twice by the FBI. The first time, in 1972, she had lied, and in 1974 she had refused to cooperate.

The second problem was the fingerprint evidence. It would be helpful if they could destroy the validity of the FBI identification. After Marjorie Caldwell's acquittal that summer, Meshbesher weighed the option of again calling on Herb MacDonell. But it was less than a month before the Piper trial that he actually decided to phone. When he explained what he wanted, MacDonell laughed.

"You've got to be kidding. Disproving one identification was a phenomenon. Two would be a miracle."

"Herb, if a trial lawyer doesn't believe in miracles, he should go into another line of business."

"Would you say that again? With violins."

"I haven't much time. Actually, Bruce Hartigan is defending Larson. He's willing to bring the print out to you."

"I still haven't been paid for Caldwell."

"Neither have I. The estate's being tied up by the kids. This time, the state of Minnesota's footing the bill. You'll get your money."

"All right. Tell him to come on out here."

Bruce Hartigan was not optimistic, but he was willing to give it a shot and he flew to Corning on October 5. MacDonell took one look at the picture of the latent print and said, "This isn't the original photograph."

"The FBI assures us that it is."

"I don't care what the FBI assures you. I'm telling you that a thirty-five-millimeter fixed-lens camera doesn't take this kind of photograph. I want to see the original negative."

They called the Minneapolis–St. Paul office of the FBI. The agent to whom they spoke said that it was impossible to let the negative get out of their hands. MacDonell suggested that they send it to the FBI office in neighboring Elmira and have one of their men bring it out to him. The agent replied that he would look into the possibility.

He called back to say that they were sorry, but they could not locate an Elmira office. MacDonell replied, "That'll be news to the guys who are running it. They're good friends of mine."

"We'll look into it."

"Thank you. And while you're at it, would you please send out the print from the other side of the piece of paper?"

"There was no print on the other side."

MacDonell hung up looking very perplexed. "He just said that there was no print on the other side of the torn-off piece of paper."

Hartigan asked, "So what?"

"That's impossible. Watch." He picked up a sheet of paper off his desk. He gripped a corner of it between his thumb and index finger and tore it off.

"You see? To tear off a piece of paper, you have to hold it between two or more fingers and rip. In gripping it to make the tear—if you leave a fingerprint on one side of the paper, you have to leave a print on the other side. Unless one of the fingers was covered by a Band-Aid or something. And there's no indication that was the case. The point is, the process the FBI used to develop the print saturates the paper and, had there been latent prints on both sides, they would have appeared. Of course, we'll never know if there was a second print now. If it wasn't processed and photographed almost immediately, it's probably gone forever. Fingerprints on paper generally diffuse very quickly."

After pressure was applied by Meshbesher in Minneapolis and MacDonell in Corning, the local agent finally brought the negative out to MacDonell's laboratory six days later. It was October 11, and only four days remained until the opening of the trial. MacDonell had to work quickly.

He went into his darkroom and developed a print from the negative. It was exactly like the print Hartigan had brought out, and he was disturbed by it for the same reasons. What he had was a photograph of the piece of paper with the fingerprint on it. A portion of a ruler was positioned beside it to indicate the print's size.

Looking at the photograph and at a copy of Larson's own print that Hartigan had given to him, MacDonell saw there were only five points of identification between the two. That was not enough for a positive identification. He told Hartigan that he would testify to the fact whenever they summoned him.

Hartigan said, "Terrific. That's going to be a big help."

"That's not all. The print's been altered."

"What did you say?"

"Somebody touched up the print. Somebody faked the evidence. If only the FBI had it in its possession all this time, then . . ."

"How do you know it was faked?"

"Look at the photograph. The ruler is in sharp focus. Except for the points that they want to use for identification, the fingerprint is blurred. Out of focus. So is the edge of the piece of paper bag. If you take a picture of a stationary object under laboratory conditions—and we must assume that they did that much—there is no way to have a part of that photograph in focus and another part out of focus."

"Are you willing to testify to that?"

MacDonell paused for a moment. He had known that the question would be asked when he volunteered the information. He could have avoided it by simply saying that a positive identification could not have been made and letting it go at that. But the evidence had told him much more. He did not like going against the FBI. The vast majority of its agents were decent and honorable men doing a difficult job to the best of their abilities. Only a few of them seemed to forget that one of their basic functions was the protection of the innocent, and that all men were presumed innocent until proven guilty. Those few, he believed, undermined the bureau's good work, as well as the faith of everyone who had to look to the FBI to protect their constitutional rights. Nobody who would break

252

the law and sow chaos should be given the job of establishing law and order.

MacDonell sighed. "I'll testify. If you'd like to stick
around, I'll show you how it was done."

Hartigan replied, "Gladly. Except for a small thing
like having to be in court in a couple of days, I love
October in Corning. I wouldn't dream of spending the
month anywhere else."

MacDonell shouted up the stairs, "Phyllis, would you
please bring a garbage bag down here?" He paused before
adding, "An empty one."

She came down with it. "Do you really think it was
necessary to add that?"

"In the interests of science, my dear."

MacDonell tore a piece of paper from the clean bag
and processed his fingerprint on it with a MAGNA Brush.
He then processed the other side. He said, "You will
notice that there are prints on *both* sides of the piece of
paper."

After placing a ruler beside the print, in the same
relationship to it as the one in the FBI photograph, he
took a picture and developed it. He showed the result to
Hartigan and asked, "What do you see?"

"It's the same as the evidence photo, only the fingerprint and the edge of the paper are as sharp as the
ruler."

"You get an A for the course. Now, I'm going to take
the negative of my photograph, project it slightly out of
focus, and make a new print."

After completing this step, he had a photograph in
which everything was blurred. He took a pencil and carefully sharpened some of the lines used for fingerprint identification. He deftly altered some of the other lines. He
placed the actual ruler over its blurred reproduction in

the picture and took another picture. The result was a new negative of the original fingerprint, now doctored, and including a ruler very much in focus. The print developed from it resembled in every detail the FBI photograph that Hartigan had brought with him.

Hartigan said, "They weren't even offering the original negative in evidence, were they?"

"Nope. A negative can be destroyed at any time. A new negative can be made at any time."

"If they went to all that trouble, why didn't they do a better job? I mean—after all that, you still see only five points of identification."

"If that FBI expert went on record twice that the print on this piece of paper had not been made by Larson—and then, just before the expiration date of the statute of limitations, he reversed himself and found thirteen points of identification—thirteen!—if it wasn't a tough identification to make, he'd look like an idiot."

"But it still didn't get by you."

"As a fingerprint, it was not good enough to identify. I think a lot of experts would agree on that. As a photograph, it was obviously a fake. It was the photograph that first struck me."

MacDonell went to St. Paul and testified before Judge Donald D. Alsop. Lynda Lee Billstrom also testified. On Thursday, December 6, the jury brought in verdicts of not guilty for both Donald Larson and Kenneth Callahan. They had deliberated for only three hours.

Nobody was ever found guilty of kidnaping Virginia Piper, nor was the bulk of the ransom money ever found. By this time, those original twenty-dollar-bills have probably been retired from circulation. Before then, they might have been among the twenties in anybody's wallet.

The statute of limitations had run out, and the FBI marked the case "closed." The kidnaping had cost the Pipers a million dollars. The investigation and two trials had cost the taxpayers many millions more than that. The only person who had really been punished was Virginia Piper. After an ordeal that had lasted for more than seven years from her abduction through the final trial, she probably was equally relieved to mark the incident "case closed."

On Friday afternoon, August 21, 1981, Herb MacDonell received a long-distance phone call.

"Herb, it's Ron Meshbesher."

"Hey, Ron, how are you?"

"Fine. You'll never guess where I'm calling from."

"Montreal."

"How the hell did you know?"

"Elementary, my dear Meshbesher. The long-distance operator spoke English with a French accent. But she pronounced MacDonell MAC-duh-NELL, which is how the other Canadians pronounce it. Voilà, you're in French Canada. If you were in a small town, you probably wouldn't ask me to guess where you are. That meant Montreal or Quebec. If it was Quebec, the operator would've been more truculent about speaking English. So, Montreal, it is."

"Terrific. I'll tell you why I'm calling. The National Association of Criminal Defense Attorneys is having its annual meeting up here. The banquet is tomorrow night, and our keynote speaker's conked out. How'd you like to fill in? Bring Phyllis. We'll have a ball."

"Wait a minute. Let me check it out." He shouted to Phyllis. "How'd you like to go to Montreal?"

"When?"

"In an hour. A gaggle of lawyers are convening up there. Meshbesher wants me to speak to them."

A vision of a restaurant in Vieux Montreal flashed through her mind. On the table, French bread and rich onion soup sealed in a thick gratiné. She said, "I'll start packing."

The Bonaventura was one of the largest hotels in Montreal. It featured a swimming pool, several restaurants, meeting rooms, ballrooms, and endless corridors of bedrooms and suites. It floated high above the city on the uppermost floors of a commercial complex that occupied a square block at the juncture of old and new Montreal.

The hotel lobby was awash with attorneys clad in variations on a uniform of gabardine trousers or jeans topped by alpaca cardigans or blazers. There were more alligators on legal breasts than could be found in the Florida Everglades. MacDonell looked for Meshbesher. He was amazed at how many of these fellows he had worked for and worked against during the previous ten years. One of them approached and greeted him effusively. They reminisced about a series of cases. The lawyer shook his head. "I've called you in four times, and I've never gotten you into court. One of these days, you're actually going to testify for me."

"One of these days, you're actually going to have an innocent client."

Laughing heartily, the lawyer went off to repeat MacDonell's crack to his friends. In addition to their acumen at their profession, these men were a good lot of showmen and gamblers. The odds were always against them; about seventy percent of all criminal cases were returned with verdicts of guilty. Outsiders often wondered how they could defend certain obviously guilty people. If they did not, the system would fail. They were not judges. Their job was to ensure their clients' rights to the presumption of innocence. That was where they parted company with MacDonell. He listened to the evidence, and they waited for the verdict.

Most of these men were liberal reformers. It went with the territory of working for the underdog. That night, at the cocktail reception before the banquet, they could easily have been mistaken for a gathering of Wall Street tycoons. Their elegant suits were of such somber hues that banker's gray looked garish. Their wives were tasteful, elegant, and understated. Chiffon flowed as freely as the liquors at the bar. In her muted pastel silk print, Phyllis MacDonell could easily have passed for the wife of a successful attorney, until one took a look at the man on whose arm she entered. It was true that he was tall and of distinguished mien with a dashingly trimmed pepper-and-salt beard, but that was where any resemblance to the others ended. In a bright arterial-red jacket, he stood out like a pool of blood on a bolt of dark silk. If the others were showmen, MacDonell seemed determined to be the ringmaster.

Meshbesher was a vice-president of the association and, after the meal, he had the unenviable job of introducing MacDonell to a group who knew him, some only by reputation, almost as well as he did. Bruce Hartigan was out there, and Jim Montgomery of the Black Panther case, and a score of others.

MacDonell was seated beside him on the dais but out of his line of vision. As Meshbesher was describing him not only as an expert in fingerprints and firearms but also as the Sherlock Holmes of bloodstain evidence, MacDonell reached into a plain brown paper bag that Phyllis had discreetly placed at his side. He removed a deerstalker

257

hat, a calabash pipe, and a magnifying glass. When he turned in profile, he got his expected laugh. He often courted the resemblance to the great detective that had first been pointed out derisively by the sheriff in the Ferry case but, with each passing year, there were more people who tended to take his joke seriously. Some of the lawyers who had come up against him and lost would decidedly have preferred to encounter him in fiction rather than in a courtroom.

When he rose to speak, the Holmes gag was put aside, and he addressed them at some length on how and when best to utilize the services of a criminalist. The underlying message was to let the truth be told. Although he would name no names, he observed wryly that there were some in that room who still owed him money for cases long over. He paused and added soberly that, though he liked to be paid, he could not be bought. Under the showmanship, his professional integrity remained what it had been from the beginning.